Boundary Spanners of Humanity

Boundary Spanners of Humanity

Three Logics of Communication and Public Diplomacy for Global Collaboration

R. S. ZAHARNA

OXFORD
UNIVERSITY PRESS

OXFORD
UNIVERSITY PRESS

Published in the United States of America by Oxford University Press
198 Madison Avenue, New York, NY 10016, United States of America.

© Oxford University Press 2022

Library of Congress Cataloging-in-Publication Data
Names: Zaharna, R. S., 1956– author.
Title: Boundary spanners of humanity : three logics of communication and
public diplomacy for global collaboration / R.S. Zaharna.
Description: New York, NY : Oxford University Press, 2022. |
Includes bibliographical references and index.
Identifiers: LCCN 2021035115 (print) | LCCN 2021035116 (ebook) |
ISBN 9780190930288 (paperback) | ISBN 9780190930271 (hardback) |
ISBN 9780190930318 | ISBN 9780190930295 | ISBN 9780190930301 (epub)
Subjects: LCSH: Communication in international relations. | International
cooperation. | Diplomacy. | Intercultural communication.
Classification: LCC P96.I53 Z35 2022 (print) | LCC P96.I53 (ebook) |
DDC 302.3—dc23
LC record available at https://lccn.loc.gov/2021035115
LC ebook record available at https://lccn.loc.gov/2021035116

DOI: 10.1093/oso/9780190930271.001.0001

1 3 5 7 9 8 6 4 2

Paperback printed by LSC Communications, United States of America
Hardback printed by Bridgeport National Bindery, Inc., United States of America

For Samih Nazmi Zaharna and all the boundary spanners of humanity who make the world a better place.

Contents

Figures

Acknowledgments

If only books could write themselves. But then, self-writing books would take from authors much of the joy of discovery of research and writing, as well as the wonderful discussions and insights from others who shape the journey.

This work began innocently enough with a prod from the late U.S. Senator Richard Lugar, who, with the then-Senator Joe Biden, grilled me on the continuing mishaps in U.S. public diplomacy. Later he would ask, Why was the United States a giant in communication and yet "all thumbs" in communicating with the Islamic world? In trying to answer that question, I wrote *Battles to Bridges* on post-9/11 U.S. public diplomacy, arguing that the United States needed to move from fighting information battles to building relational bridges. That book led me to the relational and network approach.

But I knew that the answer to these communication problems went beyond building relations—a term that, strangely, seemed to mean different things to different global actors and publics. Communication also seemed to mean different things to different actors.

I also knew it wasn't just the United States that was all thumbs. Denmark was taken aback by the uproar over what it described as "Muslim cartoons." China, when it was preparing to host the 2008 Olympics, was similarly caught off guard by the string of protests that followed the torch relay around the world. How could everyone be all thumbs?

How could everyone be all thumbs especially when the stakes were so high—and rising? At first, the public diplomacy mishaps were disappointing for national interests. However, as the world's problems seemed to be growing in frequency and severity—climate crisis, water scarcity, the Ebola outbreak—the limits of communication and public diplomacy appeared more pronounced. The threat of a global pandemic, which I wrote about, wasn't even on public diplomacy's radar screen. Rather than engage in collective problem solving to tackle the growing list of global challenges, public diplomacy appeared caught up in a global competition to see which country had the most soft power.

Was it possible that the very same tools needed to tackle global problems—communication and public diplomacy—were actually undermining our best efforts to collectively solve the challenges facing humanity and the planet?

At first, I turned to my academic roots in intercultural communication for answers. On the surface, I thought all communication misunderstandings were tied to different cultural patterns of communication which, according to theory, clashed. I am indebted to the intercultural scholars who shaped my thinking and laid the foundation for the book. First is my advisor, Prof. Louis Forsdale at Columbia University, who introduced me to the field. Then, most notable, is the founding scholar Edward T. Hall, with whom I had the opportunity to go on memorable after-lunch strolls during a symposium in Seattle. Prof. Hall, aside from having the most delightful, gentle humor, encouraged creativity and a drive to explore buried assumptions: Question what you thought you knew. William Starosta, a colleague at Howard University and co-author with Guo-Ming Chen, deepened my intercultural thinking and pushed me out of my shell and into a community of scholars and their mentors, all of whom shaped my thinking: Yoshitaka Miike, Guo-Ming Chen, John C. Condon, Wimal Dissanayake, Molefi Asante, Fred Casmir, Darla Deardorff, Shelton Gunaratne, Satoshi Ishii, Young Yun Kim, Hamid Mowlana, Peter Nwosu, Georgette Wang, and Silvio Waisbord.

While Senator Lugar's questioning during congressional testimony provided the initial impetus, the journey was fueled by the opportunity to participate in several projects and invited forums such as the NATO Defense College (Italy), RUSI-Derasat (Bahrain), Islamic University of Malaysia, and Confucius Institute Conference (China). The international settings and informal discussions exposed assumptions in my thinking that led to deeper insights. I remember a conversation in Singapore during which I used the expression "Yin versus Yang," and was politely corrected that it is yin-yang; the two are not in opposition but connected. They are one circle. Why would I assume they are oppositional? That insight was over a decade ago, but it provided the seed for the Holistic logic. At another forum, an Indian practitioner questioned my assumption about the importance of messages in communication; for her, communication begins with personal connections. Why would I assume messages instead of relations? That insight would germinate the idea of the relational bond and "contact points" that underpin the Relational logic.

Of the many forums, I am particularly indebted to the Otago Foreign Policy School in New Zealand, and the late Anthony Deos, and Paola Voci, Brett Nicholls, and Balazs Kiglics, who invited me to speak to practitioners and policy advisors in the summer of 2016. That was where I first presented the three logics. Admittedly, my ideas were a bit sketchy. The most charitable comment I received—or perhaps remembered—was "how refreshingly naïve" my presentation was. I lived to write another day.

Another significant opportunity was the two-year project "Diplomacy in the 21st Century" sponsored by the Berlin think tank Stiftung Wissenschaft und Politik (German International and Security Affairs), led by Ambassador Volker Stanzel. Amb. Stanzel, like Prof. Hall, encouraged creativity and suggested I explore the emerging prominence of emotions in public diplomacy, and how digital and social media appeared to be shifting communication from a fact-based foundation to a socio-emotional dynamic. As the only communication scholar at the table, I was indebted to the pushback from the participants from the German Foreign Ministry, as well as the engaging company of esteemed diplomatic scholars Jan Melissen, Christer Jönsson, Corneliu Bjola, Andy Cooper, and Iver Neumann. Special thanks go to Christer, who suggested Amarna diplomacy, which led to the foundation for the chapter on Relational logic.

Alongside these the forums were several writing projects. I am extremely grateful for the continuing engagement with the University of Southern California's Center on Public Diplomacy, first as Research Fellow, and then as Faculty Fellow. I give special thanks to Stacy Ingber, Sherine Badawi Walton and Naomi Leight-Give'on for their assistance, and editing of the *Cultural Awakening in Public Diplomacy* CPD blog series. My thinking on relations and collaboration was constantly shaped and reshaped while working on the book project with Amelia Arsenault (who first proposed the three public diplomacy layers of monologue, duologue, and collaboration) and Ali Fisher (who wrote the first book on collaborative public diplomacy).

I appreciate Kim Johnston and Maureen Taylor, editors of *The Handbook of Engagement*, for their careful and encouraging critique of the first written presentation of the logics. Nancy Snow and Nick Cull provided another opportunity to refine the logics in their edited collection of *The Routledge Handbook of Public Diplomacy*. I am grateful to Jan Melissen and Jay Wang, editors of the special edition of the *Hague Journal of Diplomacy* on public diplomacy in the 21st century, for prodding my thinking on the need to expand public diplomacy's vision from state-based goals to those of humanity-centered public diplomacy. I also must thank Jan as well as Natalia Grincheva and Robert Kelley for bringing me in on their special edition of non-Western public diplomacy, in which I speculated about assumptions of diplomacy as fellowship rather than "estrangement."

A final series of forums and thanks go to my public diplomacy colleagues at the annual gatherings of the International Communication Association and International Studies Association. Again, the informal casual conversations have been the most memorable in reflecting on assumptions. My thanks go my colleagues, Amelia Arsenault, Robin Brown, Narin Chitty, Noe Cornago, Daryl Copeland, Nicholas Cull, Alina Dolea, Alisher Faizullaev, Kathy Fitzpatrick, Eytan Gilboa, Sarah Ellen Graham, Guy Golan, Elizabeth Hanson, Craig Hayden, Ellen Huijgh, Diana Inhoffman, Robert Kelley, Spiro Kiousis, Teresa LaPorte, Emily Metzgar, Thomas Miller, Alister Miskimmon, Donna Oglesby, Ben O'Loughlin, James Pamment, Geoffrey Pigman, Steve Pikes, Shawn Powers, Kishan Rana, Gary Rawnsley, Laura Roselle, Michael Schneider, Phil Seib, Anbin Shi, Daya Thussu, Nur Uysal, Yiwei Wang, and Wil Youmans. I thank

Costa Constantinou as well as Yiqing Qin, whose works have greatly shaped my thinking.

A super special thanks to those who participated in the ISA and ICA Emerging Scholars in PD panels and have gone to shape the field, including, Sohaela Amiri, Philip Arceneaux Kadir Ayhan, Tainyi Bai, Lindsey Bier, Alexander Buhmann, Senem Cevik, Anthony Deos, Tania Gomez-Zapata, Natalia Grincheva, Falk Hartig, Zhao Alexandre Huang, Luigi Di Martino, Ilan Manor, Theo Mazumdar, Yelena Osipova, Andrea Pavon-Guinea, Anastasia Remes, Efe Sevin, Sonali Singh, and Deborah Trent, Eriks Varpahovskis, Willow Williamson and Di Wu.

For the production of the book: First and foremost, I thank Hallie Stebbins of Oxford University Press, who was a bright ray of encouragement from our meeting in Washington to reading the book proposal on the train back to New York; that meant the world to me. Thanks also are due to Holly Mitchell and Emily Benitez for helping me prepare the manuscript for OUP production and Anitha Jasmine and Debra Ruel at Newgen. Thank you, Simon Anholt, Nick Cull and Bruce Gregory for reading the book project—twice! Thank you, Kate Washington, for graceful editing and Ana Isabel Reyes Lam for the skilled graphics. I am indebted to the doctoral students for their invaluable research insights, proofing, and references: Erica Diya Basu, Kate Holthouser, Brian Hughes, Samantha Dols, Sindhu Manjesh, and Marwa Maoz.

Finally, there are those who shared the journey most intimately, my family, some of whom I have lost along the way but whose spirit helped carry me and the project to its completion: Amti Hind, Kamal, Dad, Nick, Nod, Rima, Yahya, Hadeel, Mohammad, Liz, and Dorene.

This book is dedicated to my late father, who came to the United States to study. He embodied the spirit of the boundary spanners, those who would find commonality alongside the rich diversity of humanity. His motto: Enjoy.

Reflected in these acknowledgments are the blessings of why books, thankfully, do not write themselves. Instead, they reflect the thinking, care, and nurturing that surround the author. I have tried to pass that care on to you, the reader. As you flip or scroll through the pages, I hope you will sense the journey of discovery and warm encouragement within which the ideas took root and grew. May you enjoy.

Introduction

Call to the Boundary Spanners

The World is in desperate need of diplomacy in the public realm. Thanks to advances in transportation and communication technology, we can connect with other people almost instantaneously worldwide, crossing barriers of time and space that once limited human contact. However, rather than reaping the benefits of the global pool of human resources and intellectual wealth, nations are experiencing unexpected public discord, resurgent nationalism, polarization, and crises that tear at the social fabric. In an age of unprecedented global connectivity, some are even resorting to the most primitive of communication barriers: they are building walls.

Perhaps nothing speaks to the 21st-century dilemma of human connectivity and diversity more than the Covid-19 pandemic. The virus's quick spread spoke to our connectivity. As the humanitarian organization Refugees International wrote, "The scale and speed of the pandemic underscore how deeply interconnected the world's populations are."[1] Unfortunately, efforts to halt the pandemic revealed our diversity, as nations sought to close territorial borders or vaccinate only their own against a microbe that had little regard for such national distinctions.

As even a tiny microbe shows, we already are connected. What we appear to lack are the skills and mindset to navigate the tension between that connectivity and our diversity. Both communication and public diplomacy would seem to be necessary tools working together globally. But paradoxically, the very tools needed for mediating diversity and bridging connections—communication and public diplomacy—may be inadvertently reinforcing and perpetuating divisions.

I argue that they are. Both communication and diplomacy appear still tethered to assumptions of separateness that are increasingly out of synch with 21st century connectivity and diversity. We need to fundamentally shift the way we think about ourselves and our tools. To explore how we might make such a shift, I sought to rethink communication from the ground up, undertaking a cross-cultural, pan-human study of communication—a global trek, if you will, to better understand the field's blind spots and assumptions about communication and diplomacy. This book both exposes the limits of conventional notions of communication and diplomacy and introduces a new framework—the three logics of communication—that we can use as a tool in harnessing our connectivity and diversity to respond collectively to the needs of humanity.

Wicked Problems, Synergistic Problem-Solving

The challenges we face are more interconnected and complex than ever—making it all the more disconcerting to see people resorting to walls. Global warming, forced migration, and deadly pandemics are what Horst Rittel and Melvin Webber call "wicked" problems.[2] We are used to solving "tame" problems, or those that can be tackled individually in a sequential manner. Wicked problems, as the scholars caution, are so mired in complexity that efforts to solve one aspect only create more problems. Multiple entities working independently can multiply the problem. Writing nearly a decade ago, Ben Ziegler, who studies collaboration, cautioned that the accelerating frequency and severity of global problems were outpacing our capacity for cooperation.[3]

Building walls also, ironically, cuts off a powerful antidote to wicked problems: global diversity. For many, working with others who are different means friction and frustration (Box I.1). The tendency is to gravitate to the familiar, which makes communication easier. But the problem with interacting with those who look and act like us is that they tend to think like us as well. That think-alike mentality often leads to seeing and trying to solve problems in the same way. Creativity is sacrificed for the sake of communication.

Box I.1

The frantic and even competitive efforts of nations in the face of a virus—which has no sense of national or cultural borders—exposed the repercussions of our diversity on our capacity to collaborate.

Thinking alike may work well for tame problems. However, when it comes to complex wicked problems, diversity of perspectives is precisely what is needed. Friction and frustrations may be the wellspring of creativity and innovation in problem-solving. As Scott Page wrote in *The Difference*,[4] different perspectives, modes of thinking, and approaches enable us to see a problem from multiple angles and generate synergic problem-solving strategies. Tapping into different wisdom traditions and practices is key to unraveling complex problems. The critical challenge, however, as Page noted, is learning how to "leverage diversity."

This book argues that radically expanding our view of communication is a key to leveraging diversity. Communication has been called "the fundamental social process."[5] Indeed, it is fundamental to all the social sciences. Diplomatic scholars

Christer Jönsson and Martin Hall describe communication as "the essence of diplomacy."[6]

My goal is to expand our vision of communication from an individual-level perspective to a humanity-level perspective. As we will explore in this book, current views of global communication are actually a continuum of individual state-based and culture-based notions of communication that divide humankind into separate, even mutually exclusive categories—prompting us to question how communication is even possible.

Critically, the individual-level perspective focuses on the immediate needs of an individual actor within its own time frame of a past, present, and future. A humanity-level perspective focuses on survival and perpetuation of the species across an evolutionary time horizon. How has communication enabled us to survive as a species? What are the pan-human aspects of communication, apart from our shared communication tools? In exploring a global and evolutionary perspective of communication, I introduce three relations-based communication logics that underlie a pan-human experience: The Individual logic, based on individualism, reflects the power of speech and expands collaboration through storytelling. The Relational logic, based on the paired or dyadic relation, reflects the power of emotion and expands collaboration through empathy. The Holistic logic, based on the relational universe, reflects the power of interactivity and expands collaboration through synchrony and synergy. By expanding the way we view communication from an individual- to a humanity-level perspective, we can develop a pan-human understanding of communication. Such a view is key to using communication as tool to mediate identities, leverage our diversity, and tackle complex wicked problems together.

That may sound aspirational now, but it is possible. If Covid-19 laid bare our struggle to cooperate, it also exposed our drive to collaborate, or synergistically create and problem-solve together. During the pandemic, people worldwide spontaneously reached out to each other, finding creative ways for singing, playing, dancing, and painting virtually together. As nations closed their borders, scientists open-sourced their findings on the virus and its spread. Emerging research suggests collaboration is an inherent part of our nature as "the social animal." This book makes a forceful case for us to move beyond cooperation to collaboration. Cooperation reflects the limited aspirations of assumed separateness. Collaboration draws upon the synergistic effect of diversity and connectivity to engage in creative problem-solving that may let us keep pace with the accelerating rate of wicked problems.

Before we begin that journey, it is important to appreciate the human capacity for cooperation. Although states and institutions may struggle to work together, the capacity for cooperation appears to be part of our evolutionary success as a species.

Evolutionary Human Capacity to Cooperate

Norwegian diplomat and scholar Iver Neumann called diplomacy "the hard-won triumph of the species . . . the recursive result, and the cause, of cooperation between human polities."[7] Neumann, an anthropologist by training, took an evolutionary perspective of diplomacy, beginning with the emergence of big-game hunting during the Pleistocene revolution. Rather than being eaten as prey individually, by cooperating together humans could hunt prey.

Neumann cautioned that "cooperation" was a positively loaded word. Even so, the idea of cooperation—rather than competition—as a defining element in contentious international politics seems odd. It runs counter to the well-known phrase "survival of the fittest"—often attributed to evolutionary biologist Charles Darwin—which embodies the idea of individual strength, not collective cooperation, to ensure survival.

The phrase is not actually Darwin's, but that of his contemporary, British sociologist Herbert Spencer, who in *Principles of Biology* (1864) suggested the phrase, arguing that progress was based on struggle and competition. The concept could not have been more apt for the era's dramatic transformations. It gave impetus to the Industrial Revolution, capitalism, racism, immigration, health policies, and colonialism, and justified dominance over those perceived as weaker. The idea of progress through strength—and the fear of its opposite, devolution through degradation—were woven into popular literature, such as Robert Louis Stevenson's classic, *Dr. Jekyll and Mr. Hyde*.[8]

The mantra "survival of the fittest" is still heard today. It permeates the international studies discourse that privileges discussion of power, anarchy, and estrangement. Writing on *Global Cooperation and the Human Factor*, global governance scholars Dirk Messner and Silke Weinlich observed that if one relies on political or economic literature, cooperation is an "especially scarce and fragile" commodity.[9] However, they found "an astounding" breadth of research from other fields that gives precedence to cooperation in human behavior. They suggest that we could address the cooperation deficit in global governance by exploring other disciplines' views of cooperation.

Darwin's work is relevant here. In *On the Origin of Species* (1859), Darwin spoke of plants and animals, not humans. He turned to humans in his second book, *The Descent of Man* (1871), characterizing humans as the "social animal" whose habits of cooperation enabled us to overcome our vulnerable bodies and survive in the face of larger creatures in the wild. Darwin identifies "the feeling of sympathy which gives the first impulse to benevolent actions"[10] as key to human evolutionary survival: ". . . those communities, which included the greatest number of the most sympathetic members, would flourish best, and rear the greatest number of offspring."[11]

Russian scientist and philosopher Peter Kropotkin, writing in 1906, expanded on Darwin's work, substituting the idea of "mutual aid" for sympathy. He argued that cooperation, not competition, was the foundation of survival. Like Darwin, he believed that it was a natural instinct.

Few today have heard of Darwin's *The Descent of Man*. Fewer still know of his third book, *The Expression of the Emotions in Humans and Animals*.[12] Though both books were bestsellers, Darwin's ideas ran up against dominant scientific sentiment that would prevail through much of the twentieth century. As we discuss more in Chapter 6, it wasn't until the end of that century that his ideas would find a more hospitable academic and social climate, and researchers would have the technology to explore the brain.

Today, more and more works are emerging on the evolutionary capacity for cooperation.[13] Some even describe humans as engaging in "hyper-cooperation," enabling "the emergence of such uniquely human traits, including complex cognition, morality and cumulative culture and technology."[14] Works by evolutionary scientists,[15] as well as popular texts such as Douglas Rushkoff's *Team Human*,[16] relate how cooperation enabled *Homo sapiens* to beat out other humanoids, including the Neanderthal. Species dominance emerged not from the brute strength of individuals but their combined strength, thus enabling *Homo sapiens* to not only survive but thrive.

In his evolutionary look at diplomacy, Neumann identified a series of tipping points, each reflecting a graduating increase in the capacity for cooperation.[17] As human societies grew in complexity, so too diplomacy and the capacity for cooperation grew in size and scope. He suggested that with our digital technologies and globalization, which has compressed spatiality and temporality, we are reaching a new tipping point. I would agree. Covid-19 offers an example: even as it exposed strains in our capacity to collaborate, it also showcased our spontaneous drive to build connections, even in forced isolation.

Public diplomacy appears to be transitioning from state-centric advocacy, digital technologies, and a competitive quest for soft power to a more expansive humanity-centered focus on problem-solving. When I started this book, I originally envisioned public diplomacy in terms of states, traditional diplomats, or organized non-state actors. The more I researched evolving global communication dynamics, the more I realized the future of public diplomacy was about people—people who are simultaneously engaged on a local as well as global level. They may implement their everyday acts of diplomacy locally, but the effect is ultimately global. In exploring ways to enhance our evolutionary capacity for cooperation, it is important to highlight the mindset or conceptual barriers that might limit us. We look at those barriers in the next section.

Assumptions of Separateness

If our human capacity for cooperation has been evolving throughout history, why are the strains becoming so pronounced now? Has this happened before in human history? As I explored the many disciplines that inform communication—from ancient cosmologies to artificial intelligence—I stumbled across an insight from neuroscience: There are ten times more neurons going from the brain to the eyes than the reverse.[18] What the brain thinks, the eyes look for. Metaphorically, we can extend this insight to the realm of scholarship: our mindset and conceptual tools steer us (scholars and practitioners) toward what we look for in our world. This realization gave me pause about public diplomacy. Do our conceptual tools align with the world we are trying to describe? Do our conceptual tools align with our growing connectivity and inherent diversity? If we are struggling to collaborate, are our conceptual tools aligned with our needs? I would suggest we have an alignment problem. Our mindset and conceptual tools are not aligned to connectivity; but rather, separateness is the dominant mindset.

Assumptions of separateness fit with an earlier world. For most of history, people have been physically separated by distance, time, and technological limitations, despite links forged by trade and its flows of innovation and ideas. Transportation was expensive and laborious. Communication had limited reach. Even mass media were tied to national structures (such as broadcasting companies) that reinforced separation. Interaction between disparate cultural groups, as Arjun Appadurai noted, were "bridged at great costs and sustained over time with great efforts."[19] He cited warfare and invasions as ready examples.

The assumption of separateness flourished during the 19th and 20th centuries, coinciding with increasing social density within nations.[20] Efforts to navigate between increasing connectivity and human diversity appears to have been tackled by efforts to erase differences—by either removing the people who were different or removing the differences among people. Colonial conquests exemplified the efforts to divide and separate peoples. Similarly, growing nationalism promoted the novel idea of a distinctive people with a shared heritage within territorial borders.

This era also coincided with the flourishing of the social sciences, which reinforced more subtle mentalities of separateness. At the heart of all social sciences was the creation of concepts which could be used for theory building.[21] Strong concepts—including those such as "race" and "culture"—were defined by the clarity of their borders. As John Gerring noted, "A classification aims to carve up the universe into comprehensive, mutually exclusive, and hierarchical categories."[22] Conceptual schemes from social sciences spread to popular parlance. The idea of distinctive, mutually exclusive cultural categories, for example, bolsters the idea of "clash of civilizations."

The assumption of the naturalness of separateness, even in an age of globalization, may explain the recent drive to build walls. More border walls separating countries and peoples have been built in recent decades than at any time in history.[23] Even on social media, people have adapted new connective technologies to self-select by friending and unfriending. The desire to return to an age of separateness or restrict connectivity only to those similar to us is understandable. Preferences for others who look and behave similarly has been documented in studies on infants as young as six months old, according to researchers at the Infant Cognition Lab at Yale University.[24] Some researchers speculate that human experience is rooted in communities rather than abstract notions of nations.[25] These tendencies make the nostalgic call for a *return* to an earlier era all the more understandable.

But such a return is unlikely. The technology, and the societal organization it promotes, is already out of the box, and future trajectory is toward increasing connectivity.[26] With that increased connectivity comes again greater interaction with diversity of every kind. Dealing simultaneously with both the growing interconnectivity that pulls people together and diversity that can push us apart requires careful navigation. It requires re-examining assumptions of separateness and developing a mindset of connectivity.

Developing a Mindset of Connectivity

If the world is experiencing stress, it may be because the old mindset of separateness clashes with today's new dynamics of global interconnectivity *and* diversity. The mindset of separateness that undergirds the social sciences no longer works for our connected world. Developing a global mindset that can increase the capacity for cooperation begins with a fundamental shift in thinking. We need not only a new mindset, but conceptual tools built on the dual assumption of growing connectivity *and* inherent diversity.

Changing mental constructs will not be easy. Assumptions of separateness run deep in social-scientific theories. Separateness, for example, underlies conventional conceptions of diplomacy such as Der Derian's widely cited *On Diplomacy*, which described diplomacy as "mediating estrangement,"[27] or Paul Sharp's concept of diplomacy as a response to "a common problem of living separately and wanting to do so, while having to conduct relations with others."[28] The combined effect of that conceptual foundation and aggressive theory-building is a cocoon of reinforcing assumptions, making the logic of separateness seem airtight and invisible.

This book seeks to deliberately and mindfully shift from assumptions of separateness to that of connectedness in order to build new conceptual frameworks. As forces of interconnectivity and human diversity intensify, we will need to radically pivot to assumptions of connectedness to maintain our evolutionary capacity for collaboration. In the following section, we begin this shift by critically re-examining the core premises of four critical areas: public diplomacy, culture, communication, and identity. These interrelated phenomena serve as the pillars for this book.

Public Diplomacy

The first pillar is public diplomacy. While public diplomacy is a relatively new field of academic study, its proximity to conventional diplomacy means it too presumes separateness, beginning with the view of international relations as relations and communication between sovereign territorial units.[29] As Geoff Pigman noted, contemporary diplomacy co-evolved with the nation-state, in, we should add, the European context.[30] Whereas traditional diplomacy was government-to-government communication, public diplomacy denoted government-to-public communication.[31] Both were tools of states; diplomacy was statecraft.

The prominence of non-state actors in the public arena brought actors beyond the state to public diplomacy, as we see in Robert Kelley's study of diplomatic agency.[32] Scholars have also sought to move beyond the Eurocentric perspective with studies of non-Western diplomatic practices.[33] While these efforts expand the sample, they still view both non-Western diplomacies and non-state actors through the analytical lens of conventional (Eurocentric) diplomacy. We see repeated discussion of actorness, interests, power, and legitimacy and diplomatic practices focused on differences in negotiations, representation, or advocacy and image. Constantinou highlights the limited vision—"an avalanche of exclusions, marginalizations, and exoticizations"—of the conventional, state-centric perspective. Swept away in this avalanche are "all kinds of pre-Westphalian polities . . . all kinds of pre-colonial encounters . . . all kinds of unofficial mediations and innovations . . . all kinds of human ways and means of dealing with others within and across cultures."[34] These exclusions mean pre-colonial diplomacies of peoples in Africa, Asia, the Pacific, and North and South America—as well as of ancient civilizations such as China, India, Egypt, and Ethiopia—are not part of our conceptual foundations for diplomacy. We are missing their diplomatic logics.

Constantinou's reference to "all kinds of human ways" is particularly notable. Diplomacy based on the *ways of the states* are not necessarily the *ways of human societies*. Consider one defining feature of the state: its status as an identifiable, fixed territorial entity. By contrast, mobility marks human history and evolution. A full understanding of diplomacy would necessarily reflect the diplomatic practices of nomadic societies of the Asiatic steppes, non-territorial political configurations of South Asian mandala politics, or even contemporary digital diasporas. Or consider emotion, a defining human trait—but one missing from the Western concept of states as "rational actors." What diplomatic logic embraces empathy? Spirituality is another powerful dimension of the human condition. While the gods were ever present in diplomacies across the ancient world, faith-based diplomacy, as Johnston's pioneering work demonstrated,[35] has been an overlooked aspect of conventional diplomacy. Public diplomacy echoes these omissions.

Not only does the assumption of separateness in conventional diplomacy overlook some of the most distinctive features common to human societies, but it also misses a functional imperative of diplomacy. The functions of state-based diplomacy respond to the needs of the state—traditionally identified as negotiation, representation, and reporting—but do not necessarily address human needs. Diplomat and scholar Tran van Dinh provides insight into an overlooked diplomatic function of problem-solving in an example from his native Vietnam:

> Whenever a crisis such as flood, fire, or drought occurred, the villagers would communicate among themselves through lengthy discussions to reach a consensus as to how to deal with the disaster collectively. They would negotiate to resolve whatever individual or group antagonisms might exist, and to devise a common strategy for collective action. Often, this collective action, depending on the extent of the problem, would spread to several villages.[36]

The example of the villagers resonates today, as many have likened our world to a global village, and we share growing wicked problems, like the flood. The diplomatic imperative arises when one cannot solve a problem individually but must do so collectively. If individuals or societies were self-contained entities that could meet all of their own needs, neither communication nor diplomacy would be necessary.

Humanity-Centered Diplomacy

Humanity-centered diplomacies reflect and respond to the needs of human societies, centering our capacity to collaborate for collective decision-making and problem-solving. In this book, I make a considered break from the dominant focus on state-centric and other "actor-centric" public diplomacy. Instead, I would like to shift attention to what I term humanity-centered public diplomacies.[37] Whereas state-centric diplomacy's focus on individual states represents the mindset of separateness, humanity-centered diplomacy, driven by our shared needs, vision, and goals of humanity, offers a mindset of connectivity and diversity.

The field of public diplomacy does not lack for works focused on how individual states can promote their image or policies. What the field needs, and more importantly what people need, are studies on interactive processes of collaboration that focus on rapport building, collective information gathering, problem-solving, and action to address the wicked problems that humanity and the planet face.

Public diplomacy scholars have been calling for such a shift. Manuel Castells emphasized that public diplomacy ought to be "the diplomacy of the public," contrasting private interests and values against a shared public interest.[38] Juyan Zhang and Brecken Chinn Swartz suggested the idea of "public diplomacy for Global Public Goods (GPG)."[39] Similarly, Kathy Fitzpatrick proposed "public diplomacy in the public interest" that is "more socially-conscious with increased focus on global issues, problem-solving, and shared goals."[40] Simon Anholt, who originally advanced the idea of nation brands and developed a ranking of countries based on their image, has long emphasized the importance of principled and collaborative national behavior. In 2014, he launched the Good Country Index, which ranks countries based on their contribution to humanity.[41]

In this book, I use diplomacies in the plural, because, as noted by Noé Cornago, there is no singular approach, but many.[42] Costas Constantinou and James Der Derian advanced the idea of "sustainability diplomacy," a shift from narrow strategic calculations of national interests to a larger view of diplomacy focused on regional or global interest.[43] Similarly, cosmopolitan diplomacy promotes values such as tolerance, friendship, and respect.[44] We see assumptions of finding commonality and mediating diversity in "everyday diplomacies," which build relations even if the participants are not aware of the diplomatic repercussions.[45]

Several aspects of humanity-centered diplomacies suggest advantages for navigating connectivity and human diversity. We can briefly highlight those related to complex problem-solving.

First, humanity-centered diplomacies assume a broad, global perspective of human and diplomatic relations. Humanity is "the fundamental survival unit" and core to diplomatic vision and practice.[46] By contrast, state-centric diplomacy focuses on individual political actors. Second, humanity-centered diplomacies assume diversity as a core dynamic, underscoring the plurality of diplomacies. Third, humanity-centered diplomacies tend to be issue-driven; initiatives address a specific wicked problem rather than the needs of any one actor. Humanity-centered diplomacies are also inherently process-oriented, as indeed they must be in order to collectively work through the complexity to find solutions rather than impose them. While traditional state-centric diplomacy relies on negotiations to gain a competitive advantage, humanity-centered diplomacies seek to foster a cooperative environment and privilege collaboration for collective problem-solving.

Perhaps the most important distinction of humanity-centered diplomacies is the element of emotion. Humanity-centered diplomacies are rooted in awareness of being connected to others and feeling a part of the larger family of humankind. Akira Iriye calls it "a greater global consciousness . . . that individuals and groups, no matter where they are share certain interests and concerns."[47] The feeling of shared humanity underlies the African concept of *ubuntu*, "one is human through others." Polynesian traditions express humanity in terms of family that extend not only to fellow humans but also to natural elements. Fellow feeling and connection to others is core to Confucian philosophy and the concept of "ren" in guiding relations. Even the origin of the English word "humanity," from the Latin *humanitas* for human nature and kindness, echoes a relational affinity. Emotional connections and global consciousness distinguish humanity-centered diplomacies from the diplomatic premise of an emotionally neutered rational actor, national awareness, or strategic statecraft.

The Copenhagen and Paris climate-change talks, COP15 and COP21, offer a ready example of the distinction between state-centric and humanity-centered diplomacies. Donna Oglesby, in her review of the COP15 talks, described the event as public diplomacy on parade with intense positioning by the individual states in pursuit of securing their interests.[48] COP21 talks, by contrast, were defined by their spirit of collaboration, and they resulted in outcomes that were previously unattainable.[49]

Humanity-centered diplomacies align with the prevailing trends of interconnectivity *and* diversity. We see these trends in the prevalence of multidimensional networks and the communication dynamics of connectivity in social media, which are overtaking the mass media era's single-actor, hierarchal, top-down communication. Another trend is pairing diplomacy with global governance, which represents a shift from individual goal-orientation to a process-orientation of multiple-actor governance.[50] Aligning also with the trends in communication technology and global governance is the rise in the number, diversity, and strength of international non-governmental organizations.[51] While state-centric and even actor-centric diplomacy may dominate the immediate term, the long-term trajectory favors humanity-centered diplomacies that aligns with our growing connectivity and diversity. This view of public diplomacy is intimately tied to changes in how we think about three other pillars: culture, communication, and identity.

Culture and Human Diversity

Prevailing notions of our second pillar, culture, also emerged during the era of accentuated separateness. Framing culture as a bound entity associated with a group or nation, for many, became a bedrock of identity. In contemporary public diplomacy, culture and the nation-state are so intertwined that notions such as "national culture" or culture as a "soft-power resource" (as Nye suggested) have gone unquestioned. But research reveals that the link between culture and nation-states is not only a fairly recent phenomenon but also one that plays a critical role in maintaining divisions. In this work, we explore assumptions of separateness tied to culture, attempting to move beyond divisive categories of "culture" to re-envision diversity of thought and traditions as a shared resource to connect and enrich humanity.

Throughout human history, diversity and cultural exchange were the norm. Beginning with the mutual discovery of ancient river civilizations, cross-fertilization of cultural artifacts has enriched and rejuvenated societies and advanced humankind. The Sumerians along the Tigris and Euphrates rivers developed and shared mathematics, irrigation, and agricultural techniques with the Harappa civilization in the Indus valley and the ancient Egyptians in the Nile valley, where later Thales and other Greek sages would study. Diplomacy, along with trade and religion, played a boundary-spanning role in transmitting innovation. From the invention of the wheel to the discovery of penicillin to the appeal of iPhones, this trend continues. If anything, social media is accelerating cultural sharing on a global scale.

In contrast to millennia of cultural diversity and exchange, singular, nationally bounded cultures are a modern construct. As natural as the link between culture and "national identity" may seem today, that link was forged during 19th and 20th century state building.[52]

Culture made its debut at a unique juncture of Western history. Between 1750 and 1918, expansive kingdoms and empires began to dissolve, and the modern state emerged.[53] State sovereignty, which laid the basis for the inter-state system, meant establishing control over both land and people. Previously, empires such as the Hapsburg or Ottoman ruled over diverse ethnic and religious groups. Identities and loyalties were local. To shift loyalties and forge the nation-state, we see the emergence of nationalism and with it the ideal of cultural unification: "The people must be united; they must dissolve all internal divisions; they must be gathered together in a single historic territory . . . and share a single public culture.[54] Under the banner of nationalism, the idea of unified culture was created to appear natural. As one historian notes, "governments assiduously promoted myths of shared ancestry, despite obvious differences even in physical appearances."[55] National symbols such as flags and mottos, as well as myths and memories, were promoted to dissolve internal division.[56] Language emerged as a pivotal marker, integral to the "imagined community" that Anderson identifies.[57] As nationalism spread throughout Europe and North America, the norm of cultural unity and assimilation gradually replaced cultural diversity. Anderson's "imagined community" of virulent nationalism gradually glided into what Michael Billig called "banal nationalism," where national symbols became commonplace features interwoven into the social and political fabric.[58]

This idea of a distinctive national character closely parallels the academic discovery of "culture" as a conceptual scheme for defining as well as dividing. Sir Edward B. Tylor, a British anthropologist, introduced the term in 1871 as "a complex whole which includes knowledge, beliefs, arts, morals, laws, customs, and any other capabilities and habits."[59] This conception is remarkably similar to popular notions today. For individuals afloat in an era of dislocation wrought by globalization, evoking perceived shared cultural traits provides a stabilizing if illusory identity anchor.

Culture did not just coincide with nationalism. In *Culture and Society*, Raymond Williams links the spread of "culture" with industrialization and democracy.[60] Lila Abu-Lughod points out that the idea of culture flourished during the era of imperialism and colonization.[61] Academic practice, as she notes, "otherized" the people of study. Scholars worked to document cultural features, traits, beliefs, and behaviors. Cultures were given labels, making whole groups of people static entities to compare and contrast.[62] Over the years, academic research in disciplines as diverse as management, diplomacy, and communication cited "culture" and "national culture" to solidify the idea of separate groups. The result has too often produced stereotypes rather than cultural insights.[63]

The idea of culture as a static, fixed thing fit well *in theory* (if not reality) with the era's emerging state-centric, carved-up view of the world. But what appeared "natural" in the 19th and 20th centuries has become a liability in today's interconnected global world. Anthropologists have been among the most vocal critics.[64] As William Sewell observed more than two decades ago, "it is no longer possible to assume the world is divided up into discrete 'societies,' each with its corresponding, well-integrated 'culture.'"[65] Discussions of "hybridity," such as that of Homi Bhabha or Marwan Kraidy, highlight the problematic nature of singled culture and speak of blending to create expanded spaces of identity and meaning in the face of connectivity.[66]

This book eschews the conventional approach—based on assumptions of separateness—of comparing individual or Western and non-Western national cultures, communication, or diplomatic practices. Today the diversity within national borders may be as pronounced as it is across borders. Humanity-centered diplomacies assume connectedness and cross-fertilization of ideas. Expanding to a global mindset means shifting assumptions from culture as a fixed attribute of the state to diversity as a shared global resource of humanity-centered diplomacies.

Human Communication

The third pillar, communication, perhaps most epitomizes assumptions of separateness and is most in need of a humanity-level perspective—which is why it represents the core of this book. In this book, we break from the idea of "communication" in the singular and instead explore a pan-human view of communication based not on culture or national entities but on three distinct relational premises found in the human experience.

Over the past decade in researching this book, I have come to realize that the notion of a single "communication" is actually a forced vision. It assumes that actors are separate (rather than joined) and different (rather than similar). As we explore in Chapters 1 and 2, contemporary communication may masquerade as "universal," but in reality it represents only one vision of communication. It is a template or metaphor of separate and disparate entities: a sender and receiver, divided by an abyss which can only be imperfectly bridged. Different societies, cultures, and nations are but variations in this one template.

Intercultural communication is supposed to provide a "global" vision of communication. Yet the very term "intercultural" reinforces the idea of separate entities and disparate cultures and a mindset of separateness. The social-scientific understanding of intercultural communication draws heavily from culture and anthropology, resting in a cocoon of assumptions of individualism. Individualism, as many have noted, is shortsighted in that it overlooks larger social dynamics, focusing instead on the individual needs or purposes of communication: how to protect and preserve the individual autonomy through persuasion and control. Given the imperative of autonomy, power becomes an ever-present element of communication.

However, the greatest shortcoming assumption of individualism in contemporary communication is not the narrow focus on the individual goals per se but rather the unspoken time frame—past, present, and future—of the individual. Communication research has focused intensively on how to meet the individual goals within an individual time horizon. Public diplomacy has echoed this individual actor focus and narrow time horizon. What has been overlooked is the longer time frame—the evolutionary perspective of communication for humankind.

This evolutionary perspective on communication is the concern of this book. How does communication contribute to the survival and evolution of humanity? What role does communication play in our evolutionary capacity for collaboration? Speech and media tools, for example, are prominent dynamics in human communication, but there are other dimensions. Throughout this work, we will explore those dimensions through three complementary logics of communication.

I came to this broader evolutionary view of communication only as I put my "communication" books aside and began a wildly interdisciplinary exploration of what happens when humans come together. I found a distinction between conventional notions of communication and the human experience of communication. In the course of researching this book, I began with intercultural communication, as I had been trained in my studies in the United States. When I realized the glaring inconsistencies of the intercultural models, I turned to relations, and specifically relationalism, as a lens for viewing how humans communicate. The three primary relationship patterns—the individual, paired, and relational universe—in turn undergird the Individual, Relational, and Holistic logics of communication.

Initially, the relational patterns appeared to be tied to intellectual heritages. The Individual logic reflected the Greeks; the Relational logic echoed with the Mediterranean and greater Middle East; and the Holistic with Asia and Africa. However, the more I studied the heritages, the more I started seeing overlaps. For example, the value of harmony, which is prominent in ancient Chinese texts, is found in ancient Greeks texts, such as Isocrates's writings on *homonoia* in *Nicocles*.[67] Similarly, the value of individual agency and autonomy often associated with the Greeks is aptly captured in the Confucius saying from *The Analects* (9/26): "One may rob an army of its commander-in-chief; one cannot deprive the humblest man of his free will."[68]

These overlaps became glaring in the ancient cosmologies. Although the ancient societies were spread across different continents, similar themes emerged, notably the dual forces of chaos and harmony in birthing the cosmos. One might attribute the recurring idea of chaos to links among the ancient Greeks, Egypt, India, and Sumer, but this dual theme also appears in ancient Central and South America, Polynesia, and China. This string of similarities across the ancient cosmologies suggested something deeper about communication and relations. More remarkable still, elements of ancient cosmologies resonate with cutting-edge research. The ancient cosmologies spoke of "life energy" or "harmony of the spheres," of the earth, humans, and celestial bodies resonating in harmony, which is found in ideas of energy and vibrations of quantum physics.[69]

Neurobiological and social neuroscience research also offers insights for expanding other views of communication. If there is a remarkable coincidence in human relational patterns, creation myths, and intellectual heritages, humans appear to share underlying neuro-biological mechanisms that scientists link to our evolution.[70] These neurological and biological imperatives help shed light on some of the coincidental similarities found in ancient as well as modern societies. Even more remarkable—if not ironic—is to see emerging technologies, such as artificial intelligence and robotics, trying to emulate "human communication," and in the process stumbling over some of the same communication, relational, and even ethical dilemmas that consumed the ancients. Programming speech and language is relatively easy. Coordinating conversational turn-taking or empathetic cues that foster relations and community is a much greater challenge.

The core of this book focuses on sketching out the relational premises and dynamics of the three logics: Individual, Relational, and Holistic. The logics are inherently global and pan-human, resting on assumptions of connectivity and diversity. The goal of this work is to propose a model for global pan-human communication based on shared relational patterns, intellectual heritages, and neurobiological features that have contributed to the survival and evolution of the human species.

Identity Constellations

A final pillar of interrelated concepts is identity, which resonates across diplomacy, culture, and communication. In state-centric public diplomacy, identity is usually thought of at the macro level of singular, unified national identity and image. Much has been written on the cultivation of national image in the nation-branding literature.[71] Notably, macro-level conceptions aim to present a unified, cohesive identity—which is often rigid, overlooking internal diversity. "National identity" or "cultural or ethnic identity" suggest shared, definable traits among groups comprising a thousand, a million, or even a billion people. Such was the case of post-9/11 U.S. public diplomacy targeted at the "Islamic world," which suggested a monolithic view of the identity of 1.7 billion people. We know that, even within families, siblings have distinctive identities.

Popular discourse around such identities, once defined, can be rigid. Kwame Appiah described this tendency as the "Medusa syndrome."[72] Like Gorgon Medusa whose stares turned others into stone; so too can a narrow, fixated gaze on a singular identity transform human complexity into solidified stereotypes.

Humanity-centered diplomacies can depart from such rigid, macro-level categories, enabling a micro-level view of identity in public diplomacy. Such identity is multi-dimensional and dynamic. Each of the communication logics, for instance, offers different dimensions of what might be a constellation of identities. The Individual logic highlights the unique attributes that give each individual personal identity. The Relational logic highlights how our bonds to others create multiple relational identities such as "mother," or "spouse," or "colleague." The Holistic logic exposes another layer of identities tied to social roles as well as hierarchies. As scholars have long noted, individuals accrue diverse identities. In humanity-centered diplomacy, identity is dynamic and even fluid: when people interact, different aspects of identity become more and less salient according to the situation. Identities are local, grounded in immediate human bonds, and also global, inasmuch as what makes us human is shared worldwide. While each of us is as unique as our individual fingerprints, shared human traits tie us together.

Call to the Boundary Spanners

This book is written with a specific reader in mind: the boundary spanners. Noted diplomatic scholar Brian Hocking uses the term "boundary spanners" to suggest diplomats who serve as bridges spanning the boundaries of different nations, ideologies, interests, or traditions.[73] Traditionally, professional diplomats mediated relations between peoples and states. Wherever there are boundaries of identities to be crossed, says Costas Constantinou, there is diplomacy.[74] Professional diplomats represented the interests of states and negotiated at the state level, primarily behind closed doors.

That rather staid view of diplomacy—the boundary spanners about whom Hocking speaks—has changed. #Diplomacy, as Phillip Seib notes, is increasingly public, done under the glare of the media and public scrutiny.[75] Daryl Copeland speaks of "guerrilla diplomacy" for diplomats who are as comfortable in formal corridors of power as in the public bazaar.[76] Moreover, professional diplomats representing states have been joined by non-state actors, including civil society, corporations, and transnational advocacy networks, social entrepreneurs, and even citizen diplomats. As Robert Kelley argues, diplomacy is less about an institution, such as the diplomatic corps, and more about agency.[77]

Although some traditions associate boundaries with lines of demarcation, Boundary Spanners must not focus only on what separates us. Perspectives from other heritages can expand our associations. In Africa, for example, boundaries are often places of connection. Leo Otoide of the University of Benin explains how pre-colonial African diplomacy differed from European colonial powers:

In the traditional African society, the boundary did not imply as in the European sense a point of separation. Rather, it was seen as a point where the interest of one state attained a type of union with the interest of the other. It provided opportunities for interethnic contact since both communities could come together to offer common sacrifices at the boundary for their general good.[78]

As shared points of connection, boundaries were seen as more fluid than fixed. In traditional African societies, people flowed freely across agreed-upon boundaries, which were often locations for markets and meeting places.

In an age of globalization, Chris Rumford and Andrew Cooper suggest that growing interconnectivity is transforming traditional state borders into cosmopolitan borders.[79] Borders, they opine, "can be thought of as connective tissue" that offer opportunities for spanning overlapping loyalties rather than binary us-and-them dichotomies. As Box I.2 notes, boundary spanning is not about bridging or negotiating between separate parties. That assumption of separateness is of a mindset from the last century when the "other" implied differences rather than similarities. Boundary spanning in an age of connectivity will be driven by an ability to identify commonalities.

Box I.2

Boundary spanning is not about bridging or negotiating between separate parties. That assumption of separateness is of a mindset from the last century when the "other" implied differences rather than similarities. Boundary spanning in an age of connectivity will be driven by an ability to identify commonalities.

If diplomacy in the public realm is needed now more than ever, so too are Boundary Spanners to leverage diversity. Although diversity brings creativity and innovation, its familiar downside is friction, resistance, and frustration. That can lead some to retreat to like-minded groups, where communication is decidedly easier, but where creativity suffers.

This book is for the Boundary Spanners. It is a roadmap and a toolbox for tackling the dual global challenges of interconnectivity and diversity. It is for those who are willing to leave the think-alike comfort of familiarity and take on the challenge bridging differences to mediate diversity, facilitate communication, and engage in complex problem-solving for the benefit of all on our planet.

Overview

The goal of this book is to expand our vision of communication, and by extension public diplomacy, to a global perspective. That means moving beyond the mindset of separateness inherent in both international and intercultural conceptual schema. A global perspective spans the range of human variations, yet it cannot be divided into separate entities or categories. It is pan-human, all-inclusive, and indivisible.

This book is short, and deliberately so. My wish is that each time you pick up this book or scroll its pages, your vision of public diplomacies, human diversity, and communication expands a little more and grows a little broader.

The first chapter, "All Thumbs at Communication," looks at how the concurrent rise of public diplomacy with the proliferation of social media exposed the fallacy of a singular notion of "communication" and the countervailing forces of separateness in a climate of connectivity and diversity. The chapter explores how U.S. public diplomacy was a giant in the field of communication, yet by relying on a singular vision of communication, found its communication efforts falling flat or backfiring with global publics. The chapter introduces the three logics of communication and how relying on one vision of communication can produce blind spots that can make one clumsily "all thumbs" when communicating in a global arena.

Chapter 2, "A World of Relations, World of Communication," traces the backstory of the communication logics, beginning with the appeal of prominent intercultural models and the inconsistencies that plague them. In an effort to break out of the circular argument of using "communication" to define "communication," this chapter uses the analytical lens of relationalism to explore the many varied assumptions about "relationships" across intellectual heritages, beginning with individualism and moving to individuality and then relationality. For the Boundary Spanners, the chapter ends with questions about the validity of cultural models and shares ideas for traversing these ideas of individualism, individuality, and relationality.

The next three chapters explore the three communication logics as they appear in ancient times. While we tend to think of communication and public diplomacy as contemporary phenomena, they have always been foundational to societies—even in prehistory. Practices from the ancient world offer insights for the digital era.

For "Individual Logic—Aristotle's Legacy" (Chapter 3), we visit the public square or *agora* (Ἀγορά) of ancient Athens. We see Aristotle's legacy of rhetoric in notions of the individual communicator, often a stateman, engaged in a rhetorical battle to win hearts and minds—a window into the Individual Expressive logic.

For "Relational Logic—A Royal Bond of Brotherhood" (Chapter 4), we venture to the ancient Near East and a brotherhood of the kings of Egypt, Assyria, and Mesopotamia. Their reciprocal exchange of gifts, greetings, and brides, known as "Amarna diplomacy," reveal the Relational or Associative Logic.

For "Holistic Logic—Cosmic Circles" (Chapter 5), we explore the cosmologies and cosmograms that ancients used to explain the universe. Their elaborate creation myths and icons echo the holistic premise of the relational universe, with its focuses on maintaining the integrity and continuity of the whole.

Chapter 6, "Enhancing Collaboration—Speech, Emotion, and Synchrony," returns to the question of how to leverage diversity to enhance our capacity for cooperation. It examines each logic's forte and then, through a technique of blending, adds the dynamics of the other logics to expand our capacity for collaboration. Blending the diverse elements of the three logics brings us full circle from the all-thumbs communication of a mindset of separateness to an expansive, pan-human vision of communication in a diverse, connected global arena. The final chapter, "Boundary Spanning Agenda for Global Collaboration," concludes with key takeaways and implications, as well as future trends for globalizing communication and public diplomacy.

1

All Thumbs at Communication

"Americans are brilliant at communication. Why in the world we're all thumbs in this particular area just strikes me as one of the anomalies of history," exclaimed an exasperated Senator Richard Lugar, Chair of the U.S. Senate Foreign Relations Committee, two years after the attacks of September 11, 2001.[1] Lugar's frustration with American struggles with public diplomacy was understandable. In the aftermath of the 9/11 attacks that shocked the nation, the United States launched one of the most aggressive communication campaigns in its history. U.S. public diplomacy issued a "Factbook" on terrorism, created a national branding campaign, published a glossy lifestyle magazine, and launched several radio stations and a satellite television venture. But despite these efforts, America had not won hearts and minds; instead, anti-American sentiment had intensified and spread globally.

Fast forward to a decade later and replace government-sponsored mass media tools with a proliferation of mobile devices and digital and social media in the hands of the public. Terror groups now were trying to woo youth in the West. The U.S. battle for hearts and minds turned to counter-narrative strategies and sophisticated infographics. Yet, despite the immediacy of the terrorism threat as well as the concerted communication efforts, the results seem uncannily similar—and unwanted. Western and non-Western youth alike appear alienated by government communication. While the ideological divide of "us versus them" remained, the targeted publics were no longer only foreign but domestic as well.

How could a country's best efforts to communicate produce such unwanted and indeed unexpected results? In this age of global communication technology, with decades of communication research, how could a communication giant be all thumbs?

The failures of U.S. public diplomacy were painful—but, as this chapter argues, instrumental in exposing buried assumptions about "communication." Since the founding of communication as a contemporary field of study, ideas about what it means to "communicate" have spread as if they were universal. While scholars widely acknowledge that different cultures have different worldviews, these worldviews were inserted into a template that provided variations of patterns, styles, and approaches. Such an approach never questions the validity of the actual template as a universal model.

After 9/11, the increased public diplomacy activity by states to communicate with publics, combined with a rapid proliferation of social media tools that allowed publics to communicate with each other as well, provided a fresh vantage point to reconsider human communication in real time and on a global scale. This chapter examines this unique intersection, but also cautions Boundary Spanners who seek to bridge difference as well as similarities to be alert to blind spots.

More Global Mis-Communication

When it comes to diplomacy in the public arena, many officials assume that all nations, societies, and publics share the same notion of what it means to communicate—an assumption that has gone unchallenged. Nations continue to communicate furiously, and yet often feel painfully misunderstood by global publics and other nations. The United States was not alone in trying and often failing to make its case to foreign publics in recent decades.

In late 2004, the Danish government found itself at the center of an international communication firestorm over political cartoons published in an independent newspaper. Where Danish officials saw a free-speech issue, many Muslims saw a vilification of Prophet Mohammed. The more the Danish government tried to explain its position, the more discontent it appeared to generate. Foreign publics reacted with an intensity that was neither expected nor entirely understood. Communication was no longer just about messages but also about images and identities. A decade later, on the streets of Paris, a similar narrative battle would take hold with the hashtag #JeSuisCharlie to express solidarity with the violent attack on the satirical magazine *Charlie Hebdo* after it published cartoons of Prophet Mohammed. Within days, counter hashtags emerged.

Further east, Chinese public diplomacy officials have also found themselves struggling to understand how their best intentions could be so misunderstood and maligned. In anticipation of the global spotlight surrounding their hosting of the 2008 Olympics, the Chinese government rallied the domestic public to put on its best face. No detail appeared to be overlooked, as even Beijing taxi drivers were given instructions on how to interact with foreign visitors. Much to the government's surprise, not only were their efforts mocked, but such attention to details was presented in foreign media as examples of the country's authoritarian style.

Why were the best efforts of countries to communicate on a global level result in unwanted and unexpected outcomes? In the past, would-be communicators have blamed problems on cultural differences, but officials surely knew about such gaps. Research on public diplomacy was also mushrooming after 2001. The problem may not have been just a matter of cultural differences in style or content; as we've seen, various countries had many different styles and approaches, yet all struggled. These global examples suggest a deeper, more fundamental disconnect over what constitutes and defines "communication." We can probe this possibility of buried assumptions further by turning specifically to U.S. communication, which was instrumental in establishing the field and has been a global leader in communication.

Public Diplomacy Window

In the early years after 9/11, the coinciding rise of states' activity of public diplomacy with the public use of social media, which allowed nations and publics to interact in real time, provided a window into the global miscommunication not only from the government perspective but, more importantly, from the public's perspective. During research for my first book, *Battles to Bridges*, on U.S. public diplomacy in the Arab and Islamic world, it became increasingly clear that U.S. officials and the public appeared to have fundamentally different views of "communication."[2] U.S. officials appeared to be operating on the assumption that "communication" was about designing and delivering information that could persuade or win over an audience. The problem, they thought, was lack of information. As then–U.S. President Bush declared: "I am amazed that there is such misunderstanding about what our country is about. We have to do a better job of making our case."[3]

As noted previously, U.S. public diplomacy immediately launched an intensive communication campaign targeted at publics in the Arab and Islamic world. The factbook "The Terrorist Network" on the al-Qaeda network was just the start. It was translated into more than thirty languages and distributed through U.S. embassies worldwide. Under the direction of the new Under Secretary of State for Public Diplomacy, the United States developed the first-of-its-kind "Shared Values" branding campaign and a web-based electronic pamphlet, "Muslim Life in America,"[4] featuring mini-documentaries, photos, statistics, articles, and statements by American Muslims designed to counter perceptions that America was not a friendly environment for Muslims.[5] A new Arabic-language radio station, Radio Sawa (*sawa* meaning "together" in Arabic), was called the "star" of the U.S. efforts.[6] The new station featured an unprecedented mix of 50% Western and 50% Arabic pop music with brief newscasts designed to appeal to Arab youth. In one of the most ambitious and costly ventures, a satellite television station, Al-Hurra ("The Free One" in Arabic), was launched to counter the popular Al-Jazeera station.[7] There was even a glossy lifestyle magazine named "Hi," which was intended to open a conversation with Arab youth.[8]

The problem was no longer a matter of not having enough information; there was a flood of information. All of the initiatives were met with controversy and criticism.[9] It seemed the more that the United States adapted its communication to fit the audience, the more anti-American sentiment grew. Public opinion polls showed the extent of the damage.[10] According to Pew Research, support for America dropped among the Muslim population in Nigeria from 72% to 38%; Indonesia dropped from 61% to 15%; Turkey from 30% to 15%; and Jordan from 25% to 1% between the summers of 2002 and 2003.[11] Many found U.S. communication alienating and even offensive.[12] As Rami Khouri, a prominent Lebanese journalist, summed up the sentiment, "Where do they [the United States] get this stuff? And why do they keep insulting us like this?"[13]

Concerns emerged over how the U.S. communication style presented information. Critics chided U.S. public diplomacy for its one-way, media-driven approach, which seemed culturally out of alignment with the intended audience.[14] America's aggressive efforts to get its message out, as Nancy Snow noted, had fueled perceptions of U.S. arrogance.[15] The prominent Council on Foreign Relations expressed concerns over perceptions of Americans as "unwilling or unable to engage in cross-cultural dialogue" and stressed the importance of listening as way of reducing negative perceptions.[16] Nicholas J. Cull (2008) increased the salience of listening by including it as the first element of his much-cited taxonomy of public diplomacy.[17] In another early and prominent piece on post-9/11 public diplomacy, Geoffrey Cowan and Amelia Arsenault called for a move in public diplomacy from monologue to dialogue and collaboration.[18]

U.S. officials tried to adopt a more relational approach that emphasized engagement strategies with the public.[19] "Engagement" soon made its way into U.S. public diplomacy discussions after a prominent State Department commission report inserted engagement into the traditional definition of public diplomacy: "the role of public diplomacy has taken on critical importance in the effort to understand, inform, engage, and influence people."[20] The U.S. State Department soon after included "engage" as one of the "Four Es" (along with exchange, educate, and empower) of U.S. public diplomacy. Youth engagement components were added to English-language programs, and new programs, such as the "Partnerships for Learning" (P4L), were developed for high school students from the Middle East and South Asia.[21]

The term "engagement" was also used to suggest a more relational and participatory approach to building relationships with the public. Kathy Fitzpatrick called relationship management the core of U.S. public diplomacy.[22] Engagement fit with the relational turn that characterized what was called "new" public diplomacy.[23]

Despite the vocal claims of "engagement" in policy documents and statements, the results were less glowing. Rather than creating the intended dialogue,

U.S. public diplomacy appeared stuck on monologue, even when using social media.[24] Despite the concerted communication effort, America's favorability remained low, particularly across the Islamic world. Comor and Bean called the gulf between the conceptualization of engagement and its actual application a "dangerous delusion."[25]

The mismatch between U.S. efforts and audience response suggested that the solution to the communication problem lay deeper than just increasing the quantity of information or even modifying communication styles, messages, or approaches. While many have critiqued U.S. public diplomacy from a policy perspective, one of the central tenets of public diplomacy is to communicate policy.

There is also an important question left unanswered. On the surface, U.S. public diplomacy had followed the theoretical prescripts for communicating with global publics by studying the audience and adapting messages and approach accordingly. The audience was perceived as having a "relational" worldview, so U.S. public diplomacy adopted a relational approach to communication. What should have worked, in communication theory, was not working in communication practice with global audiences. This gap between "communication" theory and practice is significant. The problem appeared to be more than a matter of different communication *approaches*, and instead suggested fundamentally different notions of *communication* itself.

Hidden Communication Template

The mishaps of U.S. public diplomacy were more than miscalculations. We are witnessing an evolving global paradigm shift in assumptions about communication. Models and theories of communication—which emerged as a field of study in the United States in the mid-20th century—have spread from the U.S. context around the globe, with the assumption that they were universal. Much as in the case of U.S. public diplomacy, scholars have attacked one-way communication, arguing instead for a more dynamic view of communication as a co-creational, relational process. While the shift to more relational perspectives intensified with the rise of social media, it also coincided with the globalization of communication and social science research. The dominance long held by U.S. scholars is expanding to include those originating beyond U.S. shores.

Pioneering scholars in non-Western communication, such as Molefi Asante, Guo-Ming Chen, Wimal Dissanayake, Shelton Gunaratne, Satoshi Ishii, Youich Ito, Min-Sun Kim, Mawlid Mawlana, Yoshitaka Miike, Silva Waisbrod, Georgette Wang, Kim Yun Young, June Ock Yum, and others have long questioned many of the assumptions and applications of dominant theories of communication.[26] These scholars raised concerns about individualism and proposed more relation-centered perspectives. The field witnessed the rise of Western and non-Western divisions of communication scholarship.

Remarkably, the dominance of ideas of what "communication" is appears to be quite similar, at least on the surface, resting on the notion of communication as a process of exchange of ideas, information, or symbols between entities. This core focus on exchange between entities has been a thread running through contemporary communication since its founding.

Wilbur Schramm, often called the father of communication, wrote, "In its simplest form, the communication process consists of a sender, a message, and a receiver."[27] In one of the most widely cited early communication studies, scholar Frank Dance identified fifteen main themes from definitions of communication. Yet upon closer examination, all suggest variations on communication as a process of transmitting and receiving information between separate parties.[28] More recently, the World Council of Social Science, which includes international scholars from multiple disciplines, defined communication as "the study of verbal and non-verbal *exchanges* of ideas and information" (emphasis mine).[29] Similarly, in its recent conference, the International Communication Association (ICA), the largest international professional association devoted to communication study, focused on what it called communication power: "Communicating power is about communicating—both *sending and receiving*—powerfully or forcefully" (italics mine).[30] The National Communication Association (NCA), the second largest professional association of communication scholars, had an image of a "transactional model" of communication that featured both parties as "sender/receivers".

These scholarly definitions align closely with the popular definition available in the Merriam Webster dictionary online (see Box 1.1).

The assumption of communication as *sending* and *receiving messages* was carried over and remains central to intercultural communication scholarship. The most popular intercultural communication text, *Intercultural Communication: A Reader*, recently published its 40th anniversary edition,

---

Box 1.1

Communication: the act or process of using words, sounds, signs, or behaviors to express or exchange information or to express your ideas, thoughts, feelings, etc., to someone else: a message that is given to someone: a letter, telephone call, etc.

Communications: the ways of sending information to people by using technology

Source: Merriam Webster Online Dictionary

offering this foundational definition: "Intercultural communication occurs whenever a person of one culture *sends a message* to be processed by a person from a different culture."[31] Another popular text by Chen and Starosta introduces the idea of relationships but retains the assumption of exchange: "Intercultural communication is an interdetermining process in which we develop a mutually dependent relationship by *exchanging* symbols" (emphasis mine).[32] Even international communication scholars who are critical of the U.S. communication models use similar language in defining intercultural communication. The eminent Japanese intercultural scholar Satoshi Ishii advocated for a distinctive Asian perspective, yet defined intercultural communication as "the culturally interrelated cognitive, affective, and behavioral activity process of interactively *sending and receiving* verbal and nonverbal messages between or among persons from mutually different cultural backgrounds" (emphasis mine).[33]

If we look closely, this sender-message-receiver assumption represents in effect a hidden template, which gets modified according to different worldviews. Variations of salient features of the sender, or the message, or the receiver get plugged into the template to produce different communication patterns. The patterns change, but the template remains. For example, if one plugs a U.S. "sender" into the template, various characteristics would generate a particular profile of communication behaviors, perceptions, and messages. Plugging an Arab "receiver" into the template would generate a host of different communication behaviors. These differences between the sender and the receiver help explain the inevitable problems in intercultural communication between U.S. senders and Arab receivers. On the surface, the template is eminently logical.

Because cultural differences between the sender and receiver were seen as the root problem of communication misunderstandings—not the more basic sender-receiver template—research focused on cultural differences between senders and the receivers. Over the years, scholars have identified broad cultural patterns or continuums to help explain cultural differences between senders and receivers of different cultures. Prominent cross-cultural models, which are discussed in more detail in Chapter 2, include individualism-collectivism,[34] activity-orientation and being-orientation,[35] direct and indirect,[36] and oral and literate.[37]

Despite the extensive use of these models, pronounced inconsistencies and Western cultural biases have surfaced. For example, one of the most cited and extensively used intercultural models is Individualism/Collectivism (IDV/COL). Individualism, at one end of the cultural spectrum, privileges individual perspectives, actions, and goals. Collectivism, at the opposite end, privileges the group perspective, actions, and goals. The model's powerful explanatory value helps drive its popularity,[38] as well as controversy.[39] The dichotomous nature of individualism/collectivism, for example, suggests a binary, mutually exclusive view of cultures.[40] Yet, scholars have found individualistic traits existing in societies labeled as collectivist,[41] and individualistic cultures displaying collectivist features.[42] The depersonalized "collective" has been faulted for failing to capture the personal nature of relations.[43]

Most important for our discussion here, when one plugs these IDV/COL variations into the sender-message-receiver template, it does not always result in eliminating communication problems. In fact, it can exacerbate the problems by producing an overlay of cultural stereotypes.

Without calling Western-centric models templates, scholars have introduced Afro-centric[44] and Asia-centric models of communication.[45] These studies provide rich insight into culturally mediated conceptions of communication. However, they too suffer in one critical respect. Their geo-cultural regional specificity raises the dilemma of being too narrow; the particular perspective only applies to the region from which it originated. If these perspectives of communication are rendered so different that they are not applicable to other cultural regions, how can different nations, cultures, or publics communicate? Is Huntington's "clash of civilization" really a hopeless "clash of communication"? It would seem that in order for communication between people of different cultural backgrounds to interact, there would be shared elements. There must be overlap, as Ghanaian philosopher Kwasi Wiredu opined, for communication to occur.[46]

As a result of these dual and at times dueling perspectives of "communication," scholars appeared caught in extensive comparative cross-cultural research that serves to reinforce rather than expand our understanding of communication. As Georgette Wang remarked, "over the past few decades, globalization of the field has basically stopped at the data level, and seldom reaches into the realms of methodology, theory, or paradigm."[47] What is needed is a new approach for breaking out of current theoretical molds and viewing the communication experience from different—as well as shared—vantage points. The next section suggests the idea of relationalism as a tool for such an approach.

Breaking out of Assumptions

In this study, I take a radically different approach to communication by discarding all assumptions about "communication." After studying and teaching communication theory for more than four decades, that was not easy to do. But, as I found, using *either* Western *or* non-Western "communication" to understand how people understood "communication" only produced circular arguments. More critically, neither perspective intersected with the other to provide an expansive, global understanding of communication and neither enabled an escape from the template. I found myself (and the field) left with an endless variation of senders and receivers with all their cultural misunderstandings—never addressing the question of *why were there senders and receivers in the first place*?

So, I paused to re-think communication.

Beginning in 2010, I decided to set all notions of communication aside and embark on a global, interdisciplinary tour through the world's major intellectual heritages to try to understand what happened when people came together. What did they focus on? What terms did they use and how did they use them? As Wimal Dissanayake observed in his pioneering work on Buddhist ideas of communication, "communication is the life blood of society." Thus, he reasoned that in order for ancient societies to survive, their "cultures contained traditions of thought which address the questions of human communication."[48]

Initially, I started with contemporary "communication"-related literature in U.S. scholarship. Then I moved to non-Western scholarship, then to specific cultural regions and intellectual heritages. The further I moved from U.S. academic shores, the more frequently the word "relationships" kept surfacing. Not only were discussions of relationships pronounced, they were also quite varied in their focus and assumptions. That observation raised the possibility of using relations—specifically human relations to oneself, others, and society—as a means for understanding both the distinctive and yet shared notions of communication.

During my trek, I came across "relationalism," an analytical lens that Western and Asian scholars have used to explore the nuances of relationship and relational dynamics.[49] Relationalism provides an analytical lens for what Krog described as learning "to read interconnectedness."[50] Using "relationalism" revealed a world of relations, and with it a world of communication.

Relationalism exposed the long shadow of individualism within U.S. ideological thinking and scholarship. As many have noted, individualism has been a defining and enduring feature of the United States, linked to survival in its founding and settling.[51] Alexis de Tocqueville first coined the term during his visit to America in the 1830s. Nearly two centuries later, despite the influx of immigrants from different cultures, individualism continues to distinguish Americans in global attitude surveys.[52]

While the relational assumption of individualism was pronounced in the U.S. context, notions about relations appeared to be much more varied than most contemporary scholarship assumes, as we discussed in the next chapter. Outside the U.S. context, scholarship is laced with assumptions that individuals are not separate from others but inherently connected. Scholars found that communication practitioners in twenty-five European countries tended not to distinguish between communication and relationships, using the terms interchangeably.[53] Latin American scholarship's relational emphasis on the family as the center of social gravity[54] suggests that relationships do not occur in a social vacuum but are part of a circle of other relations, or relational spheres. Across the café cultures of the Mediterranean and the greater Middle East, the affective dimension comes to the fore in defining relational connections. The early Arab sociologist Ibn Khaldun (1332–1406) suggested the concept of *assabiyah*, or "group feeling" and "group consciousness."[55] Relational bonds were emotional bonds.

Venturing through pan-African traditions, one gets a sense of the relational universe of humankind reflected in the idea of *ubuntu*, which suggests "the interconnected humanness" and that a person is a person through other persons.[56] Traveling on to South Asia, scholars reflected on Western notions of "human *and* society" and "human *in* society" as distinct and separate entities, from an Indian view of "human-society," as an inseparable, symbiotic relationship.[57] A salient assumption of East Asian scholarship was the complexity of relationships, including relational differentiation and hierarchy. For example, the Five Cardinal Relations found in Confucian philosophy—parent/child; elder sibling/younger sibling; husband/wife, friend/friend; ruler/subjects—are different from each other, like the fingers on one's hand. In this context, rather than using communication to "create" or "build" relations, one uses communication to navigate a relational universe.[58]

As I continued on my trek of intellectual heritages and encountered an expanding array of nuanced relational assumptions and configurations, I found the idea of relational dichotomies—relations/no relations, or individual/collective—increasingly suspect. Those dichotomies exposed a missing third dimension, namely, the paired relation.[59] Relationally, people don't jump from the autonomous individual to the anonymous "collective" or even "mass" audience; rather, they form intimate bonds with others. These intimate relations provide the foundation for the larger relational constellation of society in much the same way that the relational bond of marriage between two individual creates relational bonds between the extended families, and relational bonds between the families becomes interwoven into the larger relational constellation of society. Even complex social networks such as *guanxi* in China appear to be based on the foundational dyadic pairing.[60]

What also became increasingly clear in this exploration was a realization that, as assumptions about relations changed, so too did assumptions about communication. If one assumed that individuals are separate, then the necessity of sending something between separate parties may appear as the only logical explanation for communication. However, if people are not separate but instead are inherently joined, the need for sending anything makes little if any sense. Instead of focusing on separate individuals and how to connect them, communication is fundamentally about the relationship. The pivotal role of the relationship in shaping communication is why in some research traditions, such as Europe, relations and communication are used interchangeably. Alternatively, if one assumes that individuals are connected with others within a larger relational universe, then communication competence is not about individual expression but contextual and relational sensitivity.

The link between assumptions about relations and assumptions about communication helped explain the "all thumbs" observation of U.S. communication efforts: if the relational assumption of individualism is the exception rather than the rule, then contemporary "communication" study might also be an exception and have limited effectiveness in the global arena. Although contemporary communication scholarship, with its U.S. contextual bias, may be *the dominant explanation of* communication, the variety of relational assumptions suggested that it is not the only logical explanation.

Three Logics of Communication

What ultimately surfaced from this global tour of cultural heritages and interdisciplinary scholarship were three distinctive, co-existing, and global views of "relations," which in turn suggested equally credible logics of communication. Each logic stems from one of three foundational conceptions of relationships: no relations, paired relations, and holistic relational structures. Each relational premise suggests a web of interconnected assumptions and dynamics that are so airtight as to make communication appear logical or even the only reasonable explanation of "communication."

One logic, the Individual logic, rests on the paradoxical relational premise of no relations. This assumption of no relations directs attention to the singular individual and, by extension, the individual's attributes and skills. Individual agency is critical; the individual *communicator* is responsible for *communicating* or expressing himself. Because each individual is separate from the other, communication is by necessity a process of exchange (Figure 1.1). The assumption of exchange is mirrored in the importance attached to message content and message delivery (i.e., medium), as echoed in Marshall McLuhan's prominent dictum, "The medium is the message."[61] Because the Individual logic rests on the communication dynamics of self-expression, this logic may be qualified as the Expressive logic.

A second logic, the Relational logic, rests on the premise that humans are inherently connected to others as relational beings. Because this logic presupposes a relational link of some kind, the communication focus shifts from the

Figure 1.1 Individual logic of communication. Author-supplied line art.

Figure 1.2 Relational logic of communication. Author-supplied line art.

individual to the dyadic, paired relation. The infinity sign (Figure 1.2) captures the notion of communication participants being inherently joined. The communication weight in this logic falls where the eye falls—on the center overlapping bond. In the Relational logic, the quality of the relational bond acts to define the nature of communication, and the nature of the relationship in turn defines communication. Thus, the concepts of communication and relationship become logically interchangeable. Additionally, because of the powerful influence of the relational bond on communication, the salient dynamics in this communication logic are those that define, maintain, and strengthen the relational bond. These include critical contact points, co-presence, emotion, perspective-taking, reciprocity, and symbolism. In that the Relational logic presupposes fellowship and association, and equates communication to the nature of that association, this logic might be qualified as the Associative logic.

A third communication logic, the Holistic logic, moves from the dyadic or paired relational focus to a relational universe that includes all relations. Here communication rests on the relational premise that individuals are embedded in a complex, pre-existing relational structure.[62] The familiar yin-yang symbol (Figure 1.3) reflects this relational whole: whereas the Individual logic may focus on the black and white as two separate opposing entities, and the Relational logic may see a complementary pair of male and female, the Holistic logic may see but one circle.

Because this holistic relational structure precedes the existence of the individual, the relational constellation shapes communication for all individuals. Also, because the relational structure is based on inherent connections to others, the Holistic logic includes dynamics from the Relational logic that help maintain the bonds of paired relations as well as additional dynamics that help maintain the integrity and continuity of the larger relational structure. It is noteworthy that one cannot rely solely on verbal dynamics; action and inter-action are required. These inactive communication dynamics include: expanding connectivity, preserving diversity, practicing contextual sensitivity, mutually adapting (synchrony), change and continuity; and cooperative orientation. Because communication rests on maintaining the integrity of the whole, or a harmonious

Figure 1.3 Holistic logic of communication. Author-supplied line art, adapted from yin-yang.svg, released to public domain by Gregory Maxwell. https://commons.wikimedia.org/wiki/File:Yin_yang.svg

balance among differing elements, the Holistic logic might be qualified as the Harmony logic.

These visual representations underscore the distinctiveness of the three logics and their relational premises. Yet, as the yin-yang symbol illustrates, it is possible for each logic to look at the same phenomenon and make different relational assumptions. This tendency to view the same phenomenon but make different relational assumptions, and by extension communication assumptions, helps explain why each logic assumes its logic is "obvious" to all. Indeed, the relational formations—individual, paired, and relational whole—of each premise are obvious and ever-present in the human experience. So, too, are the communication dynamics. This shared but distinctive aspect of human relations is what also makes communication shared but distinctive among different intellectual heritages and traditions.

For the Boundary Spanners

Senator Lugar's observation about the United States being "a communication giant" but "all thumbs" in communicating with others was astute. U.S. public diplomacy was vigorously communicating with global publics under the assumption that there was only one vision of communication. But the ongoing struggles to be understood suggest that it was contending with multiple understandings of communication—as well as the possibility of conceptual blind spots. Rather than having a global perspective, U.S. public diplomacy appeared to be locked into a singular, narrow vision.

This chapter opened with the failings of state actors as they tried to span the boundaries of diplomacy in the global public arena. However, as mentioned in the Introduction, the need for boundary spanning in the global arena is no longer reserved solely for state actors. For humanity-centered diplomacies, non-state actors from civil society, corporations, and even individual citizens play a pivotal role in mediating between identities and navigating cultural differences.

To take on that challenge, Boundary Spanners will need to expand their awareness, knowledge, and competence across the three communication logics outlined previously. The chapters ahead address that need by discussing each of the three distinctive logics, highlighting their relational premise and salient dynamics in more detail. First, however, let's highlight several key points about the logics that help bypass the communication traps of Western and Eastern scholarship mentioned earlier, which can inadvertently keep one limited to a national perspective and cause one to miss the global picture.

Distinctive Logics, Not Variations of Styles

First, the logics are fundamentally distinctive rationales for understanding communication based on their underlying relational premise. The Individual logic is at present the dominant logic in contemporary communication studies, and by extension public diplomacy. The Individual logic's dominance may make it appear universal, obscuring the other logics' distinctiveness and legitimacy.[63] But the Relational and Holistic logics are not merely non-individual variations of the dominant Individual logic. It is not about the sender or the receiver; individual self or relational self. Because Relational and Holistic logics represent distinctive views of communication, the Individual logic cannot overcome communication hurdles by tweaking messaging strategies, narratives, or approach. To view the logics as different relational worldviews or patterns only produces *variations* of the Individual logic and restricts public diplomacy.

Boundary Spanners need to focus on underlying relational premises—not superficial differences in messages or approaches—so as not to slip into that dominant, Individual logic. U.S. public diplomacy reflected the underlying premise of the Individual logic that views entities as separate. It has thus focused on designing and delivering messages to try to "create" relations or "engage" with other entities, in the case of U.S. public diplomacy, the publics in the Arab world. However, not all of those publics shared the assumption of the Individual logic of separate entities. Many assumed the premise of the Relational logic, which views communication through the lens of the relational bond. The nature and strength of the relationship between the parties give meaning to the words and actions. Viewed from the lens of the Relational logic, what made U.S. communication meaningful to these publics was the legacy of U.S. involvement in the region and the cultivated relations with the region's leaders, which were sometimes at the expense of relations with the people. This deeper relational premise for understanding communication is what U.S. public diplomacy missed and why it was so out of alignment.

Mutually Enhancing, Not Mutually Exclusive

Second, in a break from conventional thinking, the logics are not mutually exclusive but, as we see in Chapter 6, mutually enhancing. Contemporary (Western) communication has tended to view cultures and even countries through a lens of differences that often leads to contrasting opposites. Intercultural models, such as Individualism/Collectivism discussed earlier, may suggest a continuum. However, in comparative studies, one culture characteristically seems to fall at one end of the spectrum, with its cultural "opposite" at the other end. Countries or cultures with opposite tendencies are seen as naturally conflicting.

While the logics are distinctive, based on the relational premises, they are inherently co-existing because the three relational premises represent the three basic relational forms common to human societies. The three relational forms— the individual, the paired dyad, and the larger universe—are foundational to the functioning of human societies. Because these relational forms co-exist, so too do the logics. A focus on the individual does not necessitate excluding the social dimension. Not only are these relational forms co-existent, but so too are the dynamics (e.g., messages, emotions, synchrony, etc.). Messages are not exclusive to the Individual logic any more than emotions are exclusive to the Relational logic.

Boundary Spanners must therefore move beyond "either/or" thinking about human diversity. Rather than viewing differences as opposites, they might instead be necessary complements that help round out a global vision. The Individual logic might be faulted for being too focused on messaging and miss relational cues. Yet, the Relational and Holistic logics may also suffer from limitations if they focus too narrowly on the relational aspects at the expense of messaging and media strategies. For instance, China missed effective messaging strategies for the international media during the 2008 Olympics. It has since devoted energy to building its "discourse power."[64]

Global, Not Geo-Cultural

The logics are distinct in themselves, overlapping in their presence, and global in their resonance with diverse publics. In another departure from the dominant thinking about communication—both Eastern and Western— the logics do not appear to be the product or exclusive domain of any one country or intellectual heritage. One of the most remarkable discoveries in researching this book was seeing how the very same works that Eastern or Western scholars cite to highlight defining features of one particular human society also include ideas that are supposedly defining features of other societies, even supposedly cultural opposites. For example, Asian scholars cite Confucius' *The Analects* when speaking about the importance of relations in society. Yet Harry Triandis, who wrote extensively on the individualism/collectivism divide, noted: "When reading Confucius one is struck by the extent to which some of his statements urged people to be individualists."[65] Indeed, one finds the importance of individual agency. Central to Confucian thinking, alongside the notion of harmony, is the idea of self-culti-vation. It is through diligently cultivating oneself that the individual can achieve harmony within the self, with others, and ultimately with the cosmos. Another saying from *The Analects* reflects the importance of individual agency and voli-tion: "You can capture a general from three armies, but you cannot capture the free will of a single man."[66]

Not only are elements of individualism present in ancient Eastern philos-ophy, but elements traditionally associated with Asian cultures can be found in the ancient Greek texts that scholars tie primarily and sometimes exclusively to Western cultures. The Greeks, for example, whose works inspired the rig-orous pursuit of truth through intensive questioning, known in Western legal studies as the "Socratic method," also wrote about harmony, or "*homonoia*."[67] Isocrates' discussions of chorus laid a foundation for choric communication, which relies on synchronous verbal and/or nonverbal action that promote har-mony. Choric communication was successfully deployed in the 2008 U.S. pres-idential campaign to rally disparate individual voter groups into a cohesive whole.[68]

For Boundary Spanners, the legacy of ancient ideas and the wealth of con-temporary ones about communication provide ample resources for globalizing public diplomacy. Rather than circumscribing observations of cultural traits to a particular geo-cultural region, a more advantageous approach is to transfer and even combine those insights to creative applications that is pan-human and in a way that enhances the capacity for collaboration. We do just that in Chapter 6.

Guarding against Blind Spots

A final critical step in rethinking communication is recognizing one's own preference for a particular logic. Each of us has a preference or strength in one of the logics. A focus on message, media, or individual actors, for instance, suggests a preference for the Individual logic. A focus on emotions, nonverbal behaviors, or reciprocity that strengthen the relational bond suggests a preference for the Relational logic. A focus on expanding relations, contextual awareness, or interaction synchrony within relational universe suggests a preference for the Holistic logic.

It is important to recognize such preferences because unrecognized preferences tend to become strengths over time through their constant use and mastery. Yet such strengths can become so dominant that that they create blind spots, obscuring the vision and awareness of the other logics. When a preference becomes so dominant that it obscures the other logic, that strength becomes a liability. A strong preference for the Individual logic can create the blind spot that casts the relations or interactions of the other logics as features of the message, media, or actor. Rather than perceiving relations or actions per se, they are viewed in terms of spoken words or text and analyzed through the lens of discourse.

A strong preference for the Relational logic can ignore explicit messaging attempts in a futile effort to manipulate relational dynamics. A strong preference for the Holistic logic can precipitate attention to relational dynamics that appears overwhelming and controlling to others. As the U.S. "all thumbs" experience demonstrated, a forte in one logic will not compensate for a blind spot that obscures the other logics. Sophisticated efforts to perfect message or narrative (critical to the Individual logic) will not be enough if they overlook the relational bond (critical to the Relational logic) or larger relational structure (critical to the Holistic logic).

For Boundary Spanners to be effective in a global context, they likely must develop awareness of their preferences and blind spots before they can expand to a global vision and cultivate a competency in the other logics. A truly globalized view of communication, and by extension public diplomacy, reflects awareness and competency across the logics. In Chapter 6, we touch upon several national leaders who garnered wide and favorable international recognition. Nelson Mandela, who was one of them, was the most recognized icon globally of the 20th century.[69] He also appeared to be a master of the three logics, demonstrating a keen awareness of the underlying relational premises that define the human experience and that make communication meaningful to people globally.

Summary

This chapter has exposed an underbelly of buried cultural assumptions in public diplomacy, which can keep diplomats and scholars locked into narrow national perspectives that miss the global public dimension of diplomacy today. Breaking with a tradition that views other perspectives on communication and diplomacy as variations on the theme of senders and receivers, or as complex models exclusive to specific geo-cultural regions, this chapter offered insights into three distinctive, overlapping, and global logics of communication. Because the three visions are based on basic relational formations that support all human societies, all three perspectives are necessary and complementary to each other. As I have argued, no one logic is universal in its ability to capture what makes communication meaningful to diverse publics. Moreover, a lack of awareness or a dependence on one logic can overshadow the other logics and create blind spots in global communication. Understanding how these logics overlap and what we can learn from each is key to developing an expansive global vision of communication. This broad vision is the basis for globalizing public diplomacy. Taken together, these logics hold the communication key to public diplomacy's emerging role in finding similarities, mediating identities, negotiating differences, and tackling global problems collaboratively.

The next chapter takes a closer look at the link between relations and communication, providing insight into diverse public diplomacy practices around the world. We then turn to the logics, viewing them through the lens of humankind's ancient heritages. For the Individual Expressive logic (Chapter 3), we return to the *agora*, or public square of ancient Athens, where diplomats engaged in verbal combat. For the Relational logic (Chapter 4), we travel back to Mesopotamia, where a royal brotherhood of kings developed flourishing diplomatic alliances. For the Holistic logic (Chapter 5), we gather cosmograms from across the ancient world to graphically illustrate the complex dynamics that act in harmony to maintain the integrity and continuity of a relational universe. In Chapter 6, we look at how blending the logics together can enhance the capacity for collaboration on a global level.

2

A World of Relations, World of Communication

How we think about relations is linked directly to our assumptions about communication and diplomacy. If we can appreciate that there are multiple ways of viewing relations, we might expand our vision of both communication and public diplomacy. This chapter explores dimensions of individualism, individuality, and relationality.

It is hard to imagine that something so intimate and vital as communication can be experienced so differently by people. Yet, as the novelist Virginia Woolf wrote in *Three Guineas*, "though we see the same world, we see it through different eyes."[1]

I learned this firsthand, growing up with parents from opposites sides of the globe. I was fascinated by how two grown-ups (i.e., my parents) could have completely different views of an identical object or event, each convinced that there was only one *logical* view. The phenomenon was similar to Danish psychologist Edgar Rubin's famous illusion of the two-faces/vase picture (Figure 2.1). The white space in this image is clearly a vase. The black space shows the profiles of two people facing each other. It is very difficult to see both images at once, much as my parents were each blind to the other's perspective.

This chapter begins by tracing the academic practice of studying the Other to understand intercultural communication problems—an approach, as I argue, that is fatally flawed. I then offer the backstory of how the communication logics emerged, first using Western intercultural models, and then by compiling non-Western perspectives. As discussed in the preceding chapter, the more I tried to apply intercultural models and the binary of Western and non-Western thinking to expand my understanding of communication, the more I realized that the intercultural models—much like the idea of "culture" itself—were limiting my vision. Moreover, relations, not culture, increasingly seemed like the truly global pan-human way to understand the plurality of communication and diplomacy. The assumptions we make about relations directly impact how we think about communication and diplomacy. In this chapter, we dispense with

Figure 2.1 Rubin Illusion.
Source: John Smithson, 2007, at English Wikipedia, released to public domain. https://en.wikipedia.org/wiki/File:Rubin2.jpg.

the rigid models that categorize others. Using relationalism as an analytical lens, I embark on a global trek to explore wide-ranging assumptions about the nature of relations. Whether you, the Boundary Spanners, first see a vase or a face in the image of the other, I hope your vision will be altered and expanded by the end of the chapter.

Studying the Other: Contemporary Intercultural Communication

Like most other intercultural communication scholars, when I first began studying U.S. public diplomacy aimed at the Islamic world, I turned to dominant intercultural communication models. On the surface, the intercultural models or continuums offered compelling insights—and initially, I drew from these insights to map out different understandings of communication.

Some of the most prominent cultural continuums are those developed by Edward T. Hall. Hall's prolific writings and trained anthropological eye provided a model for studying and writing about the communication behaviors, patterns, and perspectives.[2] While Hall has been widely cited as the "father of intercultural communication," his scholarly work actually has its origins in traditional diplomacy, training U.S. diplomats about culture.[3]

Among the cultural communication patterns that Hall identified was the concept of "low-context" and "high-context" cultures.[4] He described low-context cultures as ascribing little meaning to the context or setting of communication, instead focusing on the code or message. Low-context communication tends to be specific, explicit, and direct,[5] to have a linear organizational pattern,[6] and to stress accuracy and precision.[7] The Individual logic reflects the low-context focus on content or message, in which communication is primarily about sending and receiving messages. Solutions to communication problems are similarly seen as "fixing" errant messages.

High-context communication, on the other hand, assumes that "most of the information is either in the physical context or internalized in the person, while very little is in the coded, explicit, transmitted part of the message."[8] In other words, in high-context communication one cannot rely on message content alone for understanding. According to Hall, audiences in high-context cultures draw upon well-honed skills to decipher nonverbal and contextual cues to discern the speaker's intent.[9] The Holistic logic reflects the strong focus on context, as relations among communication participants are part of the high-context orientation.

Another widely cited intercultural model is the individualism-collectivism continuum. Psychologist Harry Triandis's intensive global research gave credence to the continuum.[10] Geertz Hofstede's multinational study, *Culture's Consequences*, categorized different national cultures and helped maintain the currency and popularity of the continuum.[11]

The individualism/collectivism continuum originates in a seminal 1953 essay by U.S. anthropologist Florence Kluckhohn on "value orientations."[12] One of the five basic value orientations Kluckhohn identified was "man's relation to other men." She proposed three modalities of relationships: individualistic (nuclear, immediate family), collateral (kinship group, living members), and lineal (kinship lineage, living and dead). While all societies have collateral, and extended group relations, the distinction "is always that of emphasis," according to Kluckhohn. "If the individualistic is dominant," she writes, "individual goals will have primacy over the goals of the collateral or lineal group."[13] Individualistic and collectivist differences in communication can be seen in terms of whether the focus is on the individual or the group. The Individual logic reflects the focus on the individual, while both the Relational and Holistic logics focus on relational bonds and the larger social context.

Another continuum, which also initially informed the logics, is Kluckhohn and Strodtbeck's distinction between activity- and being-oriented cultures.[14] The activity orientation places a premium on "measurable accomplishments through action."[15] Edward Stewart described the differences between the two orientations as "doing" and "being" cultures. Individuals from activity-oriented cultures stress the importance of achievement, visible accomplishments, and measurements of achievement—results.[16] In "being cultures," however, what one *is* carries greater significance than what one *does*.[17] The Individual logic reflects a view of communication as purposeful, instrumental, and goal-oriented; it is an assertive action of establishing one's voice. By contrast, the Relational and Holistic logics reflect the *state of being* in a relationship or relational structure, not necessarily with an intended outcome.

A final communication parallel that contributed to the logics of this book stems from the ideas of Canadian scholars Harold Innis and James Carey. In the early 1950s, Innis, a political economist by training, suggested a distinction between "heavy, durable time-based media" associated with religious empires and their conquest of time and "light, portable space-based media" associated with militaristic empires and their conquest of space.[18] Carey developed Innis's ideas into "transmission" and "ritual" views of communication. According to Carey, at the heart of the transmission view is "the transmission of signals or messages over distance for the purpose of control."[19] Whereas the transmission view seeks to "impart information," the ritual view focuses on "the representation of shared beliefs."[20] The ritual view is rooted in the metaphor of religious rituals, or the "sacred ceremony that draws persons together in fellowship and commonality." While Carey highlighted rituals as communication activities, he viewed them through the lens of exchange, noting that "very little information is transmitted."[21] The Relational logic reflects this idea of communication as a social lubricant. However, as we see, the Relational logic spans much more than rituals.

These models are still widely used across the various areas of communication studies, from advertising to marketing to organizational communication, public relations, and strategic communication. The assumption remains that if one can understand the particular worldview that shapes cultural patterns of perception and behaviors, then one can use these patterns to "communicate" despite cultural differences. This was the thinking behind post-9/11 U.S. public diplomacy: if the United States could understand cultural differences and tailor its messages and approach to the particular audience, then the "communication" would be effective.

In retrospect, it is embarrassing how remarkably short-sighted this assumption is. Even as scholars studied the "culture" and "communication" of different others, they often overlooked their own role in their research as we see in the next section.

Overlooking the Self, Creating the Other

Contemporary intercultural communication appears to be as much a product of Western academic traditions as the scholars who study it. Much as with the failings of the individualist/collectivist model discussed in Chapter 1, the continuums are uncannily similar in their assumptions and patterns. In studying the Other, it appears that the scholars discounted their own cultural assumptions.

First, all of the models mentioned previously are presented as continuums, which suggests a range or gradient. However, in scholarly studies and training exercises, they are often presented as opposite extremes: High-context versus low-context, individualism versus collectivism, past-oriented versus future-oriented. The assumption of binary extremes is that they are mutually exclusive. A culture is either one way or the other.

This binary structure makes the continuums vulnerable to the inevitable contradictions of human nature and, by extension, human societies. Every continuum mentioned previously is riddled with contradictions. The contradictions are especially glaring in the popular individualism/collectivism model. Studies often juxtapose seemingly monolithic cultures, labeling Western cultures as individualistic and Eastern cultures as collectivist. Yet the concept of a depersonalized "collective" fails to capture the intensely personal nature of relations within so-called collectivist cultures.[22] Individualism similarly fails to capture collectivist behaviors within Western societies. Sharp in-group/out-group distinctions, for example, have long been cited as a marker of collectivist cultures. Yet, researchers more than twenty years ago suggested that Western societies may be just as, if not more prone to making such distinctions.[23] Consider the very vocal anti-immigration debates and policies in Western countries, which draw clear in-group/out-group distinctions of nativism, as a case in point.

Viewing the intercultural models as binary often prompts scholars to speak in relational extremes. Discounted is the possibility that individualistic societies may have collectivist traits[24] or that both dimensions may exist simultaneously.[25] In fact, rather than being mutually exclusive, individualism and collectivism may be mutually compatible, even desirable: "In every society people must be able to satisfy both individual and collective needs, that is, no culture, group or society is per se 'individualistic' or collective."[26]

What is most notable about all the models from a communication's perspective is how they focus on the exchange of messages between separate actors. The models center on two actors: Self and Other. In looking critically at "intercultural" communication, we see this assumption of a separate self and the studious focus on the culturally different Other. The features of the actors and modes of messaging may change, but the basic assumption of *separate* Self and *different* Other does not. This focus, which may appear perfectly natural, is in itself revealing. It speaks to an underlying assumption that permeates contemporary communication study.

The premise of a separate Self is at the core of individualism. Scholars have been clamoring for years about the dominance of the U.S. perspective in contemporary communication studies, even identifying "individualism" as the distinguishing feature.[27] It seems that in studying the Other, intercultural scholars assumed a neutral self. This assumption is, however, hardly surprising, as Min-Sun Kim observes: "One does not question a fact that appears to be self-evident or natural."[28]

This assumption of separate actors and focus on their behaviors and outcomes reduces communication to a template for inserting different cultural patterns. The appeal of the template and these cultural continuums is their simplicity. What makes these cultural continuums lethal, however, is that they never question the underlying premises that constrain our understanding of communication.

Lens of Relationalism

As the limitations of the intercultural communication models grew increasingly clear to me, I also noted how frequently references to relationships or assumptions about relations kept popping up in the literature. Relations appeared pivotal. The importance of relations raised the possibility of using relations—specifically a person's relations to themselves, others, and society—to conceptualize a pan-human understanding of communication. Could relations be the key to understanding communication?

As I began my survey of interdisciplinary scholarship on "relations," "relationships," and "communication," I first used the broad cultural categories "Western" and "non-Western." Later, I narrowed my focus to specific geographic regions and prominent cultural heritages (e.g., African, Asian, Arab, European, Latin, etc.). The literature was rich. As Indian scholar Durganand Sinha argued in 1965:

> Long before the advent of scientific psychology in the West, India, like most countries of the developing world, had its own religious and metaphysical systems that contained elaborate theories about human nature, actions, personalities, and interrelationships in the world. . . .[29]

The notion of relationalism further enriched my study. Ritzer and Gindoff proposed methodological relationalism as a meta-theoretical lens parallel to methodological individualism and methodological holism.[30] Methodological individualism focuses on the individual as the unit of analysis and privileges the individual perspective, whereas methodological holism focuses on the society or group as the unit of analysis and privileges the macro-level perspective. The third dimension, methodological relationalism, focuses on relationships and privileges the relational perspective.

Relationalism offers a nuanced view of relations, including the multiple dimensions and types of relational ties, relational contexts, processes, and structures. Ho, for example, used relationalism to distinguish between "person-in-relationS" (a person engaged in multiple relations simultaneously) and "personS-in-relation" (multiple people in one relation).[31]

While relationalism appears relatively new to communication studies, it has appeared with growing frequency across the social sciences. In Western scholarship, relationalism is found in social psychology[32] and sociology.[33] Asian scholars have also spoken of an Asian—and specifically Chinese—theory of relationalism, stemming from the Confucian emphasis on relationships.[34] With the discovery of relationalism as an analytical lens, I returned again to re-examine individualism, as a mode not for designing messages but for exploring underlying assumptions about relations and communication.

By developing lists of distinctive terms, prominent features, and recurring themes in various intellectual traditions, relational themes began to emerge. The next section uses relationalism as an analytical lens to view notions of relations. From assumptions of individualism tied to U.S. cultural heritage, which spawned contemporary communication scholarship, I move to cultural milieus and heritages considered close to the United States, such as Western Europe, then to those considered more culturally distant, such as East Asia.

Individualism

Robert N. Bellah and his colleagues' study of American society in *Habits of the Heart*, argues, "Individualism lies at the very core of American culture."[35] Larry Samovar and his colleagues further link individualism to individual survival in the founding and settling of the United States: "The more people were able to accomplish on their own, independent of others, the more able they were to survive the unsettled land... self-reliance was paramount."[36]

Alexis de Tocqueville, a French nobleman, is credited with coining the term "individualism" during his visit to America in the 1830s. Among his many reflections on American characteristics, he notes the "one which predominates over and includes almost all the rest ... [is that] each American appeals to the individual exercise of his own understanding alone," later labeling that characteristic "individualism."[37] De Tocqueville then defines this "novel expression":

> Individualism is a mature and calm feeling, which disposes each member of the community to sever himself from the mass of his fellow-creatures; and to draw apart with his family and his friends; so that, after he has thus formed a little circle of his own, he willingly leaves society at large to itself.[38]

Remarkably, this predominant American characteristic morphed into a *Western* assumption that would permeate scholarship. Writing about 150 years later, noted U.S. anthropologist Clifford Geertz provides one of the most comprehensive visions of individualism. However, he does not call it American individualism but rather a *Western* view of the individual:

> The Western conception of the person as a bounded, unique, more or less integrated motivational and cognitive universe, a dynamic center of awareness, emotion, judgment, and action organized into a distinctive whole and set contrastively both against other such wholes and against its social background...[39]

Within Geertz's conception of individualism are several important assumptions about relations, which I tease out in the following subsections.

Individual as Separate and Autonomous

First, we see the idea that the individual is separate and autonomous. For de Tocqueville, equality was a pivotal and recurring principle undergirding individualism: "Equality places men side by side, unconnected by any common tie."[40] He contrasted this lack of ties to the "chain" of aristocracy: "Aristocracy has made a chain of all the members of the community, from the peasant to the king."[41] In this chain, "all the members of the community are connected with and dependent upon each other."[42]

Yet for the individualist, no connections means no obligation to others. Separateness and autonomy became the norm, and relations the antithesis of independence. As de Tocqueville observed: "They owe nothing to any man, they expect nothing from any man; they acquire the habit of always considering themselves as standing alone, and they are apt to imagine that their whole destiny is in their hands."[43] This observation was echoed almost verbatim in a 2007 Pew Research poll of Americans that found that Americans were most likely to believe that they were in control of their situation.[44]

The premise of individual autonomy sets up the lone individual as the natural state of being in the world. Because individualism suggests that autonomy is the natural state of being, being joined or connected to others is anathema, or unnatural. Assuming autonomy places a premium on individual liberty. Scholars have highlighted tensions between the desire for individual pursuits and commitments of social groups. If one does connect with others, it should be of the individual's own choice and for a good reason. Relations are voluntary and instrumental; they serve a purpose. Otherwise, why would an individual make an extra effort to go from the natural state of autonomy to an unnatural state of relinquishing it?

Individual as Bounded and Complete "Whole"

The second dimension of the autonomous individual is that of the individual's inherent completeness, a bounded whole unto himself or herself. As Geertz notes, this aspect of the individual is an "integrated. . . universe" and "distinctive whole."[45] Not only is the individual bounded and complete, but so too are others. Here the assumption of equality takes on additional relational significance. Condon and Yousef found a "fusion of individualism and equality," and pointed to its manifestation in the U.S. flag, where the "sense of individualism [is] symbolized by the individual stars—each state independent but equal."[46] The high value placed on equality leads to a corresponding preference for horizontal, peer-to-peer relations.[47] The assumption of "relations among equals" makes relational inequities and asymmetries, such as hierarchies, suspect.

Equality, or parity, also sets up the familiar and even predictable dynamic of self and other. Relationally, from the individual perspective, the Other exists in contra-distinction to the Self. Each entity has its own unique set of attributes, which are assumed to set it apart from others. The bounded wholeness of each individual, in turn, implies that opposites must be mutually exclusive.

Geertz's conception, crucially, posits that individual attributes are "set contrastively both against other such wholes and against its social background," suggesting a focus on differences as a means of distinguishing the Self from the Other. When relations or alliances are broached, it is assumed to be on the basis of similarities—what one might have in common with the other. When the attributes of the Self align with those of others, there is the opportunity for cooperation. Cooperative relations among equals is the ideal, and the assumption of being "bounded and complete" becomes problematic when two bounded individuals who are unsimilar come into contact. Such an encounter inevitably causes friction. This stance perceives conflict as natural, if not inevitable.

Justifying and Maintaining Relations

If autonomy is the preferred and even natural state of individualism, then joining with others is its antithesis. To willfully go from autonomy to the unnatural state of relinquishing one's liberty and join with others thus requires justification. De Tocqueville suggests that an individual might join with others out of both self-interest and necessity. Whereas the lone individual may have considerable freedom from social connections and command of their destiny, individualism also "exposes him alone and unprotected," according to de Tocqueville.[48] De Tocqueville's words are searing: "In ages of equality every man naturally stands alone; he has no hereditary friends whose co-operation he may demand—no class upon whose sympathy he may rely: he is easily got rid of, and he is trampled on with impunity."[49]

At times, we find individuals joining with others out of necessity to meet either their own and larger social goals. Again, justification is required. Not surprisingly, the "exchange theory" is the most prominent theory in contemporary interpersonal relations.[50] According to exchange theory, individuals form relations because each receives something of benefit from the other. Relations have utility value, providing a means to a greater end. This "rational choice" is also prominent in models of international relations. Individuals search for common ground or mutual interests, fostering an expectation that enduring relations are inherently positive and mutually fulfilling.

Relations Created by Individual Agency

Because individualism suggests that autonomy is the natural state of being, joining with others requires not only justification but individual agency. Relations must be created and built. De Tocqueville had several novel observations about the how individuals in early America built ties. First, he noticed the habit of association: "Americans form associations for the smallest of undertakings," he writes, attributing this habit to the lack of enduring ties. "All the citizens are independent and feeble; they can do hardly anything by themselves, and none of them can oblige his fellow men to lend him their assistance." Hence, the associations: "They all, therefore, become powerless if they do not learn voluntarily to help one another."[51]

Second was the critical importance of persuasion. The individualist must persuade other individuals to join forces. "When men are no longer united among themselves by firm and lasting ties, it is impossible to obtain the cooperation of any great number of them unless you can persuade every man who helps you."[52]

The vehicle of persuasion, de Tocqueville observed, was the media, specifically newspapers. "Equality deprives a man of the support of his connections; but the press enables him to summon all his fellow-countrymen and all his fellow-men to his assistance." So vital is the media, he adds, "if there were no newspapers, there would be no common activity."[53] He saw newspapers as particularly suited for early America, "providing the means to converse every day without seeing one another, and to take steps in common without having met."[54] Here we see the role of media as a channel and communication as a process of relationship building—and communication as the process by which individuals create, sustain, and even end relations.

Relational "Life Span"

A final significant relational assumption is that because relations are an individual choice, and autonomy is the natural state, relationships can be "broken" or "ended." Interpersonal texts frequently use the term "life cycle" to describe relationships.[55] The life cycle of a relationship, similar to the life cycle of an individual, proceeds linearly from the birth of the relationship through a flourishing maturity, and finally into a process of decay, brought about by negative, unfulfilling aspects. Despite the use of the term "cycle," which is circular and suggests continuity, the cycle is tied to the individual—not the relationship. Hence, the autonomous Self circles from autonomy, to relations, and finally back to autonomy.

Individuality

Let us hit the pause button for a moment. As familiar as these assumptions about relations may be from the individualistic perspective, they are not universally shared. Geertz qualifies his conception of the individual mentioned earlier, adding words of caution: "however incorrigible it may seem to us, it [this view of the individual] is a *rather peculiar idea* within the context of the world's cultures" (emphasis mine).[56] In other words, individualism is the global exception rather than the rule. In other societies we see the dominance of relationality: the assumption that all individuals are inherently connected to others or interconnected in a larger relational universe. Humans are assumed relational beings, even as they are individuals.

Relationality may seem to be the opposite of individualism, as in the individualism-collectivism dichotomy. However, it does not have to be so. Condon and Yousef introduced the idea of individuality, which shares with individualism the idea that every person is a unique, one-of-a-kind being.[57] Yet, unlike individualism, individuality does not assume separateness. Instead, part of an individual's unique individuality stems from relations to others. My family constellation is part of what gives me my unique individuality, as I imagine yours does the same for your unique individuality.

For Boundary Spanners and scholars, the critical aspect of Individuality is that it creates a space for thinking about identity and individuals as being *a part* of a group (having connections) rather than *apart* from others (being separate). Relations are integral to the human experience. The Māori concept of *whakapapa* (genealogy) helps illustrate the uniqueness of the individual within an intercon-nected universe.[58] *Whakapapa* is important because each person is linked to other Māori in an interconnected chain of past, present, and future generations and the world around them. To miss one link—one unique individual—would disrupt the interconnectedness. Each person is uniquely valued precisely be-cause of their connection to others in the universe.

The most critical aspect of relationality is that it is not an inherent property or attribute of any one individual. Relationality is not, as in the case of the cul-tural continuums, a "worldview." Relationships, not individuals, are the basic unit of analysis. To understand individuals, including their attributes and espe-cially their behaviors, one has to understand their relationships. From this van-tage point, communication and diplomacy for any individual entity begins by looking at their relationships.

Relationality

Relationality is the assumption and condition of being in a relationship. As an analytic lens, relationalism provides a more nuanced view of relations as connections and inter-connections in a rich variety of patterns. While the term "relationality" does not yet appear in the English-language dictionary, the con-cept is ever present in societies, traditions, and scholarship around the globe, including in the United States.

Relations as the Natural State of Being

Relationality assumes relations as the natural state of being for individuals. From this perspective, the human experience is predicated upon and defined by rela-tions. People come into being through relations (parents), they are born into a web of relations (family) and exist within a web of relations (society).

Across many traditions, "family" emerged as a pivotal and central theme. In Europe, family as the basis of social and political structures is foundational to de Tocqueville's discussion of aristocracy. Similarly, the Latin perspective acknow-ledges the individual-level perspective—but always as tied to the family as center of social gravity and communication. As Korzenny and Korzenny state, "[there is] thinking of the family and the groups to which they belong, as essential elem-ents to the functioning and enjoyment of their lives."[59] Even some national constitutions inscribe the family, not the individual, as the fundamental unit of society, as in Article 1 of the Chilean constitution: "The family is the basic core of society."[60]

The assumption of being connected to others makes being in relations the norm. In contrast to individualism, in relationality the state of being *un-linked* requires justification. The very idea that individuals "are somehow detached" from others, as one scholar put it, is suspect.[61] Several African traditions express the primacy of relational connections. Mentioned earlier is the pan-African concept of *Ubuntu*; a related idiom is *umuntu ngumuntu ngabantu* (a person is a person through other persons).[62] As Antjiehi Krog explains the idiom, "one's human-ness manifests itself in one's relations with others."[63] Not only is one human by being in relationship, being severed from critical relationships can be equated with death.[64] The Igbo people of Eastern Nigeria would say, "*Onye ya na Umunna ya a akwuro ga eli onwe ya*": a person who is not with his or her extended family must bury himself.[65]

Noteworthy for Boundary Spanners is the expanse of what a family can mean. Notions of family range from parents and children, to extended kinship of grandparents and relatives, to tribes. Such notions of family assume direct relational links or a bloodline. For some traditions, however, all humans are members of the human family, hence the practice of referring to others as "brother" or "sister." For still other traditions, the notion of "family" extends to non-human entities. For example, in Native American and pan-Polynesian lore, family includes not only animals and plants but also mountains and rivers as well as natural forces such as the wind and sky. All are related, and all are family.

Relational Contexts and Spheres

The importance of relational contexts and connections also emerged from my survey. While individualism focuses on the individual actor and agency, the idea of an audience introduces the potential for relationship. A focus on the actor-audience dyad, however, misses the critical social context. Where is everyone else? What relationship exists in a social vacuum? If relationality is assumed as the norm, then analysis naturally begins as the relational level, with relation itself, not individuals, as the focus. One cannot study the individuals or communication between individuals apart from the relation within which they are embedded.

Many scholarly traditions foreground relationships in context. In European scholarship, the social context emerges quite prominently.[66] German sociologist Jürgen Habermas' writings on the "public sphere,"[67] for instance, presumes that relations do not occur in a social vacuum, but within a public context. Verčič and his colleagues suggested that the concern with the "public sphere" distinguishes European public communication from the American focus on "publics."[68]

Indian scholars point to culture as an essential context for understanding relations. "The culture remains for the Indian, all pervasive, a kind of ruling principle, an intangible order of values and relationships," says Usha Vyasulu Reddi.[69] The importance of culture relates to the great diversity of India's public sphere, which, as Reddi describes, is "a highly complex jigsaw puzzle of fourteen major languages, at least five major religions and races, different music and dance forms."[70]

While the idea of the public sphere and social context provide a backdrop for relations, both are rather abstract. The Latin perspective introduces the idea that relationships often form or extend from other relationships, creating an ever-expanding circle of relations, or what might be called "relational spheres." For example, a relationship with a friend can extend to include relations with the friend's family and other friends. The idea of using relations to build relations undergirds the practice of professional and social networking. Years ago, Chinese scholar Fei Xiaotong suggested the image of interpersonal and social relationships—like that of a stone cast in a lake—which radiate out in concentric circles from each individual entity and which overlap with the relational circles of others.[71] This image puts individuals at the center of an ever-expanding circle of relationships, that moves from close, strong relations to more distant and weaker ones. Notably, Asian literature presupposes that relational distance is not solely physical or cognitive, but primarily emotional proximity or intimacy.[72]

Relations as Emotional Bonds

Emotions and feelings emerged as another dominant theme in discussions of relations, alongside that of family. In many ways, family was a metaphor for relations as emotional bonds. People are connected not only genealogically but emotionally, through attraction and attachment. Emotions provide the glue that bonds people. The prominence of family as a metaphor for the assumption of emotional ties extends even to those who are not family. For instance, the kings of Amarna diplomacy, whose relational bonds I discuss in more detail in Chapter 4, used familial terms among themselves and professed love for their "brothers" in their diplomatic communications.

The primacy of emotion in relations undergirds the concept of *ubuntu* as embodying the idea of humanism as "a feeling for others." June Ock Yum likens the emotional affinity in *ubuntu* to *ren* in Confucian philosophy, which similarly suggests humanism as an inner feeling for others.[73] Unlike the term 'collective,' which has an emotionally sterile connotation, emotions and feelings for others are personal and specific in the discussions of relationships.

We see another aspect of the personal and relational nature of emotions in scholarship from the Arab world. Emotional ties in relations lay a foundation for identity. The founding Arab sociologist Ibn Khaldun (1332–1406) linked the strength of human social organizations to the concept of *assabiyah*, or solidarity, group feeling, or group consciousness. *Assabiyah* could be built within a tribal clan or politically across an entire geographic region.[74] Echoing this observation regarding nations today, John Mercer observed, "Emotions structure relationships. A group without emotions is a mere collection of autonomous individuals."[75]

Relational Differentiation

In individualism, all relations appear the same, or equal. Relationalism provides a nuanced view of relations. In an expansive relational context, differentiation of relations would appear natural. Like the fingers on one's hands, each is different in position and function relative the others. We might return to Fei's image of expanding concentric circles, representing relations with graduating degrees of intimacy and obligation, or what he called "manners of different orders." The Confucian five cardinal relations exemplify such differentiation: (1) father-son (relation of love); (2) emperor-subject (the relational of righteousness); (3) husband-wife (the relational of chaste conduct); (4) elder-younger (the relation of order); and (5) friend-friend (the relation of faithfulness).[76]

While Confucius saw the maintenance of proper relations as foundational to Chinese society, relational differentiation is prominent across societies. Differentiation is often readily recognized through nonverbal cues of status or power. Differentiation may also be acknowledged through language and word choice: informal language for more intimate relations and more formal language for more distant relations. Many languages reflect this in verb conjugations, with their formal and informal forms of address, such as French *vous* (you formal) and *tu* (you informal).

Hierarchy is an implicit assumption of relational differentiation. As we will discuss later, even in societies where peer relations dominate, hierarchies thrive as a means of attaining social stability and individual identity. For diplomatic Boundary Spanners, signs of hierarchy in both traditional and public diplomacy abound, albeit perhaps subtly. The elaborate rules of diplomatic protocols, such as who stands where in the receiving line or even if there is a receiving line for a visiting official, are acknowledgments of relational differentiation. Within public diplomacy, relational differentiation is reflected in the idea of elite publics and influencers.

Relational Roles and Commitments

We see the idea of pre-existing connections as well as commitment in the traditional value of communalism found across Africa. Communalism assumes primacy of the community over the individual: "The individual is born out of and into the community and therefore will always be a part of the community."[77] As Peter Nwosu explains, "Communalism represents commitment to interdependence, community affiliation, others and the idea of we."[78] The "we" of community is the basis for "I," or the individual. Hence the African saying "I am because we are, we are because I am."

Communal membership carries specific duties and obligations. The intent of the relational responsibility is reflected in the oft-heard saying "It takes a village." The contribution of each member in the community, from children to elders, is captured in the African proverb "A child's hands are too short to reach a high shelf, but the elder's hands are too big to enter a narrow gourd." This expression also illustrates the idea that relational obligations position each individual not in opposition to others, but in alignment and complementarity to one another. The natural relation of Self and Other is assumed to be fellowship. Failure to fulfill relational expectations can be socially costly in terms of loss of face or reputation in letting down the community.

From the perspective of Individualism, which views relations as choice rather than condition, being embedded in a network of pre-defined relations might be viewed as a limitation, a restriction, or even a threat.[79] From this perspective, the relationship between the individual and society turns oppositional: the individual *versus* society. The assumption of an oppositional stance is alien to many traditions.[80]

Relations within a Relational Universe

The idea that individuals are an inseparable part of a larger relational universe brings us to another important relational assumption from my global trek. Indian and other Asian scholarship emphasizes the idea of an interconnected relational universe. In U.S.-based texts with assumptions of individualism, one may find entire discussions of relationships without any mention of links within a larger social context. In public diplomacy scholarship, one sees discussions focused almost entirely on one state and a target audience. One might ask, Where is the rest of the world? As we saw in European, Latin, and Arab scholarship, there is an assumed social *context*, such as the public sphere or family. In Asian scholarship, one gets the sense of a social *system*, and relationships are viewed from a systems perspective. From systems perspective, everything is interconnected. The individual is not the unit of analysis, but the larger system—the whole relational universe—is.

Scholars from Asian traditions have likened the relational universe "to a running river without a beginning and an end."[81] D. Sinha tried to capture the distinction between "human *and* society," "human *in* society," and the indivisibility of "human-society."

> The model of human . . . in the West is "human in society," as "human and society"—the two being conceptualized as distinct and separate. As far as Indian thinking goes, the model is "human-society," i.e., the two being in a state of symbiotic relationship where you cannot separate the one from the other.[82]

Within this worldview, although each human is unique, one cannot understand or study any individual apart from the larger relational universe.

Relational Being and Non-Agency

A final relational assumption that emerged in Asian literature is the idea of a "relational being."[83] The perspective of human-society or relational being deflates the necessity of human agency in creating or controlling relations. Jo and Kim, for example, discuss the Korean concept of *yon* in communication: "*Yon* is related to the belief that relationships are formed, maintained, and terminated by uncontrollable external forces, not by an individual's conscious efforts."[84]

The premise of a relational being represents a paradigm shift from "building" relationships through individual agency to "being" in relationships, which does not require agency. Miyahara points out that English-language literature uses words such as "create," "build," "manage," or "end" when speaking about relations with others.[85] From the perspective of "relational being," such vocabulary appears not only alien but redundant: how can one "create" what already exists?

While one does not have agency in creating the larger relational structure, each individual has responsibility by virtue of their relational position. Indeed, this perspective views relational positions in terms of relational responsibilities rather than individual power. Again, however, the larger relational universe is the guide. As Uichol Kim notes, "specific obligations and duties are attached to roles and status, but not to individuals."[86] The interconnectivity of different roles and duties are part of the responsibilities of relational beings within a relational universe.

A World of Relations and Communication

In a radical break from trying to use either Western or non-Western "communication" models to explain "communication," I turned to different modes of relations that are foundational to the pan-human experience. The importance of relations is not a novel insight. What is novel is the attempt to understand how relations can alter assumptions about what happens when people relate with each other, or "communicate." Seeing the communication through a relational lens reveals that assumptions about communication can vary as relations vary. Understanding differing relational assumptions as shared aspects of the human experience is at the heart of envisioning, practicing, and cultivating different views of "communication."

To understand the foundational importance of relational assumptions, consider the following distinct relational perspectives in defining and solving "communication problems."

Say that one assumes that individuals are separate, bounded autonomous entities. Communication then becomes inherently about passing *something*—a message—back and forth in order to create and build relations. Communication also becomes by necessity a transmission process of designing and delivering information. Individuals bear the responsibility for the clarity and persuasiveness of their messages. From this perspective, a "communication problem" occurs when the message the individual sent is not understood (or received) by the other person. The individual tries to solve the "communication problem" by trying to find where or how the transmission process failed. Perhaps, one might think, *The other person doesn't understand what I meant.* The individual might try to fix the message or try another medium. *How can I change the message? Maybe we can meet in person rather than talk by phone?* Efforts to solve the communication problem rest on individual agency and the ability to find the source of the transmission failure to fix the "communication problem."

Yet, how might the perception of a "communication problem" change if one assumes that individuals are not separate but are inherently bound to others? If people are inherently linked, transmitting messages no longer applies. Rather than sending messages, the relational bond becomes the defining feature of "communication." The nature of the relationship shapes the nature of communication. A "communication problem" emerges when there is a strain or break in the relationship. For example, if one has a falling out with a close friend, one may try to fix the "communication problem" by repairing the relationship. Solving the communication problem rests on fixing the relationship.

Alternatively we can ask, What if one assumes that individuals are inter-connected to others in an all-encompassing relational universe that governs communication? From this perspective, individual agency or ability to fix a "communication problem" might seem overwhelming. Communication is not defined solely by the individual or the relational bond, but by and within the larger relational universe. If that relational universe defines "communication," then "communication" for the individual is about learning and preserving that relational universe. "Communication problems" arise when the individual does not know or is out of alignment with the communication dynamics of the rela-tional universe. The awkwardness of feeling of out of place or out of sync in a new or unfamiliar social setting can precipitate a "communication problem." Fixing the communication problem rests on learning and getting in sync with the new or unfamiliar relational universe.

Most people will recognize these "communication problems" to some degree in all three of the relational positions—and that is the point. People are able to identify with the different relational perspectives. I hope it is apparent, also, that the different relational perspectives are not mutually exclusive. It is not a matter of either/or, or Western/non-Western. The three relational modes—individual, relational, and holistic—define human existence and indeed are necessary for the procreation, perpetuation, and survival of human societies. We see the pri-macy of the individual in the universal act of naming offspring. The institution of marriage epitomizes the sacredness of the relational bond. The experience of living and working in society mirrors the idea of the relational universe we in-habit together.

As discussed in Chapter 1, I used the three relational modes presented in this chapter to develop three corresponding communication logics: Individual, Relational and Holistic. This chapter has shared the backstory of how the logics developed. The remainder of the book explores how each logic begins with one of the relational premises and weaves a web of assumptions, producing the com-munication logics.

For the Boundary Spanners

There is an expression, "A foreigner sees what a foreigner knows." In many ways, we are all intimate strangers to each other's understandings of communication. We are intimate because communication is fundamental to our shared existence. We are strangers in that we bring our different assumptions to our shared social space. Each of us tends to focus on what is familiar and what makes sense to us. The rest flies by unnoticed. As with the face/vase drawing that began this chapter, we may get fixated on only one vision. Just as U.S. individualism helped shape a particular view of communication and, by extension, public diplomacy, alternative assumptions about relations help expand the vision of communication and public diplomacy. For Boundary Spanners, developing a global vision and globalizing habits means seeing both face and vase: that is, moving from rather simplistic and exclusive visions to ones that are more complex and inclusive. Several closing points are worth noting.

Recognizing Habits of Seeing

A first step for Boundary Spanners to move toward globalizing their vision is to recognize their own habits of seeing. As the global tour revealed, assumptions about relations vary. There is no single universal view of relations but rather a world of relational assumptions. Individualism as a relational assumption is significant in communication because it helped establish the notion of autonomy as the norm. What de Tocqueville identified as an *American* trait in the 19th century had become *Western* by the 20th century. Because many communication scholars fail to credit individualism as a perceptual bias, theories of communication based on individualism continue to spread *as if* they are universal. However, as we have seen, this far from the case.

Boundary Spanners would do well to be mindful of how the concepts of individualism, individuality, and relationality can restrict or expand conceptual space in how we think about ourselves and others. Whereas individualism assumes separateness, individuality privileges uniqueness, regardless of whether one is separate or connected. Some individuals may even view their connections as part of their unique individuality. Additionally, whereas individualism is associated with the geo-cultural context of the United States and collectivism is often associated with Asian cultures, individuality is pan-human—one can be separate as well as connected.

In much the same way that individuality expands our thinking beyond individualism, relationality can augment our thinking beyond collectivism. Relationality provides an expansive view of relationship formations, from the intimate paired relationship to an all-encompassing relational universe. Relationality is not a property of any one individual or one particular society, but global. However, just as U.S.-based assumptions of individualism slipped under the radar of awareness, assumptions regarding relationality can also go undetected. The most skilled Boundary Spanners will be those who are alert to relational assumptions in communication and diplomacy.

Retiring Intercultural Continuums

One of the goals of this chapter was to make a compelling case for expanding—rather than mutually canceling out—other ways of seeing. The value of the intercultural models is that they provided sharp contrasts and insights on very different ways of seeing. It is possible to draw upon those insights. The risk is always in getting stuck on one vision and not realizing the presence of another way of seeing. Boundary Spanners would do well to look warily at intercultural communication "patterns" such as Individualism/Collectivism, High-context/Low-Context, and so forth. Rather than being patterns of distinct views of communication, they appear to be a variation of the still-dominant individualist template of communication that views the Self and the Other in separate, mutually exclusive categories. Relying on these intercultural models, as Georgette Wang observed, leaves researchers repetitively collecting data that reinforces a limiting vision rather than reaching into new realms of methodology, theory, or paradigm of communication.[87]

I would go further and suggest that the intercultural models developed in an earlier time are rapidly becoming obsolete and it is time to think about retiring them. Not only were these intercultural categories developed primarily by Western scholars, but they were also developed during a very different stage of research development. As Nelson and her colleagues point out, when the field of intercultural communication was young, identifying patterns of cultural differences was important and the models served a "useful purpose." The scholars added, "No single characterization can adequately describe the communication patterns of any one group in every context."[88]

More problematic still is that these cultural categories of communication have morphed into "national cultures," which suggests how all the people in a particular nation communicate. Hofstede's models, still widely cited today, were based on research conducted on "national cultures" between 1967 and 1973—the height of the bipolar world of the Cold War. Dividing up the world into cultural dichotomies mirrored the dichotomy of the international political arena. In today's globalized, interconnected world, such rigid, monolithic cultural categories make little sense. Today, national cultures often contain multiple ethnic traditions, while cultures can span multiple nations. As Ingrid Piller noted, the intercultural models may actually reinforce cultural biases and misunderstandings, particularly when culture is ascribed to nations. For Boundary Spanners, it is just as important to think about differences *within* nations and cultures as it is to look solely *across* them.

Relationalism

While the intercultural models may no longer be as useful as they once were considered to be, learning to understand the relational dynamics in an interconnected world will be increasingly important. Developing relationalism as an analytical tool can help cultivate new ways of seeing. The word "relationalism," as I type it, appears in red on my screen as a spelling error. It is not yet part of the standardized English vocabulary. That, I hope, will change in the coming years as the field of communication globalizes and a diversity of scholars share additional insights on relationality in their work. Not only does social media favor connectivity, but scholars now have the computational technologies to map these connections using network analysis tools. Even this, however, can be fraught: network analysis is helpful in showing relations, but visual representations can assume the primacy of separate individuals by representing them as individual "nodes." Ego networks, or networks that look at the relational dynamics of individual nations, dominate the field of international relations, while studies of whole network analyses have been comparatively rare.[89] The dynamics of relationalism proceed not from individual nodes but rather the indivisibility of the relational universe itself. That primacy of the relational universe is the basic unit of analysis; the parts cannot be studied apart from the whole. Relationalism is still in its infancy as it applies to contemporary communication. Therefore, the tools, vocabulary, and insights we develop can help us to do as Krog suggested and "read the interconnections."[90]

Actorness in Diplomacy

Assumptions about relations have important implications and insights for diplomacy, as we will see in the coming chapters as well. One outstanding observation is the emphasis that individualism places on individual entities. In communication, this means a focus on the "communicator." In diplomacy, we find a parallel emphasis on state/non-state actors. This focus on the actor overlooks how different assumptions about relations may shape the relational dynamics between actors, as well as optimal relational strategies in different situations. Yaqing Qin outlined an extensive relational theory of world politics, including in particular how relations may constrain or enhance actors.[91] Yang and her colleagues, as another example, discussed the soft balancing among actors during the Libyan crisis, to underscore the importance of being mindful of the larger relational context.[92]

Relational assumptions may be particularly important for shaping predispositions toward competition and collaboration. The indigenous Māori of New Zealand, for example, have a relational premise that encompasses all living creatures and other entities on the planet. Relational being implies relational responsibilities. This relational premise is echoed in the concept of *Kai-tia-tanga*, which translates as "stewardship" or responsibility to other entities on the planet. The New Zealand Foreign Ministry included the Maori concept of *Kai-tia-tanga* in its policy objectives and approach to diplomacy.

Viewing the "Other"

Another implication of these different views of relations are the multiple perceptions of the Other. Not only are the views the Self and Others separate in the individualistic view, but their differences are contrasted, as Geertz highlighted. We see that this assumption of separation extends to contemporary diplomatic and international studies in corollary assumptions of the need for power, control, competition and an estranged Other. James Der Derian's classic 1987 text, *On Diplomacy: A Genealogy of Western Estrangement*, is a ready example. Der Derian posits that diplomacy is about mediating "estrangement (that is, *separation marked by indifference to hostility*)."[93] Der Derian appears to make natural the idea of relations with the Other as estrangement and alienation.

Relationality, which assumes connection, spawns an alternative view of the Other that suggests fellowship. Diplomatic ideals and practice follow a much different line. Family emerges as a dominant diplomatic template. In many pre-Westphalian diplomacies, including dynasties in Europe, political relations were largely defined using familial terms, with sovereigns addressing each other as "brothers." As noted previously, such was the case in ancient Amarna diplomacy, which we discuss in detail in Chapter 4. We likewise see the assumption of world as family in the Maori example of stewardship mentioned earlier, as well as in other indigenous diplomacies.[94] Since 1987, Der Derian appears to have also expanded from estrangement to relationality. In 2010, he teamed with Costa Constantinou to edit a collection on "sustainable diplomacies."[95] Such diplomacy initiatives are sustainable because they incorporate the wide relational expanse.

Summary

In this chapter we looked at the backstory of how the communication logics evolved from intercultural categories. The categories proposed by early intercultural communication models were not only limiting but riddled with inconsistencies. In our search for alternatives paths to understand communication, relationalism emerged as a viable analytic lens. A global survey of notions of relations, beginning with individualism and moving to relationality, revealed widely divergent assumptions. In the chapters that follow, we look more closely at how a world of relations creates a world of communication and public diplomacy in the different logics.

3

Individual Logic

Aristotle's Legacy

The Individual logic is based on the premise of the bounded, autonomous individual communicator whose unique combination of attributes and agency define the communication experience.

It was the Golden Age of ancient Athens. Philosophy, art, and science were flourishing. Participatory democracy had taken root and with it the importance of oratory skills had grown. Public speaking was an "indispensable accomplishment," as citizens were expected to represent themselves in court as well as public assemblies.[1] In the public squares, or agora (Ἀγορά), statesmen and diplomatic envoys engaged in verbal combat to persuade others to their causes and win debates against equally impassioned opponents. The ability to speak in public, persuade fellow citizens, and defend oneself verbally was as vital to life as physical defense. As the great Athenian statesman Pericles (495–429 BCE) intoned, "one who forms a judgement on any point but cannot explain himself clearly to the people might well have never thought at all upon the subject."[2]

More than 2,500 years ago, Aristotle compiled his notes on *rhetorike*, or rhetoric, the technique or art of public speaking. While ancient Greece is widely recognized as laying a foundation for Western culture in general, Aristotle's *Rhetoric* may be the single most cited work in contemporary (Western) communication study. As one noted Western scholar of communication theory observed, "communication as a whole can be nearly synonymous with rhetoric."[3]

Eloquence in verbal expression is a shared dimension of the human experience; it is also the heart of the Individual Expressive logic of communication. Today, the global public sphere and social media tools have replaced the agora of ancient Greece. The rhetorical stance flourishes as verbal combatants identify their opponents, draw upon sophisticated strategies and tools, and engage in debates designed to influence audiences. Such debates—whether spoken or written—are competitive, zero-sum scenarios. Public diplomacy expressions such as the "battle for hearts and minds," "war of ideas," "information as weapons," or "strategic narratives" and "counter-narratives," all echo with the call to verbal battle.

Given the impact of Aristotle's *Rhetoric*, we can turn to it and the socio-political context from which it sprang as a window into the relational premise, interwoven assumptions, and communication dynamics of the Individual logic.

Aristotle's Legacy of Persuasion

Athens was the intellectual center of the Western world when Aristotle arrived there at the age of seventeen in 367 BCE. He studied under the philosopher Plato for twenty years. An avid researcher and book collector, Aristotle would go on to write more than two hundred treatises across a range of subjects, from agriculture to biology, botany, dance and theatre, ethics, mathematics, medicine, metaphysics, physics, and zoology.[4] His theories of logic and systematic research influenced Western scholarly traditions. Aristotle later went on to develop his own school, Lyceum, in Athens.

At the time, Aristotle was not the only one writing on the art of public speaking (Box 3.1). In Athens, "to be a politician was the rule rather than the exception."[5] Oratory skill was so critical to political participation and personal stature that its form and instruction were themselves sources of long-running debate. Well before Aristotle's day, in 427 BCE, the sophist orator Gorgias of Leontini arrived in Athens as a member of a delegation from Sicily and astonished the Athenians with his eloquence. Gorgias's orations popularized the sophist style of verbal embellishment and flattery.[6]

While the communication innovations of the sophists captured the imagination of many of Athens's youth, not all were enamored. The sophists' use of

---

Box 3.1 Ancient Greek Notables

Pericles (495–429 BCE)
Gorgias of Leontini (483–375 BCE)
Socrates (ca. 470–399 BC)
Isocrates (436–338 BC)
Plato (428/427–348/347 BC)
Aristotle (384–322 BCE)
Alexander the Great (356–323 BC)

deception and persuasion at all costs was so strongly criticized that the term "sophistry" retains a negative connotation even today. The great philosopher Socrates, a dominant force in Athenian intellectual life at the time of Gorgias's sudden popularity, called for "the veil to be removed" from the sophist's verbal deception. His pupil, Plato, was even more critical of sophistry, and introduced the term *rhetorike*, from which the term *rhetoric* derives.[7] True rhetoric or public speaking, according to Plato, should combine a search for truth with a grounded knowledge of human behavior.

Plato's protégé Aristotle took up the challenge of explicating rhetoric. In *Rhetoric*, Aristotle declares at the outset his focus on persuasion: "Rhetorical study, in its strictest sense, is concerned with the modes of persuasion."[8] He elaborated, defining rhetoric "as the faculty of observing in any given case the possible means of persuasion."[9] Orators should look for the possibility of persuasion in the situation, context, and the audience. The emphasis on persuasion is a cornerstone of the Individual logic. Communication is purposeful.

Aristotle breaks public speaking into three categories: political, forensic, and ornamental. He claimed that the political was the least studied, so he focused on the public political sphere.

Aristotle's focus on speaking in the public political arena is also noteworthy for its enduring impact on elite and then public education. Rhetoric, along with grammar and logic, was part of the classic Latinate Trivium, a required course of study for (Western) clergy, lawyers, physicians, diplomats, and other public servants engaged in a "persuasive or subtle combative mode of speaking and writing."[10] Note that diplomats are included in that list.

Aristotle's legacy of rhetoric can be seen not only in communication but also diplomacy. Diplomacy, like political democracy, was conducted in the public arena. Envoys of delegations, such as that of Gorgias of Leontini, were expected to present their cases in public. Jönsson and Hall credited ancient Athens as "the forerunner of the verbal skills and eloquence associated with modern diplomacy."[11]

The role of rhetoric in elite education would transfer to public education. Public speaking and debate were embedded in the public education curriculum. Students competed for spots on their school debate teams. In the early 1910s in the United States, teachers of public speaking and English founded what would evolve into today's major communication associations: the International Communication Association and the National Communication Association. Both were originally founded as speech associations but later changed their names to "communication" (the ICA in 1969, the NCA in 2014) with the influx of social science researchers.[12] As we see in Chapter 6, the power of speech—the written or spoken word—is a defining strength of the Individual logic.

Aristotle identified three key elements of political speeches: speaker, subject, and persons addressed. These three elements mirror the focus on sender, receiver, and message that we find in contemporary communication and the Individual logic. According to Aristotle, of these three elements in speech-making "it is the last one, the hearer, that determines the speech's end and object."[13] Audience reception of the message remains a strong determinant in gauging the success or effectiveness of communication in the Individual logic.

In discussing the possible means of persuasion of audiences, Aristotle identified what he called "artistic proofs" or appeals: *ethos*, *pathos*, and *logos*. These ancient Greek terms are still found in present-day studies, including in the digital age. As scholars Gulbrandsen and Just noted in a survey of digital studies, while digital technologies call for a radical reassessment of outdated communication theories for the "online communicator," the "classical rhetorical concepts . . . ethos, pathos and logos" are still applicable. As they reason, "people continue to act with intention and attempt to persuade each other. And conflicts of interest and attempts at domination persist."[14] The Individual logic is similarly goal-driven and influenced by these artistic proofs.

Aristotle spends the remainder of the Rhetoric elaborating on these three artistic proofs of persuasion. The first proof, *ethos*, refers to the speaker's character, including image and reputation. According to Aristotle, "persuasion is achieved by the speaker's personal character when the speech is so spoken as to make us think him credible."[15] In the Individual logic, communicator attributes remain a critical feature in defining the communication experience. In the other logics, the relational bonds as well as the relational universe carry greater communication weight.

The second proof, *pathos*, is sometimes equated with persuasive appeals to emotions. Aristotle defined emotions as "all those feelings that so change men as to affect their judgements . . . such are anger, pity, fear and the like, with their opposites."[16] However, as scholars have cautioned, this proof is more complicated than appealing to fear or anger.[17] For Aristotle, the quest was not simply evoking emotion in the listener, but also understanding the emotional state of one's audience and how emotions connected to perception and behavior.

Aristotle's powerfully nuanced observations of human behavior have crossed millennia. As one persuasion scholar noted, "the ancient descriptions of what is or is not likely to persuade seem remarkably contemporary. In fact, we could argue that most contemporary persuasion research is derived from the work of Aristotle in some way."[18] Indeed, the intensive study and development of persuasion theory by U.S. social scientists between 1940 and 1960 was known as the "new 'scientific' Rhetoric."[19] Interestingly, the Individual logic tends to view emotion through the lens of persuasion. As we see in the Relational and Holistic logics, emotion is also linked to assumptions of affinity, relational bonds, and identity.

The third proof is *logos*. Aristotle frames *logos* as a systematic and deliberate construction of an argument to appeal to the listener. Debaters must be able to deconstruct or refute the arguments of others. In the process of outlining the mechanisms for constructing and refuting arguments, we see the development of logic, including the logic of opposites (A and not A). Opposites are presented as opposing, and mutually exclusive rather than naturally co-existing or complementary—a tendency of the Individual logic which we examined in previous chapters. Aristotle has been called "the father of logic" in Western heritage because of his systematic reasoning.

Looking closer, Aristotle's systematic discussions of these separate aspects of speech, emotion, and logic appear to be characteristic of the ancient Greeks' penchant for causal modeling, which sought to categorize objects and events and then generate rules about them for systematic description, prediction, and explanation.[20] We see this chain of description-prediction-explanation as well as the construction of mutually exclusive, distinctive categories amply demonstrated in a plethora of models in contemporary communication studies. The Individual logic is built upon the idea of modeling.

The systematic view of speech, the development of verbal strategies for persuasion, the focus on logic, and the idea of categories and models to describe the world are all part of Aristotle's legacy and ancient Greek rhetoric that continue to shape notions of contemporary communication studies more than two-and-a-half millennia later. It is as if the agora of 5th Century BCE Athens lives on today. In the next section, as we dive deeper into the underlying assumptions of the Individual logic, we see parallel elements of the ancient Greeks' imprint on contemporary communication that extend to public diplomacy.

The Communicator

The Individual logic of communication rests on the paradoxical relational premise of no relations. Following from anthropologist Clifford Geertz's description of the individual discussed in Chapter 2, the individual is conceived of as "a *bounded*, unique, more or less integrated motivational and cognitive *universe*, . . . a *distinctive whole* and set *contrastively* both against *other such wholes* and *against* its social and natural background" (emphasis mine).[21]

If we unpack Geertz's description, we discover several interlocking assumptions that act to reinforce each other, making ideas about communication from the Individual logic appear airtight. First is the idea that the individual is "bounded," which suggests the individual is complete or a "distinctive whole"—a "universe" unto itself. The individual whole includes attributes (awareness, emotion, judgment) and agency (action). Boundary Spanners should note that this argument assumes that what the individual is or does is inherent in the individual—not the context or relations. The boundedness suggests definitive boundaries of the individual or the self and the "non-self," or that which is other than the self.[22] The individual self must distinguish itself from others; self-expression is critical to defining the self and boundaries of the self.

The premise of the bounded individual puts the communication focus squarely on individual. In contemporary communication, the assumption that the individual is the focus of communication and the one responsible for communication is echoed in the terminology. The individual is not just a "sender" but is often labeled "the source" or "the Communicator." In a recent, comprehensive compilation of contemporary Western communication theory, a survey of more than fifty communication-related journals over the past seven years revealed that most of them named the first element of communication as the "Communicator."[23]

In Geertz's description, we see the buried assumption of separateness: the distinctive boundaries between the individual as "a distinctive whole" and "other such wholes."[24] Geertz implicitly assumes that not only is the individual a distinct entity, but so too are all other entities. The Individual logic sees others in terms of itself, as separate and distinct. The assumption of separateness means that relationships, which are important for the survival of the individual as a social being, must be created. Relations are necessary, but they are not presupposed.

The assumption of separateness undergirds the whole idea of communication as a process. Under the Individual logic, individuals assume there are no relations and thus proceed to communicate as if there are no relations. Communication by necessity becomes what Carey described as a "transmission process" of sending and receiving between the separate entities.[25] Although many scholars may cringe at the idea of communication-as-transmission, we see this implicit assumption of separateness in the focus, common in Western communication studies, on information and descriptions of communication as "information flows," or "one-way," "two-way," or even interactive "exchange." The Individual logic's premise of separateness is evident in the explicit goals that seek to "reach," "connect," or "engage" with others. For Boundary Spanners, it is noteworthy that in the Individual logic, relations are a *by-product* of communication, not a prerequisite or state of being in communication.

Tied to the idea of wholeness and separateness of each individual entity is the idea of autonomy. Each individual is bounded, separate, and autonomous. Autonomy privileges independence, freedom of individual choice and action. Autonomy is inherent in the critical need for boundary definition and vigilance against others or the larger social group that would trespass on individual boundaries of identity expression or action. Geertz's phrasing assumes not only separateness but also an inherent opposition with others and the larger social grouping: "(1) a distinctive whole [the individual] . . . set contrastively both against (2) other such wholes and (3) its social or natural background."[26] "Contrastive . . . against" suggests a predisposition to look for differences, rather than an assumption of commonality and a focus on similarities.

The interlocking nature of these characteristics of the individual as the Communicator makes this reasoning appear airtight. It is hard to talk about one without evoking justification for the other; if the individual is a bounded whole, it is by definition autonomous and separate. If it is separate from others, it is bounded itself and thus autonomous. It if it autonomous, it must be complete unto itself, and that implies being separate.

However, if we probe deeper into these buried assumptions, we see another layer. This hidden layer once again bears the imprint of the ancient Greeks, specifically Aristotle's *Rhetoric*. An unspoken assumption that makes it possible to even entertain the idea of "the Communicator"—the very idea that one individual can be responsible for communication—is the imperative of individual agency.

Agency lies at the heart of the Individual logic of communication. The whole idea of self-definition, self-expression, and relationship building by a single individual entity implies agency. Agency, not surprisingly, was identified as one of the defining features of ancient Greece by a team of international researchers led by Richard Nisbett.[27] As Nisbett and his colleagues observed, participatory democracy imbued individuals with a sense of personal agency: "The idea of the Athenian state was a union of individuals free to develop their own powers and live in their own way."[28] Rhetoric at its core was about empowering and enhancing individual agency.

Probing further, we see another corollary assumption. Not only does the individual have agency, but that agency is tied to the power of speech. Ancient Greece was known for its contentious debates; one needed to defend oneself in the political arena as one would on the battlefield. For Aristotle, "the use of rational speech is more distinctive of a human being than the use of his limbs" as a means of defense.[29] Speech designed to affect others and one's environment privileged the goal of persuasion and influence. Aristotle's focus on "all means of persuasion" resonates with the core underlying premise of the Individual logic: an individual Communicator imbued with agency through the power of speech with the goal of influencing others and one's environment.

David Berlo aptly captures these assumptions of agency, speech, persuasion, and influence in *The Process of Communication,* one of the early texts introducing students to the field. In the opening chapter, Berlo explains the purpose of communication as an evolution of behavioral development that we begin at birth as "totally helpless creatures." He writes, "We have no control over our own behavior, over the behavior of others, over the physical environment . . . we are at the mercy of any force interested in affecting us."[30] As infants, we have zero agency. Gradually, "we form sounds and we learn that some of these sounds elicit desirable behaviors from others. . . . We can begin to *affect*, as well as be affected" (emphasis in the original).[31] Thus, we gain agency, even if we are unaware of that agency.

Gradually, we gain both greater awareness and agency. Berlo implies agency through speech: "We begin to master a verbal language . . . we learn to talk, to ask questions, to make requests. . . ."[32] We grow more sophisticated: "We interact with other people. Communication is the basis of this interaction." But, Berlo asks, "why do we communicate? What are our purposes?" Agency. It is all about agency, as Berlo forcefully argues:

> Our basic purpose in communication is to become an affecting agent, to affect others, our physical environment, and ourselves, to become a determining agent, to have a vote in how things are. *In short, we communicate to influence— to affect with intent.* (emphasis in the original)[33]

Throwing in the idea of having a "vote" may seem out of place, but it takes us back again to the *agora* of ancient Greece. Berlo invokes Aristotle: "This kind of formulation of communication purpose clearly is similar to the classical statement of Aristotle. It may appear to belabor the obvious."[34] For those with a preference for the Individual logic, it may be "obvious." For Boundary Spanners, it is important to note, as we see in the other logics, none of this is obvious—unless one begins with relational premise of the individual Communicator.

These buried assumptions that undergird the Individual logic in communication have parallels that extend to public diplomacy, including the association of speaking with agency. When the Italian city-states began the practice of exchanging diplomatic representatives, resident ambassadors were originally known as "resident orators."[35] Then, as today, "the value of a diplomat lay in his ability to communicate, negotiate and persuade."[36] In one of the most extensive discussions of communication and diplomacy, Jönsson and Hall write that "in diplomatic communication 'saying is doing' and 'doing is saying.'"[37] They add that the "semantic obsession" of diplomats, observed by Aba Eban, rests on the realization that "speech is an incisive form of action."[38]

Verbal dexterity is still valued in modern diplomatic practice. In public diplomacy, speech as a substitute for action, including violence or coercive force, is epitomized in the notion of soft power. When Joseph Nye first introduced the concept back in 1990, he contrasted "soft power"—the ability to persuade by attraction—to "hard power," the use of economic and military force.[39] The next section looks at the unique communication dynamics that help maintain the relational premise and assumptions of the Individual logic.

Winning Hearts and Minds

As we have seen, preserving individual autonomy and agency is paramount in the Individual logic. In the ways this logic's communication dynamics contribute to preserving autonomy and agency, we can hear echoes of both Aristotle's legacy and the Communicator's quest to win hearts and minds. We can highlight several key communication dynamics, most of which are familiar to contemporary Western communication models as well as public diplomacy.

Individual Attributes and Agency

Given the focus on the individual Communicator, the first salient dynamics of the Individual Logic are the attributes and agency of the individual entity. Attributes can be values, beliefs, or characteristic features. Agency aligns to the focus on communication behaviors, verbal and nonverbal. According to this logic, everything one says or does communicates; hence the early communication axiom: "One cannot not communicate."[40] Behaviors, when used purposefully, become communication skills and competencies. The skillful communicator often equates to an effective communicator. Boundary Spanners should note that according to the Individual logic, attributes and agency are qualities possessed solely by the individual Communicator.

As we have seen, Aristotle posited that *ethos*, or the speaker's character, was foundational to persuasion. Aristotle wrote of the attributes of a "good man" as virtues. What makes for a "good man"? For Aristotle, three attributes in the orator's own character can "induce us to believe a thing apart from any proof of it: good sense, good moral character, and goodwill."[41] Goodwill was an important attribute. "It helps a speaker to convince us," said Aristotle, "if we believe that he has certain qualities himself, namely, goodness, or goodwill towards us, or both together."[42] Contemporary communication studies would add personal charisma and competence to the list of attributes Aristotle identifies.[43]

In public diplomacy, the rise of the concept of soft power illustrates the focus on individual attributes as a foundation for persuasion. Joseph Nye characterized a nation's culture, political ideas, and policies as soft-power resources, or inherent attributes of the nation. Nye writes of public diplomacy in terms of "wielding" these soft power resources to attract and influence others in the international arena.[44] The idea of "wielding" relates to the importance of communication as agency. According to this logic, it is not enough to possess attractive attributes. As Rawnsley noted in speaking of the soft power competition among states, "Public diplomacy is the conscious act of communicating with foreign publics.... After all, if no-one knows about one's values and good deeds, where is the power?"[45]

Message

Wilbur Schramm captured the importance of message when he observed that "at some point in the process [the message] is separate from either sender or receiver."[46] The message is the vital link between the individual sender and the receiver. The message enables the autonomous individual to connect with others. The message is the key to persuading others. Early communication models (such as the Shannon and Weaver model) focus intently on how to encode and decode messages so that the message which the source intends is the one that the receiver understands and that the message achieves its objective. Not coincidentally, as Deibert notes, "message content and strategies have been the dominant focus in all areas of contemporary communication."[47]

For Aristotle, message was a crucial element. He laid the foundation for the expectation of a well-reasoned argument and use of logic. As Aristotle writes, "Persuasion is effected through speech itself when we have proved a truth or an apparent truth by means of the persuasive arguments suitable to the case in question."[48] He developed numerous techniques for constructing persuasive arguments. Syllogism, for example, is a rhetorical device that presents a major premise and minor premise, and leads to a conclusion reached through deductive reasoning.

In public diplomacy, message is paramount not only to persuasion but also expression. We see this in U.S. public diplomacy, where messaging has been central. This was underscored in early the 9/11 Commission Report on public diplomacy, which stated: "From the first days of our Revolution, America's security has depended on the clarity of the message: Don't tread on us."[49] The Commission's first public diplomacy recommendation was: "The U.S. government must define what the message is, what it stands for."[50] With the rise of networks, the focus on static messages has gradually been superseded by the dynamic quality of narratives. One of the most innovative theory building in public diplomacy is in the area of strategic narratives, which was introduced by the research team of Miskommon, O'Loughlin, and Roselle.[51]

Medium

The third dynamic in the Individual logic is message delivery, or communication medium. If communicators in this logic first ask, What is our message?, then the next question is, How do we get the message out? What is the most effective means for reaching and persuading the audience? Message design and message delivery are often intimately intertwined; the content of the message shapes the choice of delivery. In ancient Greece, both the message content and the message delivery were embodied in the orator; hence the importance of speaking style. An orator's style was part of message effectiveness as well as identity. Athenians, for example, were known for their elaborate, lengthy treatises and eloquent style. Spartans, in contrast, were known to be terse, mastering pithy rebuttals.[52]

Message design and delivery are likewise intertwined in contemporary communication study. Advancement in one prompts advances in the other. For instance, the advent of the mass media heralded more sophisticated message design and delivery strategies to reach a mass audience. As mass media grew, we saw the birth of marketing, advertising, public relations, and propaganda. The field of communication has had an enduring fascination with media and how it shapes messages, captured in Marshall McLuhan's often-cited phrase "The medium is the message."[53] Although McLuhan was referring to radio and television during the mass-media era, the phrase continues to resonate powerfully into the digital era.[54] A reiteration of "the medium is the message" is seen in digital media in the extensive discussion of "affordances," or perceived uses or "action possibilities," such as interactivity and collaboration.[55]

In traditional and public diplomacy, the impact of changing communication technologies has been pivotal in shifting perspectives from the "old diplomacy" to the "new diplomacy," according to Geoff Pigman.[56] The early telegraph dramatically changed the time dynamics of traditional diplomacy. In public diplomacy, early mass media tools were instrumental in reaching foreign publics. Beginning with radio broadcasts during World Wars I and II and continuing throughout the Cold War, ever more sophisticated media tools and persuasion strategies emerged. In the immediate aftermath of the 9/11 attacks, U.S. public diplomacy immediately deployed a wide-ranging arsenal of mass media tools, from radio stations to glossy magazines. With the rapid rise of digital and social media, public diplomacy was soon referred to as "digital diplomacy"[57] and quickly become an "obsession" for the foreign ministries, according to diplomatic scholar Shaun Riordan.[58]

Audience

A fourth dynamic of the Individual logic concerns the receiver, or audience. Aristotle considered the hearer as a judge who would ultimately determine the persuasiveness of the speech. He discussed different types of listeners or characteristics of the audience, what today might be considered basic demographics.[59] However, in classical rhetoric, the focus was on the *rhetor* or communicator. The audience's role was largely passive, as one scholar notes: "The Rhetor might need to learn *about* the audience in order to persuade them, but the rhetor does not learn *from* the audience."[60]

The Individual logic and contemporary communication studies share a dominant focus on the Communicator. Because both presume that the communicator is separate and distinct from the audience, the audience is not intuitively known but must be identified and studied. Analyzing one's audience and knowing human behavior resonate with contemporary Western communication studies and the Individual logic.[61] In contemporary communication, there is an extensive body of literature on how to research the audience. The corollary idea, however—that of the audience studying the communicator, as we see in many traditions—is not a given. Again, the Communicator learns *about* the audience, not from it. The Individual logic largely sees the audience as passive, the recipient of the communication. The view of the audience as passive, in a one-way flow of information and influence, mirrors early models of contemporary communication. Later models added audience feedback, making communication a loop or two-way flow of information from the receiver back to the speaker. The lack of information exchange or mutual learning helps to reinforce the view of an audience as a passive and distinct, if not distant, "Other."

Public diplomacy embeds the idea of audience as separate and "the Other" in its assumptions about who makes up the *public* in public diplomacy. Kathy Fitzpatrick, in her study of public diplomacy definitions found in public diplomacy scholarship, notes that there was common agreement that public diplomacy is aimed at foreign publics.[62] However, Ellen Huijgh, in her study of the practice of public diplomacy of some countries, found that the domestic public was the key public.[63] Chinese terms for public diplomacy, such as "diplomacy of the people," reflect this priority.[64] Similarly, national branding campaigns, such as *South Africa—Alive with Possibility*; *Colombia es Passion*; and *Indonesia Hundred Years of National Awakening* were all predicated on building a domestic buy-in before venturing to the international realm.

Goal Orientation

The Individual logic's goal orientation also relates to its presumption of agency. In this logic, communication is persuasive and purposeful with an end goal in mind. For the ancient Greeks, the goal of rhetorical training was to persuade enough people to secure the majority opinion and win a debate. Greece was distinct from other ancient civilizations in that conflicts were solved by majority rule. Debaters did not need to reconcile differences with opponents or with the whole of the community, as in consensus politics. Instead, differences between opponents might actually be deliberately accentuated in order to secure the support of the doubtful and solidify the support of those who already agreed.[65] Vigorous advocacy by separate parties fueled a tolerance for contentious political discourse.

The Individual logic reflects that ancient Greek goal orientation. What is noteworthy in both contemporary communication studies and this logic is that the individual defines the goal. Goals of communication include to inform, persuade, entertain, and educate. Uses and gratification theory, for example, is a prominent example of a theory that looks at media use by individuals.

Both scholarly and policy discussions of public diplomacy prominently assume goal orientation. Nye defines soft power, for instance, as a means "to achieve one's goals through attraction and persuasion rather than coercion and payment."[66] Scholars have even explicitly referred to public diplomacy as a genre of rhetoric. Hayden, for example, discusses "the rhetoric of soft power."[67] Jackson writes of "twisting tongues and twisting arms."[68] As Gerber notes: "Public diplomacy is, at its core, a necessarily suasive endeavor, concerned with the influence of foreign audiences and the modification of their behavior in some way."[69] State-centric public diplomacy also focuses on individual-level persuasion, as we see in the early definitions of public diplomacy as a way to inform, influence, and engage foreign publics.

Measurability

Finally, goal orientation also suggests that communication outcomes are measurable. To secure a majority in Greek politics, a party only needed one more vote than the opponent. One vote could make the difference between winning or losing the debate—a practice founded on the presumption of separate, autonomous individuals.

The Individual logic pairs two linked premises: that communication has an end goal, and that we can measure communication's success vis-à-vis that goal. We see this goal orientation in one of the earliest models of contemporary communication. Harold Lasswell's verbal model captures all the communication dynamics of the Individual logic, including the need to assess impact or effect: "Who says what to whom in which channel with what effect."[70] The tradition of quantifying the effect of communication has heavily favored quantitative assessment methods such as opinion surveys, content analysis, and, more recently, data mining over more organic, qualitative analyses. Quantitative studies ask if communication has achieved its goal and, if so, by how much.

Today, measurability has been elevated beyond its practical function to become an end in itself. Frequent mentions of 'accountability,' 'effects,' and 'effectiveness' underscore the notion that communication outcomes must be measured to have value.[71] As Cull notes, such measurements of engagement may include many different figures, such as numbers of student exchanges, cultural exhibitions, or changes in public opinion. [72]

If we look again at Lasswell's verbal model—"Who says what to whom through what medium with what effect"—we have a pithy summary of communication dynamics accentuated in the Individual logic. "Who" corresponds to the communicator. "What" is the message. "To whom" is the audience. "Through what medium" is the delivery method. "With what effect" reflects the assumption of goal orientation and measurability. Of course, these dynamics are present in the other logics, but not necessarily interpreted along similar lines or seen as equally important. For instance, a would-be communicator accustomed to the goal-oriented Individual logic may wish to gain influence or control, and thus enter into relationship-building with this goal in mind with a partner operating within the Relational logic. Their efforts may well be perceived as disingenuous or manipulative, undermining the very relationship they seek to build. The idea of "measuring" the relationship may seem similarly off putting. However, as seen in the Relational logic, partners gauge the strength of relational bonds in subtle and sometimes not-so-subtle ways.

For the Boundary Spanners

The role of Boundary Spanners is to look for the commonalities as well as the differences among the communication logics. Finding commonality is especially important for the Individual logic. As Geertz noted, because the individual is bounded and complete within itself, the tendency is to find contrasts and differences rather than similarities.[73]

Individualism and Individuality

One possible area of commonality for Boundary Spanners is noting the distinction between "individualism" and "individuality." We examined the distinction between the two from a relational perspective in Chapter 2. Here we can highlight further the communication implications of the Individual logic. Individualism—the idea of a bounded entity as separate or apart—is often associated with a Western and even uniquely American perspective.[74] Here individualism might be seen as a trait particular to a limited group of people. Individuality, on the other hand, is pan-human. Individuality is the idea that each individual is unique and distinctive from others—without necessarily being separate or apart from others. In other words, one does not have to be separate to be unique or distinctive. Individuality is common around the globe and exemplified in the common practice of naming human infants upon birth. Naming makes each individual uniquely identifiable and distinctive. Similarly, a person's fingerprints, facial features, or even the iris of the eyes are all pan-human examples of distinctive physical attributes that make each individual unique. Our distinctive personalities, too, make us recognizable to others, including when we are out of sorts or "not ourselves." Whereas individuality accentuates uniqueness, individualism accentuates separateness.

The Individual logic highlights the individual as bounded, separate, and autonomous. Because it presumes autonomy, this logic ties individuality—what makes the individual unique—to individual agency. Individualism also implies boundedness, locating unique attributes and agency *within the individual*. Soft power, for example, is an attribute of individual nations, not contextually based in the geopolitical context or relationally based in a shared cultural heritage. Individuality, however, does ascribe both unique attributes and agency to individuals, but it does not necessarily locate those features solely within the individual.

The Individualist logic prizes independence and "self-reliance" because they preserve the autonomy of the individual. In a social setting, the individual may choose to remain independent or enter into an interdependent relationship with other autonomous individuals. If autonomy is linked to identity, losing autonomy can be experienced as losing one's identity or uniqueness. Interdependence risks fusing the separate identity of the individual with the identity of the group. Because this logic posits that conformity, passivity, submission, and compromise can threaten or erode individual autonomy, individualism tends to stress equality and mutuality as well as horizontal relationship patterns.

Individuality does not imply individualism or being a separate, bounded, or even autonomous entity. Individuality is not predicated on the need to be separate in order to define and preserve distinctness. In fact, because relational contexts assume individuals are inherently connected to others, those connections provide the foundation for the individual's identity. As an Ubuntu expression relates: "One is a person through other persons." Remaining connected to the larger social grouping is an important dimension of individuality. Rather than seeking to express one's individuality as separate from the social group, individuals express their individuality *within the social context* of relationships.

While the Individual logic may stress individual agency, we see the relational and contextual features of individuality in the Relational and Holistic logics. In these, the greater risk to identity is not loss of autonomy but separation or isolation from the social group. Valued individual attributes such as loyalty, generosity, sincerity, and sensitivity are all relational-level qualifiers and underpin valued social attributes such as group solidarity or harmony. Seemingly individual-level qualities such as dignity, honor, and "face" carry immense value not as individual attributes but rather as social currency. Similarly, the notion of "public face" is not an individual attribute but rather a collective property to be safeguarded and preserved.

For Boundary Spanners, it is important to understand the nuanced distinctions between individualism and individuality in order to bridge differences, find commonality, and leverage diversity in problem-solving.

Individuality: Identity and Expression

Individuality is particularly important for Boundary Spanners in understanding the importance of human speech and the connection between verbal expression and identity. Both are key in the Individual logic.

One of the important underlying threads spanning the Individual logic is the connection between self-expression and identity. On the surface, the Individual logic may appear to have an exaggerated focus on speaking, leading to a common characterization of Westerners as talkative. Individual logic not only values speaking, but speaking up and out. Each individual is self-reliant, and that self-reliance includes communication in being able to speak up for oneself. Individual logic contains often-heard phrases such as "self-identity," "self-expression," "self-promotion," and "self-assertion." There is a competition to be heard, to be visible. Assertiveness is viewed positively, as it plainly and directly expresses feelings and requests.[75] People who lack assertiveness can take assertiveness training classes.

Why the focus on verbal expression? It is not solely about political participation or agency. If we return to the premise of individualism, expression for the individual is an existential imperative. Expression by the individual in any form is, at its core, self-expression. The only way for the individual to be "known" to others, to "connect" with others, or to maintain autonomy, is through self-expression. Hence the emphatic meaning of the Athenian statesman Pericles, quoted in this chapter's opening, that unless one can express oneself clearly, a person might well never have had the thought. Pericles equates the value of expression to that of thinking.[76] Without verbal expression, it is as if individual thought has little, if any, value.

As Kennedy noted, the most distinctive feature of Greek public address was its eristic quality. Eris, from which the word *eristic* is derived, was the Greek goddess of chaos, strife, and discord. While the ancient Greeks reveled in the contentious nature of their public debates, their sentiment is not universal. As Kennedy noted, in other rhetorical traditions "differences are usually politely or indirectly stated" and "injunctions to turn away wrath with a soft answer or even to be silent."[77]

The value of expression, of speaking up, has a corollary effect that tends to devalue silence. The Individual logic sees silence as the "absence of words."[78] Silence is often interpreted as a lack of skills or confidence in communicating with others, signaling shyness or anxiety. It can also be seen as an unwillingness to communicate, and thus signal disagreement or hostility as well as power status or control.[79] In public communication, those favoring the Individual logic may interpret silence negatively as a sign of guilt. Spokespersons are cautioned to avoid using the phrase "no comment." In a crisis situation or confrontation, silence gives the opponent the upper hand or creates a verbal vacuum that the opponent can fill. Because it is grounded in the Individual logic, contemporary (Western) public diplomacy has mirrored this negative view of silence.

For those unaccustomed to the Individual logic, the very need for such explicit assertions may be baffling and perceived as aggressiveness, arrogance, or superfluous verbiage. In some traditions, silence is privileged over words. The Korean term *noon-chi* (tact) and the Japanese term *haragei* (wordless communication) capture the positive regard for communication without verbal expression.[80] Silence is an important feature of yoga.[81] Silence is essential to communing with the self during meditation. As such, silence leads to truth. Silence is also valued in public communication. The Indian leader the Mahatma Gandhi led the quest for independence from Britain, using nonviolence and patience as virtues derived from silence. Gandhi drew from the concept of *satyagraha* (holding on to truth) to extend the value of silence from self-purification at the individual level to a mass, public level demonstrating the power of "silence as protest."[82]

In the Individual logic, negative view of silence is more than an absence of words. It may actually be a threat or risk to loss of identity. In the words of the first U.S. undersecretary of public diplomacy, when compared to the possibility of misunderstanding by speaking out, she cautioned, "Far more dangerous is silence."[83] Her successor echoed that sentiment during Congressional hearings on the public diplomacy recommendations of the 9/11 Commission: "If we do not define ourselves, others will gladly do it for us."[84] Her statement harkens back to 1911 and the famous line by Theodore N. Vail, the head at that time of American Telegraph and Telephone, who captured the rationale against not speaking up: "If we don't tell the truth about ourselves, somebody else will."[85]

Within the Individual logic, self-expression is essential for the individual's sense of identity and being in the world. In a social landscape inhabited by bounded individuals, each separate from the other, the only way that the self makes itself known to others is through self-expression. Separateness presumes no inherent intuitive sense of shared feeling. Verbal expression is the bridge that supplies the information lifeline to others and creates the emotional link that connects one to others. The implicit assumption of the relation between expression and identity underlies the necessity of speaking. It is the trigger that sparks an immediate reaction to preserve and protect "freedom of expression" as a sacred individual right. Individual (self-) expression is essential to (individual) identity.

Sharing and Preserving Heritages

One last note for the Boundary Spanners is the importance of the intertwined nature of intellectual heritages. The Individual logic, for example, appears to originate in ancient Athens, with Western culture as its obvious inheritor. Yet, if one studies the timeline of rhetorical study, there is an obvious gap of several centuries. What happened? When the Greeks fell to the Roman empire, entire collections of works were pillaged, destroyed, or stolen. Some found their way to Constantinople (present-day Istanbul), where they were translated by Christian, Assyrian, and Jewish scholars. During the Islamic renaissance, the Abbasid caliph Al-Mansur in Baghdad sparked a "translation movement" of all the ancient Greek works, including in particular those of Aristotle.[86] In his pathbreaking research, Uwe Vagelpohl described the Greek-Arabic translation movement as "both in terms of its scale and its influence, an unprecedented process of cultural transmission and transformation."[87] The movement lasted over a century and the translated works spread throughout the Islamic empire. When the Islamic empire fell in Spain, European scholars rummaging through the libraries of Andalusia made the surprising discovery of the lost heritage of ancient Greece. This discovery would help propel Europe out of the Dark Ages and lead to its own Renaissance.[88] Boundary Spanners today can see how the synergy of cultural contact and exchange, and ultimately how the preservation of one cultural heritage, often rests on that of another.

Summary

Bounded, separate, and autonomous: taken together, these presumed qualities of individuals highlight why "rhetoric" or skilled verbal expression, indeed self-expression, is so critical in the Individual logic. The three attributes are interrelated ideas that reinforce the logical presence of the others. If autonomous, individuals must be complete or bounded; if individuals are bounded and autonomous, they must communicate to connect with others, who are likewise presumed to be separate and autonomous. Because it is something one must do, communication is purposeful and goal oriented, aiming to connect with others for self-survival and the survival of society. Though the Individual logic assumes we are separate and self-contained, the need for connecting with others is strong and persistent, because individual entities need others for their survival. The drive to connect with others is therefore one of the ironies of the autonomous self: each entity may in theory be autonomous, but survival rests on connecting with others, a charitable way of stating that the autonomous may not be so autonomous after all.

The next chapter ventures to the ancient Near East to examine the origins of the Relational logic. As scholars have noted, if ancient Greece presaged the verbal dimensions of diplomacy, then ancient Mesopotamia was the harbinger of the relational dimensions of diplomatic communication and protocol.[89]

4

Relational Logic

Royal Bonds of Brotherhood

The Relational logic of communication is based on the premise of relationality, that relational bonds constitute the foundation of humanity and communication.

It was the late Bronze Age (ca. 1500–1200 BCE) in the ancient Near East. The Mitanni king was consulting with his advisors: What to do about the aggressive young pharaoh? War would be costly. In lieu of waging battle, the king offered to engage the Egyptian ruler in a course of relations-building, similar to the ties he had cultivated with kings in neighboring Syria.[1] Instead of dispatching his troops, the Mitanni king sent greeting gifts and a letter, carefully etched in cuneiform script on a clay tablet. Surprisingly, the powerful pharaoh accepted the diplomatic overture. When the pharaoh replied, instead of using Egyptian hieroglyphics drawn on papyrus, he used the Akkadian cuneiform script etched on a clay tablet. He, too, sent greeting gifts in return. In hindsight, the kiln-baked clay tablet would weather time more readily than the fragile papyrus. More importantly, through his reciprocal greetings and gifts, he opened the door to an alliance.

Nearly 3,500 years later, in 1887, an Egyptian peasant working his fields discovered the correspondence between the ancient kings. This collection of 382 clay tablets is now known as the Amarna Letters. In the Amarna Letters, diplomatic scholars discovered a flourishing and complex system of diplomatic relations among the rulers of the five great powers of the time (Egypt, Babylonia,

Hatti, Mittani, and Assyria; see Figure 4.1),[2] and kings who called each other "brother." The notion of brotherhood was not an empty formula but a solemn bond with far-reaching political consequences.[3]

At the heart of the royal brotherhood was an elaborate practice of mutual gift-giving and other gestures that served to define and maintain not just their relational bonds but emotional ones as well. The Relational logic shines a spotlight

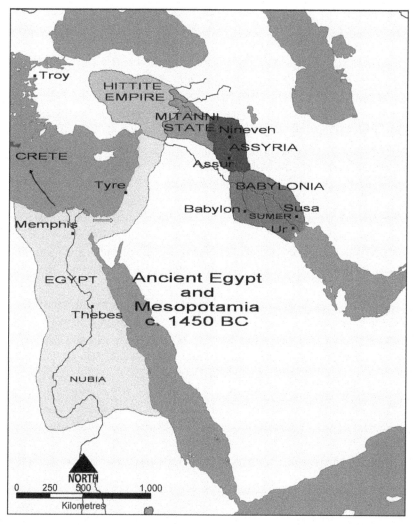

Figure 4.1 Map of ancient Near East kingdoms, 1450 BCE. Author: Свифт/ Svift 2013. Released to the public domain. https://commons.wikimedia.org/wiki/ File:Ancient_Egypt_and_Mesopotamia_c._1450_BC.png.

on the multiple roles emotions and feelings play in human communication. Because emotions reside in the wordless limbic system of the human brain, as we will see, the communication dynamics of the Relational logic do not rely on words. Communication is intuitive, rather than expressed explicitly. We can use Amarna diplomacy as a window into the Relational logic. For the Boundary Spanners, we conclude this chapter by combining insights from ancient texts and emerging research in neuroscience to ground our understanding of the premises, assumptions, and dynamics of the Relational logic.

Amarna Diplomacy: Cultivating Relational Bonds

If ancient Greece heralded verbal dimensions of diplomacy, the ancient Near East cultivated many of the nonverbal, symbolic, and relational dimensions of diplomatic communication and protocol, according to diplomatic scholars Jönsson and Hall.[4] When the Mitanni king approached the Egyptian ruler, he was drawing upon a long tradition of diplomatic practice stretching back to the ancient Syrian city of Ebla of the 24th century BCE. The letters themselves were written in the Akkadian language, the international language of diplomacy developed in Babylonia and used throughout the ancient Near East. By the time of the Amarna letters in the Late Bronze Age, diplomatic practices had been refined. "Amarna diplomacy," as it has become known, shared many features with contemporary diplomacy; it had rules, conventions, procedures, and institutions governing the representation, communication, and negotiations among the kings.[5]

We see in Amarna diplomacy many of the nuances of the Relational logic, beginning with the premise that individuals are not inherently separate but are born into the intimate ties of kith and kin. Amarna diplomacy was built on the "family metaphor."[6] Not only did the kings address each other as "brothers," but "they saw one another as family and expected the kind of loyalty that real brothers would show to one another."[7]

Once established, relationship bonds, like other organic phenomena, require constant attention and nurturing to avoid stagnation and decay. Amarna diplomacy vividly displays that necessary attention to such bonds. The constant exchange of envoys with greetings and gifts served to define and maintain relational vitality. Delay in sending back another's envoy could signal displeasure or a deterioration in the relationship.[8]

We also see in Amarna diplomacy the pivotal element of emotions. While relations may be built upon cognitive elements such as shared understanding or strategic interests, emotions often play a more powerful role in creating, defining, and maintaining relationships. Within the royal brotherhood, open and continuous expression of emotion was integral to relationship maintenance. The Amarna letters are filled with expressions of fraternity (*ahhûtu*) and affirmations of the bonds of love (the Akkadian term *ra'amûtu* and its derivatives), which connote affection, devotion, and esteem, according to William L. Moran, who translated the collection into English. "Love," as Moran observed, "had become part of the terminology of international relations."[9] Such is the profession of love in one of many letters: "Nimmureya, the king of Egypt, my brother, my son-in-law, whom I love and who loves me: Thus Tushratta, the king of Mitanni, who loves you, your father-in-law. For me all goes well. For you may all go well."[10]

The kings nurtured their relationship bonds not only through constant and attentive interaction and heartwarming supplications, but also concretely through tokens of affection. For the royal brothers, this meant gifts. The gifts were beautiful and numerous: gold chariots; daggers adorned with coveted lapis lazuli; horses and exotic animals; and multiple crates filled with personal jewelry, ornaments, figurines, cosmetic flasks, combs, bowls, goblets, and utensils wrought in gold, silver, bronze, alabaster, and ivory.[11] Each item was individually described, weighed, and recorded on a manifest of gifts, then packed in sealed crates that would be publicly opened by the receiving king. Displaying the gifts was a public pronouncement of the strength of the alliance.

Gifts expressed affection: "The more generous the gifts, the greater the love. That was at least the theory."[12] They similarly signaled the gift-giver's stature and generosity: "My brother has but to write to me asking for whatever he wants, and it will be taken from my house."[13] Gifts often indicated the strength of the relationship. One new prince, upon assuming the throne of Babylon, received not the gold statues his father had been promised by the Egyptian ruler, but instead, a wooden carving with gold plate. He knew his relationship was in trouble.[14]

At the time, it was unseemly for a king to engage in commerce. Luxury items, such as those exchanged by the kings, were acquired only by gifts—or war booty. Once an alliance was forged, the royal brothers were not shy about asking for gifts. As one king writes to his powerful royal brother in Egypt: "Gold in your country is dust; one simply gathers it up. Why are you so sparing of it? I am engaged in building a new palace. Send me as much gold as is needed to adorn it."[15] Nor did the royal brothers withhold their sentiments about gifts that did not exactly meet their expectations of reciprocity. A Babylonian king complains to his Egyptian brother: "My gift does not amount to what I have given you every year."[16]

In the exchange of gifts among the royal brothers, "no gift was more consequential than a royal bride."[17] Royal brides directly linked one king to another. While the practice of diplomatic treaties is evident in the region as early as 2400 BCE, the exchange of royal brides effectively solidified family bonds among the kings, thus proving more enduring and prevailing than written treaties.[18]

The practice of exchanging royal brides (daughters and sisters of the kings) transformed symbolic family ties into actual ones.

In Amarna diplomacy, the bonds among the brothers, as the scholars noted, corresponded to political and diplomatic alliances.[19] Yet all these familial greetings, emotional expressions, and lavish gifts were reserved for the households of the Great Kings, who had worked deliberately to establish and cultivate strong bonds.

Conversely, unless the "brothers" established and cultivated relations, communications were strained or non-existent. When one ruler took the liberty to address one of the kings as his "brother"—without having established a relationship—he was strongly rebuked and his mental state as well as his motives were questioned: "For what reason should I write to you about brotherhood?"[20] The brotherly relationship dictated both communication and identity.

Cultivating relational bonds in the ancient Near East has similarities with cultivating diplomatic alliances and partnerships in contemporary public diplomacy. Public-private partnerships, sister city initiatives, and coalition parliamentarians are among the many examples. For Boundary Spanners, building relations is a critical skill, involving attention to the relational nuances such as those embedded in greetings and gifts of Amarna diplomacy. As we will see in chapter 6, iconic global leaders such as the Mahatma Gandhi or Martin Luther King, Jr., were masters at building relations and coalitions. The next section of this chapter examines the underpinnings of the Relational logic. We then turn to the specific communication and relational dynamics that Boundary Spanners want to be alert to in the Relational logic.

The Bond

The Relational logic rests on the premise of relationality, that individuals are inherently linked to others as relational beings. As expressed by Miike, "No one and nothing in the universe exists in isolation."[21] The Other presupposes association with others in fellowship.[22] Unlike the Individual logic that presupposes that individuals are separate and autonomous, and thus seeks to "create" relations, the Relational logic begins with the idea that individuals are born into relations and live their lives in relation to others, and thus seeks to define, build, and manage those relations. This relationality in turn implies that one's identity is not singularly defined by one's own attributes or actions (i.e., self-expression) but by one's relations with others. In the Amarna Letters, we see fellowship in the expressions of brotherhood and relations among kings.

For Boundary Spanners seeking to bridge the communication logics, it is important to recognize the relational premise that distinguishes the Relational logic from the Individual and Holistic logics. The Relational logic shares with the Holistic logic this premise of relationality. The Relational logic, however, is distinct in its focus on intimate, paired relations and the communication dynamics that sustain the paired relational bond. For its part, the Holistic logic focuses on larger relational structures and communication dynamics, seeking to preserve the integrity and continuity of the whole relational structure.

The Relational logic is also distinctive in terms of its communication focus. As we have seen, the Individual logic focuses primarily on the "communicator" and assumes discrete units such as sender, receiver, and speaker/listener. The Relational logic, notably, blurs these separate categories. Muneo Jay Yoshikawa proposed an infinity sign (Figure 4.2) to visually reflect the idea of communication participants as inherently joined: "Both are no longer one or two, but both with the other."[23] The communication focus or weight falls where the eye falls— on the relational bond that links the two.[24]

The focus on the intimate, paired relation contains several implicit assumptions that shape understandings of communication. First is the assumption of mutuality. Mutuality is an inherent aspect of being joined with another; what affects one can affect the other. Mutuality is a prominent theme found in discussions of dialogue, including such notable works as Martin Buber's *I and Thou* and Mikhail Bakhtin's *The Dialogical Imagination*.[25] For Boundary Spanners it is important to note that within the Individual logic, which assumes autonomy, mutuality is a deliberate choice; hence, as Buber's and Bakhtin's works illustrate, mutuality must be argued, and its merits deliberated. The Relational logic, however, assumes mutuality, as we see in the Amarna Letters. The royal brothers are able to make demands upon each other because of the assumption of mutuality; their mutual exchanges provided for mutual benefits. In the following section of this chapter, we see the assumption of mutuality in the various communication dynamics: mutual contact points, mutuality in co-presence,

Figure 4.2

mutuality in perspective taking, mutuality in shared emotions, and mutuality in the shared symbolism of affection, power, or status.

Tied to this assumption of mutuality is the corollary assumption of reciprocity. In the Relational logic, reciprocity is both a concept and a practice. As a practice, reciprocity is included and discussed here as one of the critical communication dynamics that define, maintain, and strengthen relational bonds. Reciprocity in gifting carries with it mutual claims and "moral and sacred obligations to give and receive."[26] In Amarna diplomacy, the kings were exacting in the principle of reciprocity.[27] Each gift sent was weighed against the gifts received. The kings were not shy in calling each other out when their gifts were not of comparable value.[28] Diplomatic scholars have described Amarna reciprocity as "the sacred ground rule of exchange systems. Without it, the system fails."[29]

A final, critical assumption that undergirds both mutuality and reciprocity is buried in an even deeper assumption of fellow-feeling. At its core, the Relational logic is about a felt emotional connection with the other: shared feeling binds the relationship. Emotion pervades the communication/relational dynamics. Although relations may be positive or strained—or competitive in the case of the royal brothers—the underlying premise of shared humanity makes mutuality and reciprocity a moral obligation.

In Amarna diplomacy, the royal brothers were described as "a new kind of collectivity" based on a "common conception of humanity" that distinguished them from the barbarians.[30] In forging ties, "Above all, make him a brother. A man who recognized the ties of family would no longer be a stranger or an enemy or a barbarian."[31]

These interwoven basic assumptions—feeling of shared humanity, mutuality, and reciprocity—shaped an overarching view of "communication as relations." By the Relational logic, the relationship itself constitutes an act or state of communication. Not only does the nature of the relationship define communication, but being in a relationship *is* communication.[32] The relational bond shapes communication; a strong, positive relationship equates with strong communication, while a weak or negative relationship suggests strained communication. This direct correlation between the relationship and communication is why the terms "relations" and "communication" are often used interchangeably in some research traditions.[33]

Because of the bond's powerful influence on communication, actors devote considerable time and energy to the relationship. This focus on the bond has particular implications for viewing words or messages. The Individual logic assumes that words or rhetoric can create a relationship or be a bridge between parties. The Relational logic does not; words have little meaning apart from the relation between the parties. To understand communication from the perspective of relational logic, one must look at connections between the parties involved.

Communication implies relations; without an established relationship, communication experience suffers—if it exists at all. As one African leader put it, "Exchanging information is not the same as communicating."[34] Until a relationship is ripe, communication is limited to formalities, and without an established relationship there is no perceived communication at all. Communication dynamics, as we shall see in the following section, help define and reinforce the relational bond.

Strengthening Ties that Bind

In the Relational logic, the bond between the dyadic pair defines communication. Several prominent communication dynamics help to define, maintain, and strengthen the relational bond and, by extension, the Relational logic. These dynamics are discussed separately and in a linear sequence in this section; however, they are intimately intertwined.

Contact Points

The first and most critical dynamic of the Relational logic involves identifying contact points—either specific persons or opportunity—that anchor the relationship. Contact points form the relationship's foundation. Contact points can reside in a particular person, such as an activist or ambassador, or an opportunity, such as a formal meeting or social event. The assumption of finding the right relational connection or venue to cultivate a relation is similar to the imperative of finding the right message. One of my communication colleagues remarked on her experience in India: "I don't think about messages. Tell me what you want to achieve, what is your goal, and then I will tell you who you need to talk to. For me it is the people I need to get involved. Who do we need to connect with in order to make this happen?"[35] Some traditions implicitly acknowledge contact points as a precondition for communication. We find examples in complex indigenous social networks such as "*guanxi*" in China or "*wasta*" in the Arab world.[36] In Arabic the word *wasta* (which literally means "the middle") is both a verb and an individual who acts as an intermediator between persons to make connections. In China, *guanxi* (which aligns in meaning with "relationships") represents a similar practice of drawing upon relational connections to gain entrée with others.[37]

In Amarna diplomacy, contact points among the kings formed the relational base of brotherhood and family, which in turn defined the larger relational expectations of mutual rights and responsibilities, moral obligations, and reciprocity. The Babylonian king who initially reached out to the Egyptian pharaoh used greeting-gifts, *šulmānu*, to create a contact point. Such greetings physically and verbally establish the relational bond that constitutes "communication."

The idea of contact points and opportunities is prominent in traditional and public diplomacy. In traditional diplomacy, emissaries and ambassadors are obvious contact points in relations between states. It is worth noting that the status or personality of the contact point can play a role in shaping the nature of a relationship. High-level envoys can signal the importance the state attaches to the relationship. In city diplomacy, for instance, elected officials or business executives serve as the contact points for initiating formal connections between "sister cities," helping to lay a foundation for joint activities and exchange.[38] In lieu of specific contact persons, social activities provide opportunities for contact. Meetings or entertainment forums that encourage sustained informal interaction are often most fruitful.

For Boundary Spanners designing or assessing a public diplomacy initiative, identifying strong, durable contact points or well-thought-out contact opportunities are critical skills. Initiatives that are implemented without first establishing contact points or contact opportunities may lack the foundation to grow.

Nonverbal Behaviors

A second dynamic that emerges after sustained contact and co-presence is nonverbal behaviors. The Relational logic assumes that the two parties must be able to view each other, either physically in an in-person setting, virtually in a mediated setting, or even symbolically in a representative setting. Physical in-person co-presence is the most powerful form in that it allows a multi-sensory, embodied communication. Synchronous face-to-face co-presence, whether in-person or virtual, provides valuable cues on the emotional states and reactions of the participants. When people meet face-to-face, they actively scan each other's nonverbal behaviors and adjust their communication in real time.[39] People may shift their words mid-sentence in response to a wrinkled forehead of confusion or a raised eyebrow of disbelief. In a matter of seconds, people may shift from a relaxed to a stiff posture when they perceive a change in voice tone or eye movement that signals sarcasm and disrespect rather than trust and respect.

Nonverbal behaviors contain important relational cues that enable parties to gauge the strength of a relationship.[40] Nonverbal behaviors also play a powerful role in relational development and maintenance. While words or verbal communication contain the "information" content, nonverbal behaviors such as eye contact, facial expressions, or posture offer emotional cues that enrich or deplete relational bonds. Feelings of trust and sincerity—so foundational to the establishment, maintenance, and enhancement of a relational bond—reveal themselves through eye contact, vocal cues, and body gestures. Feelings of liking and attraction or anger and hostility often derive from subtle shifts in posture, body orientation, or physical proximity.[41]

In Amarna diplomacy, the kings never actually met each other, yet contact through messengers stood in for co-presence. The messengers and the gifts they presented in court took the place of face-to-face contact and became the embodiment of the relationship between two kings. The king's messenger was treated as if he were the king.[42] Their gifts—gold, jewels, chariots, and royal brides—were concrete and visible expressions of affection and the strength of relational bonds between the brothers. For this reason, the sealed crates carrying the gifts were ceremoniously received and opened publicly for all to witness, especially visiting dignitaries.[43] As we can see, Amarna diplomacy was very much open *public* diplomacy.

In public diplomacy, perhaps because of its importance, there are numerous examples of co-presence. Visit diplomacy, either by heads of state or groups within the public, are prominent. As Jarol Manheim noted, the welcome accorded to official guests can signal the importance of the relationship between countries even more than "pomp and ceremony."[44] Exchanges such as cultural or education programs are another prominent example, as are international conferences. Not surprising, exchanges are cited as one of the most effective public diplomacy approaches for building trust and good will among participants, and by extension, their countries.[45]

For Boundary Spanners, the critical value of co-presence lies in participants' access to nonverbal cues. Physical co-presence occurs naturally in visit diplomacy, sports diplomacy, and other intiatives in which the participants are physically present and participating in the communication experience. Urry called "meetingness" crucial for social networks. The "the rich gossipy nature of conferences" helps to provide generalizing trust and to establish and cement network ties.[46] Because of the importance of nonverbal cues, online initiatives often eventually incorporate offline gatherings to solidify relationships among participants.

Emotional Expression

A third communication dynamic is emotional expression. Emotion is central to the Relational logic and plays multiple roles. Emotion has popularly been called the glue of personal and social relations, serving the "affiliation function" of linking and binding others in relations.[47] This bonding capability of emotion through "sensing and feeling" is, in the Relational logic, distinct from emotion as an instrumental tool of persuasion in the Individual logic. In the Relational logic, strengthening the emotional connection strengthens the relationship itself. Emotions also provide a global, intuitive sense that can help define the relationship. Emotions serve as a barometer for gauging the strength of the relations, reflected in such common expressions as "strong," "weak," or "strained" relations. Emotions also epitomize the direction and "temperature" of relations, captured by expressions such as "positive" and "warm," or "negative" and "cold."

In the Amarna Letters, emotions were prominent and explicit. As Moran notes, "love" and "fraternity" were integral to the language of diplomacy of the time.[48] Bryce describes communication among the kings as "characterized by effusive expressions of the love . . . and declarations of heartfelt concern for the health and well-being of a royal brother's entire establishment, beginning with his family and extending to his magnates, his horses, his chariots and indeed to all the lands over which he held sway."[49] The brothers openly shared negative as well as positive emotions. When the young king, mentioned earlier who had been promised two gold statues, instead received only gold-plated statues of wood, he wrote to his brother, describing himself as "in pain, angry and in distress."[50] Such explicit expression of emotions acknowledged their power in defining relations.

In traditional and public diplomacy, emotion has been a powerful—yet underexplored—area of research. Research on emotion has been described as the new frontier of contemporary international studies and public diplomacy.[51] Cultural diplomacy, by contrast, readily invokes and celebrates emotions through music, art, and dance performances. Interestingly, while cultural diplomacy is often described as a vehicle for relationship building, one finds few explicit discussions of the role of emotion in cultural diplomacy.[52]

Boundary Spanners may heed Jay Wang's call for a better understanding of publics, "not only at the rational but also the emotional level."[53] We've seen how the emotional tenor of the royal brothers' relations had diplomatic and political implications. Whereas emotional expression may provide a barometer for the relationship, trust is foundational to the establishment, maintenance, and enhancement of a relational bond. We further explore emotion in the section on boundary spanning at the end of this chapter.

Perspective-Taking

Scholars have found that close relational alignment rests on perspective taking.[54] Perspective taking can occur at the cognitive level, by understanding the other's situational circumstances or perspective. Or it may appear as emotional perspective taking—the ability to accurately gauge the other's emotional states or empathizing with the other. Some scholars speak of being "listener-oriented," in the sense that the listener is responsible for attending to the other communication participant's words and behaviors to discern the true meaning of the communication experience. Edward T. Hall describes the process, using the term "interlocutor" as a substitute for listener:

> When talking about something that they have on their minds, a high-context individual will expect his interlocutor to know what's bothering him, so that he doesn't have to be specific. The result is that he will talk around and around the point, in effect putting all the pieces in place except the crucial one. Placing it properly—this keystone—is the role of his interlocutor.[55]

"Feeling with the other," as Ishii describes it, provides an intuitive sense of knowing, which makes the need for explicit self-expression less pressing in the Relational logic than in the Individual logic.[56] In fact, in some socio-cultural traditions, explicitly expressing one's ideas or intent may be perceived negatively. Doing so implicitly questions the other's communication competence, doubting their ability to accurately "read" and anticipate one's needs.

Amarna diplomacy offers an interesting example of this dynamic, in which one king appears deliberately not to engage in perspective-taking by calling out his Egyptian brother for failing to send an envoy to inquire about his health.[57] The king would have known that it took several weeks for envoys to travel, and that he had taken ill and recovered before his Egyptian brother could even know or dispatch an envoy. Such were the "metagames" of the relational dynamics among the royal brothers that tested the loyalties and boundaries of their ties.

In public diplomacy, we see perspective-taking in displays of solidarity among peoples and leaders. A vivid example comes from early 2015, when more than forty heads of state traveled to Paris after the *Charlie Hebdo* attacks. A widely circulated image of the time of the "solidarity march" showed the foreign leaders walking in locked arms with the French president to show their solidarity with the French public's feelings of both sorrow and defiance in response to the attacks.

While some criticized the photo as staged, the image is striking in that it visually captures the communication dynamics of the Relational logic. We see the element of contact points as the heads of state/government representing their respective countries and peoples. Co-presence is seen in their physical presence in Paris (rather than issuing a press statement). We see the bond expressed nonverbally, quite literally, by their walking arm-in-arm. Their shared solemn facial expressions reflect the emotional element, and we see reciprocity in the mirroring of gestures and expressions. Symbolism, the next dynamic, permeates their physical presence, locked arms, somber facial expressions, and black mourning attire.

Reciprocity

A fifth dynamic of the Relational logic is reciprocity. As mentioned earlier, reciprocity is not only an assumption of the Relational logic but also a practice that concretely manifests the assumptions of mutuality and expectation of moral equity. Reciprocity undergirds the relational dynamics of identifying shared contact points, physical co-presence, and perspective-taking. While these dynamics help anchor the relation, reciprocity often guides the relationship's trajectory after an initial meeting or sense of attraction.[58] Reciprocity may be visible, as in exchanges of gifts or visits. It may be subtle, as in the exchange of glances and then smiles across a crowded room. It can be immediate, as in the exchange of compliments or favors, or delayed in terms of borrowed time and "paying forward" for a gesture returned in kind. Jönsson and Hall call reciprocity "a core normative theme running through all diplomatic practice."[59] They distinguish between specific reciprocity, which tends to be immediate and equivalent in nature, and diffused reciprocity, which is less precise and more open. The difference between the two, they say, is often mitigated by trust.

In Amarna diplomacy, reciprocity was pivotal. However, given the assumption of trust in a familial context, one might expect the royal brotherhood of kings to display diffused reciprocity. As Jönsson opines, the strict reciprocity of gifts suggests that this dynamic played a larger and more formal role in defining international relations at the time.[60] Reciprocity among the brothers was also a relational statement of stature. Royal brides were the most valued gifts and were exchanged among the kings—with the exception of the Egyptian pharaoh. While the other kings were symbolically brothers and equal, the pharaoh saw himself as a little more equal and proclaimed that no Egyptian princess would be reciprocated in marriage.[61]

In public diplomacy, examples of reciprocity abound. Reciprocity is a cornerstone in diplomatic protocol and exchanges, as each side looks to the other to see how its efforts were received—a contemporary equivalent of the Amarna kings' attention to whether gifts matched each other.

Boundary Spanners should note the subtle nuances in reciprocity. Gouldner called reciprocity a universal norm.[62] However, different cultural heritages, and of course individuals, appear to have different expectations of reciprocity. In some traditions, delayed reciprocity may be taken as a sign of disrespect or relational neglect, and thus can weaken the relational bond. In other traditions, an immediate return would suggest a lack of trust in the long-term commitment to the relationship.[63] Finding a shared understanding of reciprocity is part of developing the relational bond.

Symbolism

Symbolism, like emotion, is a distinctive dynamic of the Relational logic with multiple roles in bonding a dyadic pair. Symbolism in the Relational logic is often most powerful when it is wordless—an important difference from the Individual logic, in which symbolism is prominent in verbal forms of self-expression and persuasion. Unlike the Holistic logic, which embeds symbolism in group enactments such as rituals, symbolism in the Relational logic is often unique to the two people in the relationship. When symbolism is co-created by both parties, it imbues their relationship with a unique personality.[64] We see the use of symbolism for defining relational bonds whenever parties assign special meaning or symbolic status to their relational bond. On an interpersonal level, two people dating may announce themselves as "a couple," or two business executives may formalize their "partnership," whereas two nations may establish a military "alliance." The kings also formalized their alliances through symbolism. The kings were not real brothers, but by referring to themselves as brothers they symbolically redefined their relationship as familial and distinguished themselves from the barbarians.

Symbolism helps maintain relations by making abstract aspects of the relational bond concrete and visible. In the Individual logic, verbal symbols, including language, make thoughts and ideas concrete. In the Relational logic, symbolism can be verbal, as when parties give each other special titles (e.g., nicknames) or co-create phrases of special significance (e.g., special greetings, stories, or cues). However, symbolism is more often a physical item or act that connects parties to their shared bond. For example, a wedding ring may be a physical symbol of the relational bond between a couple. Symbolism also plays a critical role in preserving relational bonds in diplomatic as well as personal relations, according to Alisher Faizullaev.[65] Often the symbolism entails formal, public ceremonies that involve third parties who witness the bond to reinforce relational commitments. Weddings are prominent interpersonal examples. Official signing ceremonies of partnerships, trade agreements, or treaties are examples in diplomacy.

In Amarna diplomacy, envoys symbolically embodied the physical presence of the kings. Ceremonial receptions and lavish banquets honored not the envoy but the king he represented. Similarly, gifts indicated the king's stature and wealth.[66]

On a higher level of symbolism, we find the spiritual realm. Lafont brings attention to the ever-present and prominent position of the gods in Amarna diplomacy "as witnesses at every stage of this diplomatic life" and "the guarantors of international agreements . . . every treaty, covenant and sworn oath."[67] In a world without international sanctions, as Podany reminds us, "The gods were absolutely real to the ancients" and "only the gods" could punish those who broke treaties and alliances.[68]

In public diplomacy, some of the richest symbolism is found in humanitarian aid work. Japan, for example, has used its extensive bridge-building expertise to construct "friendship bridges" in countries throughout Asia and the Pacific. The completed bridges are opened with an official ceremony, proclaiming the bridge as a physical symbol of the friendship between Japan and the receiving country. Such symbolism, like emotion, may be overlooked. Boundary Spanners can attend to this dynamic and make it more explicit, encouraging parties to draw upon or co-create symbolic expressions that define, solidify, and preserve the relational bond.

For the Boundary Spanners

Each logic directs our attention to different aspects of human communication. The Relational logic highlights the bond between people and the communication dynamics that strengthen and maintain that bond, to which emotion is pivotal. Emotion is also a central thread interwoven throughout the five communication dynamics. We can turn to the Relational logic to expand our vision of the many roles emotions play, especially in wordless communication. For Boundary Spanners, seeing the many dimensions and functions of emotion in communication is key to building competency in the Relational logic (Box 4.1).

Emotion and Relational Identities

The Relational logic highlights multiple roles for emotions in communication. The Individual logic has dominated our understanding of emotion in communication and international studies, and we see again Aristotle's legacy. In devising

---

Box 4.1

The Relational logic highlights the paramount role of emotion in the life of humans as "social animals." The communication dynamics are ever present in relations. However, because of personal preference, habit, or training, we may have overlooked them.

persuasive strategies, Aristotle distinguished between *logos* (appeal to logic) and *pathos* (appeal to emotion), suggesting an either/or vision of emotion in communication. Aristotle not only helped seed the idea of reason and emotion as separate but gave reason the upper hand—hardly surprising given Aristotle's disdain for Sophists' manipulative appeal to emotion. In public debates, Aristotle believed, the wise appealed to truth through logic, facts, and reason, whereas the desperate resorted to emotional appeals. This assumption of separate cognitive versus emotional appeals remains prominent in Western communication theories.[69] Even today, most studies in communication view emotion through the lens of persuasion and search for persuasive appeals. The "Elaboration Likelihood Model" (ELM), for example, distinguishes between a direct communicative route, which requires cognitive engagement, and the "peripheral" route which relies on emotion appeals.

While persuasive appeals may help win over audiences, they do little to explain the bonding function of emotion in human relations. Even interpersonal communication, a field that focuses specifically on personal relationships, appears heavily influenced by the Individual logic. The field views emotions primarily from an individual (as opposed to relational) perspective and as a process of exchanged messages or observed behavior.[70] The exchange theory remains a dominant theory for rationalizing why individuals form and remain in relationships.[71]

In international studies, emotion has long been largely absent from discourse; scholars have focused on states as rational actors and relied on power and rational approaches to explain political dynamics and state behavior.[72] Yet, emotion is everywhere in world politics, as Neta Crawford pointed out in her pioneering study.[73] Emotion has since emerged as a new frontier of research,[74] with scholars studying the role of emotions across a range of behaviors, including political decision-making,[75] negotiations, and mediation.[76] One area of increased study is the role emotions play in political identity and community. As Jonathan Mercer wrote in his piece "Feeling like a State," "All identities depend on social emotions. . . . Emotion structures relationships. A group without emotion is a mere collection of individuals."[77]

The link between emotion and identity is a key insight for the Relational logic. Looking at emotion helps expose yet another dimension of human identity. The Individual logic highlights unique personal attributes, such as personalities or idiosyncrasies, as well as agency, such as skills and competencies. But in addition to these individual identity qualifiers, another realm of identities exists solely because of our relations with others. One can be a brother or sister only by virtue of being in a specific type of relation with another person. While many of us may be a brother or sister, not all are mothers or fathers, grandmothers or grandfathers. These relational identities are also emotional identities. We can, like the ancient kings, extend the emotion to others to create a relational identity: to make another a brother.

What we see also from the international relations literature is how emotion can be extended to include others "who feel like we feel" as part of our identity. This feeling of connectedness to others can be as powerful as it is invisible, whether in an online community scattered across the globe or populism that draws the line between "us" and "them." Similarly, Andersen's "imagined community" and the phenomenon of nationalism cultivated a sense of shared feeling, shared heritage and identity.[78] Without the feeling of being connected to others, as Mercer notes, there is only a collection of individuals who lack a common identity.[79] Boundary Spanners will find it important to look for not just outward or observable relational identities, such as brothers in a family, but the other relational identities forged and sustained by emotional ties, such as the royal brotherhood of kings.

Emotions, Feelings, and Bonding

The focus on emotions in the Relational logic of communication highlights a distinctive aspect of human communication that is often overlooked—communication is often wordless. In much the same way that the Individual logic privileges speech and text, the Relational logic highlights communication in the absence of speech—felt emotions, silence and behaviors.

The dynamics of this logic—contact points, co-presence, perspective taking, reciprocity, and symbolism—do not rely on words. Consider contact points. We often have an emotional gut reaction to people we meet; impressions can form in less than a minute. In co-presence, nonverbal behaviors convey emotional cues about how the other is feeling as well as closeness of the relationship. Accurate perspective-taking rests on gauging the emotional state of the other. Reciprocity is often material, such as in swapping gifts, or based on actions, such as the exchange of favors. Symbolism is often most powerful when it expresses an emotional bond without using words, as in offering a token of one's affection, as the kings surely did on special occasions.

Neuroscience can help us better understand this wordless dimension of communication in the Relational logic. Neurochemical reactions in our mammalian brains reveal a very real physiological basis for the feelings of connection that shape our behaviors, identities, and alliances.[80] During moments of trust and security, for instance, the hormone oxytocin is released. Oxytocin is also stimulated by comforting touch and has been called the "bonding hormone."[81] The good feeling of having coffee and tea or enjoying a laugh with a friend comes from a chemical surge of oxytocin bathing our neural pathways. Oxytocin surges during childbirth. As the mother mammal strokes, caresses, and cleanses the infant, so too, they bond. In adults, sex can provide another oxytocin surge. Holding hands works, too.

According to neuroscientists, the mammalian brain craves oxytocin to maintain a steady, calm state. The problem with oxytocin is that it metabolizes back into the body after a couple of hours. Yes, it's true: We can't hold onto good feelings. Not only can we not hold on to the good feelings (oxytocin), but we may also get jolted by a surge of cortisol. The hormone cortisol is paired with feelings of stress, fear, and anxiety triggered by perceived threats or danger. In order to maintain a steady supply of the good feelings (oxytocin) and mitigate the negative ones (cortisol), we find the telltale characteristic of humans and other mammals to live in relatively stable social groupings such as herds, packs, and clans.

This neuroscience research offers several important takeaways for understanding the Relational logic. First, research suggests that feelings of connection and bonding are neuro-biological needs.[82] We need social companionship and comfort much as we need food. Not only are social bonds tied to our individual needs, but social constellations are also biologically part of our mammalian existence and survival. There is safety in numbers. Diplomatic alliances appear to be part of our mammalian heritage.

Second, the part of the brain where the hormones associated with feelings reside is known as the limbic system. The limbic system has no capacity for language. It is wordless. As Joseph Ledoux, a leading researcher in this area explains, the limbic system operates on the release of hormones that signal whether to approach or avoid.[83] The release of oxytocin is associated with pleasure, so approach. The release of cortisol signals pain, so avoid.

Understanding this wordless realm has critical implications for our understanding of communication. It is feelings, not words, that are used to form and maintain the social bonds that are key to our survival. We do not need words to communicate. In fact, if we want to "express" what we feel, we have to turn to another region in the human brain, the cortex, where language capacity resides. However, as most of us know, putting our "feelings into words" is not always easy. It is a learned, cognitive function. Just as Boundary Spanners learn verbal language, they will need to become more attuned to the wordless realm of communication through emotional literacy and emotional intelligence.[84]

Intuitive Communication

The Relational logic also highlights the role of emotion in comprehending our social world. This intuitive sense is the basis for how we feel about something or someone. Whereas the Individual logic relies primarily on words and cognitive explanations, the Relational logic foregrounds intuitive understanding. To better appreciate the basis of intuitive human communication, we can turn to ancient heritages as well as contemporary neuroscience. In speaking of the experience of ancient India, Durganand Sinha notes, "Long before the advent of scientific psychology in the West, India . . . had developed elaborate theories about human nature, actions, personality, and interrelationships with the world."[85] He adds that these theories were largely based on intuitive knowledge: "Modern methods of controlled observation and experimentation did not have a place, and it was not 'scientific' in the strict sense of the term."[86]

In some societies, the heart is associated with feelings of affection. However, in many traditions, the heart—not the brain—is the seat of wisdom because it combines knowledge of the head with emotion and intuitive knowing-through-feeling. Even in contemporary times and in societies championing deliberative decision-making, we find English-language expressions such as "follow your heart" or "trust your gut," advising that emotions overrule the intellect. The Japanese have a similar expression of "belly logic." Coincidentally, the upper abdomen has one of the largest concentrations of nerve cells in the human body, even more than the spinal cord. Known as the enteric nervous system, it has been called "the second brain."[87] Although neurologists speculate that this system aids in digestion, they have also found it is sensitive to sensory input. Micro movements by another—a twitch of the eye or a millimeter's shift of the lip—may escape our cognitive awareness but cause alarm bells to go off in our second brain. We suddenly lose trust in the other.

Perhaps no discussion of relationships is complete without mentioning trust. While many discussions of trust focus on behavioral indicators, we can also again turn to neuroscience for a deeper understanding of what makes us believe in one another. Neuroscientists have documented the phenomenon of mirror neurons, which enable us to sense the emotion states of others and empathize, according to Marco Iacoboni author of *Mirroring People*.[88] In face-to-face encounters, mirror neurons explain why we may feel fear by witnessing fear in another person.[89] Marcus Holmes applied the research on this mirroring capability to face-to-face diplomacy.[90] As Holmes notes, the mirror neuron system simulates feeling and intent; we simulate in our own brain what the other may be feeling and intending.[91] It is through this simulation that we are able to detect deception. This neurological capability, however, is only available in face-to-face meetings. That, he argues, is why in-person meetings have been such a staple of traditional diplomacy and why diplomats insist on face-to-face negotiations when the stakes are high. Again, Boundary Spanners can see why co-presence and nonverbal behaviors are so important in the Relational communication logic. These physical aspects, along with the neurobiological basis of emotion, are also part of embodied communication. We will look at embodied and holistic sensing of communication in the following chapter, on Holistic logic.

Summary

This chapter explored the Relational logic of human communication. The Relational logic expands our view of communication beyond the individual perspective to the second relational dimension, that of the paired or dyadic relationship. The Relational logic rests on the idea of relationality, that individuals are inherently linked to others. The impetus to form emotional bonds appears to be another pan-human evolutionary aspect shared across human societies—an impetus that cutting-edge neuroscience helps to explain. The Relational logic is pan-human and evolutionary in that the communication dynamics help define, maintain and strengthen relational bonds. Because parties are joined, not separate, this logic's communication dynamics do not rely on transmission of information. Emotions take primacy over words. The Relational logic highlights the paramount role of emotion in the life of humans as "social animals."

These dynamics are ever-present in human communication. However, because of personal preference, habit, or training, we may have overlooked the roles of emotions in communication, including bonding, shaping identities, intuitive knowing, and trust. The Relational logic opens a window into communication dynamics that lets people relate not through language or transmission of information but through intuitive feeling. Because emotions inhabit the wordless realm, we must pay particular attention to the communication dynamics that do not rely on words, such as the symbolism of a gift, the tenor of an email, or the facial expression and posture of one's counterpart. Striving to see both visible and invisible relational dynamics is key to communication competence for Boundary Spanners. In the next chapter, on Holistic logic, we explore the communication dynamics of the relational universe and explore more deeply the dynamics of pan-human embodied communication.

5

Holistic Logic

Cosmic Circles

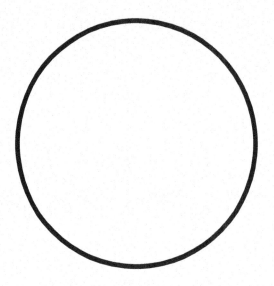

The Holistic logic extends the intimacy of paired relations to a felt sense of connection to others within an all-encompassing, dynamic relational universe. That relational universe defines communication for each individual, and each individual in turn helps maintain the integrity and continuity of the whole relational universe.

In the beginning, there was Chaos. So begins the creation myths of both the ancient Greeks and Egyptians. For the Greeks, χάος (Khaos) was the first of the primordial gods.[1] She existed at the dawn of creation as a void, a disordered and formless mass between the heavens and earth. For the Egyptians, the primeval waters of chaos of Nun was transformed into order and creation by Ma'at, the goddess of justice, balance, and harmony.[2] Maintaining order rested on right behavior with others in the cosmos, as the actions of each affected the other. From the visible world of natural and social relations to the unseen realms of ancestors and the gods, all were connected and interactive. Such interconnectivity and interactivity meant humankind had to follow Ma'at's prescripts and work in sync with all others and nature to maintain balance and harmony—lest chaos return.

The Greeks' belief system would later separate the workings of the physical realm from the whims of the gods in the spiritual realm.[3] Contemporary cosmology reflects the concentrated focus on the physical universe inherited from the Greeks. Egyptian and other cosmologies, however, retained the links between the physical, social, and spiritual realms. The feeling of connectivity with the seen and unseen was for them no less real than today's global-spanning digital connections that include unknown others, and the intersection of cyber-physical-human worlds through the Internet of things.

The connectivity and interactivity assumed in the ancient cosmologies provide valuable insights for understanding the dynamics of our hyper-connected world today. It is also a window into the Holistic logic. In much the same way that the assumption of separateness in the Individual logic raises the imperative of agency or individual action, the assumption of connectivity in the Holistic logic raises the imperative of coordinated interaction with others in a relational universe. This relational universe provides the foundation for communication for all, and all have a role in maintaining the integrity and continuity of the whole. In this chapter, we turn to cosmologies from across the ancient world to explore in depth the relational premise, assumptions, and communication dynamics of the Holistic logic. We begin with the symbolism of the sacred circles scattered across the ancient world.

Cosmic Circles: Connecting the Universe

Soon after gaining the capacity for speech, humans began exploring, naming, and explaining the world around them. According to anthropologists, all societies throughout human history have developed their own cosmology or creation myths.[4] Some ancient cosmologies, such as the Australian Aboriginal Dreamtime, were preserved orally; others visually, as stone structures or etched cosmograms; others in writing, as sacred texts. Understanding them is key to understanding the Holistic logic and its communication dynamics.

These cosmologies reveal embedded assumptions about our relations with others, and thus offer insights for communication and diplomacy, especially pre-Westphalian and indigenous practices. For example, the feather worn in the crown of the Egyptian Goddess Ma'at (Figure 5.1) was used to weigh one's actions; a good heart as light as that feather ensured righteous passage of one's spirit to the next life, indicating the interconnectedness of the social and spiritual

Figure 5.1 The Goddess Ma'at with feather.

Source: Creative Commons, public domain. https://commons.wikimedia.org/wiki/File:Maat.jpg; https://creativecommons.org/publicdomain/mark/1.0/deed.en. This file has been identified as being free of known restrictions under copyright law, including all related and neighboring rights.

realms. The prescripts of the Goddess spread throughout Africa and resonate strongly with the pan-African idea of *ubuntu.*[5]

These ancient cosmologies appear remarkably varied, from Mesoamerica's *Leyenda de los Soles* (Legend of the Suns) to ancient China's whirling yin and yang.[6] They are also remarkably similar in viewing the cosmos as an indivisible whole of interacting realms. How humans acted on earth (social realm) was witnessed by the gods (spiritual realm), who could mete out punishment through a violent act of nature (physical realm). Also linked was an aesthetic realm. In the ancient Greek texts of Homer, the term "cosmos" refers to "an aesthetic act of creating order," according to Nikos Papastergiadis, who describes artistic expression as "partly a symbolic gesture of belonging to the world."[7] Art, in this sense, expresses connection. The aesthetic realm intertwines with the social and spiritual realms in rituals involving synchronous chanting, singing, and dancing.

The unbroken connection of the different realms was symbolized by one of the most prevalent representations found in the ancient cosmologies: circles. One finds circles and circularity everywhere from Stonehenge in Europe to mandalas in Asia to the sun stone in the Americas. Speaking of African cosmologies, Fu-Kiau Bunseki called the sun circle the first geometric form given to humankind.[8] The Ba'Kongo cosmogram, he wrote, consisted of a circle with a horizontal line connecting birth to adulthood, and a vertical line connecting the living to ancestors in the underworld. Taken together, the interconnected elements reflect the circle of life.

The circle symbolically captured the cyclical nature of renewal and regeneration. In ancient Egyptian and Hindu cosmology, the ouroboros, or snake eating its tail, reflected the endless cycle of renewal and continuity. This cycle of renewal suggested a circular view of time, which, unlike linear time, had no end. The Aztecs of Mesoamerica, for example, also envisioned time as circular. Their calendars were typically round, composed of interlocking cycles.[9] The Aztec sun stone (*Piedra del Sol*), in the National Museum of Mexico, visually captures the idea of circular time as well as symbols of cosmic creation (Figure 5.2).

Within this cosmic vision of circular time, diplomatic practices required that relations receive constant attention and renewal through symbolic gestures such as ceremonies, visits, and gifts. Such were the diplomatic practices of the Iroquois nations of North America. The European diplomatic practice of written treaties, which reflected a linear view of time, held little meaning for the Iroquois. Relations could not be frozen in time but needed to be constantly renewed lest they deteriorate. Hence the Iroquois's diplomatic practice of annually "polishing the chains" that tethered the British ships to the harbor and Iroquois territory was a symbolic gesture of renewing the relational bond between the British and the Iroquois.[10]

Circles also can symbolize unity, including the emotional connections of humans to the natural, spiritual, and aesthetic realms. Traditional Hawaiian and pan-Polynesian cultures speak of such emotional connections to humanity and nature in terms of family or *ohana*.[11] Feelings of connectedness made reciprocal exchanges prominent features in indigenous diplomatic relations, such as with the Aztecs of Mesoamerica.[12] If others were viewed as extended family, then one would naturally welcome them with gifts and hospitality. The Aztecs did just that when Spanish conquistadors arrived—with fateful consequences.[13]

Circles represented not only renewal but the dynamic, ever-changing nature of the cosmos. Many cosmologies called this dynamic quality "energy," "force," or even "life-force." Ancient Chinese spoke of *chi* or *qi*, traditional Hawaiian culture *mana*, yoga philosophy *prana*.[14] For the Aztecs of Mesoamerica, a single "dynamic, flowing" life force animated "human beings, plants, mountains water, wind, light, mummified human remains, textiles, and stone structures."[15]

Figure 5.2 Aztec Sun Calendar.
Source: Creative Commons, https://commons.wikimedia.org/wiki/File:Aztec_calendar_(bronze).
svg. Licensed under CC BY-SA 3.0, https://creativecommons.org/licenses/by-sa/3.0/deed.en.

This dynamic energy, however, was not chaotic but coordinated and reciprocal. Traditional African cosmologies speak of harmonized movement in terms
of cosmic rhythm, with similar ideas found in ancient Hindu as well as Greek
texts.[16] Pythagoreans such as Plato likened a well-ordered society to a well-tuned
lyre: "While each note retains its individuality, all are proportionally linked together in a larger whole to form a musical scale, and all are interdependent."[17]

The energy and activity of the cosmos are ordered, proportioned, and in harmony with other elements, including humans.[18] According to the ancient Aztecs,
humans must "perform reciprocating actions that maintain the equilibrium and
continuing existence of the cosmos and humankind."[19] This interplay echoes
the prescripts, discussed previously, of the Egyptian Goddess Ma'at. In these
cultures, humans had a cosmic duty to align their activity with others, expressed

in the Hindu concept of *dharma*, African *ubuntu*, Māori *kia-taa-tanga*, and Confucian *li*.

Although today "cosmos" signifies the universe, originally the Greek *kosmos* meant "order" or "harmony." Harmony was valued not only by the Greeks, but also by ancient Egyptians, Chinese, Sumerians, Hindus and civilizations in Mesoamerica, Australia, and across Polynesia.[20]

The imperative of harmony was not left to chance or human temperament which, as the ancients observed, tended toward the opposite. The spiritual realm, including the all-powerful gods and ancestors, helped modify human temperament by eliciting a moral duty and responsibility to others in the cosmos. Violators would face the wrath of the gods. The aesthetic realm also promoted order. Communal art, music, and dance provided an emotional sense of belonging as well as enjoyment. Artistic expression and aesthetic interest in others, as Papastergiadis notes, is linked to our need for conviviality.[21] Thus, the ancients guarded harmony against the chaos of humankind in two ways: first, through moral duty coupled with the threat of punishment from the spiritual realm; second, through the rewards of shared pleasure provided from the aesthetic realm. These intertwined realms completed each other, and together they completed the sacred circles of the cosmos.

It may surprise us that people of the ancient world *assumed* such universal interconnectivity, given how the modern world struggles with the hyperconnectivity of globalization. The ancients' assumption was based not on visible physical or digital links but rather on invisible emotional and spiritual connections—key underpinnings of the Holistic logic. We explore some of the guiding premises of this mindset next.

An Indivisible Whole

The Holistic logic, like the Relational logic, rests on relationality: the notion that relations constitute the foundation of humanity and communication. But, while both logics assume relationality, they differ in scope and focus. As we have seen, the Relational logic focuses on the paired dyadic relationship and its emotional bond. The Holistic perspective extends and multiplies paired relations, positing an all-encompassing relational universe. This all-encompassing, indivisible relational universe defines communication and makes it meaningful within the Holistic logic (Box 5.1).

Because the paired relationship serves as the building block for the relational universe, the Relational logic's emotional dynamics also permeate the Holistic logic. The Holistic universe is not an impersonal collective of separate individuals, but a felt emotional connection with others. This fellow feeling makes the

---

Box 5.1

Just as the individual *communicator* gives meaning to communication in the Individual logic, and the relational *bond* gives meaning to communication in the Relational logic, it is the whole of the *relational universe* that gives meaning to the communication experience in the Holistic logic.

---

relational universe more than an impersonal collective or network of neutral nodes.[22] Appreciating a shared feeling of connectedness, in belonging within and to the relational universe, is key to the Holistic logic.

Additionally, because communication rests on the relational universe, it is crucial to maintain the integrity and continuity of that relational universe. Within the Holistic logic, an unstable or chaotic universe makes meaningful communication nearly impossible. As we will see, all of the communication dynamics within this logic revolve around this imperative of maintaining the integrity and continuity of the whole.

While the Holistic logic prioritizes stability and order, this relational universe is anything but static. Like the cosmos envisioned by the ancients, the relational universe is dynamic and in constant motion. This dynamism reveals three important premises of the relational universe, and with it, the Holistic logic: connectivity, diversity, and interactivity, which taken together produce the imperative of harmony.

First is the premise of complete interconnectivity. In an all-encompassing relational universe, all are connected. Connectivity expands across time and space to encompass all relations—near and far, direct and indirect, seen and unseen. Even the most distant entities are connected. Relational connectivity is unbounded by time. Past relations may be immediate, such as a felt ancestral spirit, while future relations may shift, as in the case of a hostile enemy transforming into a vital ally. While the nature of connections may change, the idea of being in a perpetual state of relational connectivity with all others remains constant. No single thing is independent: "The universe is a great whole in which everyone and everything are inter-related."[23] Indian heritage, for instance, speaks of a single spirit and frames separateness as an illusion; the greeting "*Namaste*" means "the spirit in me honors the spirit in you."

Because of connectivity and indivisibility, there are no independent entities—an important factor in the Holistic logic's view of communication.[24] Because there are no truly separate entities, there is no separate communicator to transmit information or audience to try to influence. Neither persuasion nor information transfer drives the Holistic logic. The core communication imperative for the Holistic logic is the need to align and balance diverse elements in the interconnected universe. A beautiful example of this communication imperative is the poetry or "flower and songs" of the Aztecs.[25] The purpose of this performative poetry was integration: "Well-crafted song-poems are harmonizing processes in the world alongside the singing of songbirds, the blooming of flowers."[26]

Another underlying premise of the Holistic logic is diversity—which occurs naturally in spanning the entirety of the relational universe. The ancient cosmologies vividly capture the assumption of diversity. The yin-yang symbol, for example, contains the yin elements (female, dark, night, passive) and yang elements (male, light, day, active). The presence of diversity and co-existence of opposites are natural features of the whole. As Fletcher and Fang observed, the yin-yang symbol represents "not opposing forces but rather a reflection of the paired nature of everything in the universe."[27]

To better understand communication within the Holistic logic, it is important to appreciate that while the diverse elements differ from each other, they are not separate bounded entities, but instead are contained *within* a larger whole. Because diversity is a feature of the whole, preserving diversity is important for maintaining the integrity and continuity of the whole. Gou-Ming Chen speaks of the dialectical interaction between feminine and masculine forces of yin and yang as integral to transformation and balance.[28]

A third interwoven assumption of the Holistic logic is that of interactivity, in which the diverse elements constantly realign and adjust as they come into contact with each other. In much the same way as the Individual logic highlights the agency of the individual entity, the Holistic logic spotlights the interactivity of all the diverse entities contained within the whole. Interactivity is implied in face-to-face human communication, as people are continually adjusting and calibrating their behaviors to others. This constant interaction among diverse entities is why, within the Holistic logic, relations are more aptly characterized as a verb or action. Rather than viewing network structures as a static relational grid, this logic views such networks as a circuit of energy.[29] All of the cosmologies, ancient and modern (including Einstein's equation $E = mc^2$), describe the universe in terms of energy—a critical concept in the next section on communication dynamics.

The imperative of harmony is the final overarching assumption of the Holistic logic. From the perspective of the Individual logic, harmony would seem to be an aspirational state; that logic might ask how one can possibly align the actions of individual entities, especially if they are dissimilar. In the Individual logic, harmony implies suppressing diversity to bring diverse elements into alignment. This is not the case in the Holistic logic; harmony does not assume sameness. In the Holistic logic, diverse elements align because of interconnectivity and interaction, not sameness. As different entities interact with each other, they mutually change each other. Because the elements are not separate, but connected parts of the larger whole, harmony is not only possible but, as Yaqing Qin noted, inevitable.

From a holistic perspective, harmony among diverse, interconnected, and interactive elements is key to maintaining the integrity and continuity of the whole. Whereas emotional connection is the defining feature of the bond in the Relational logic, harmony is the defining quality of the whole in the Holistic logic. This defining imperative of harmony, or balance and order, occurs prominently in the cosmologies, from the ancient Greek philosophers to the Chinese sages.

In the Holistic logic, harmony or what Marsh called "dynamic equilibrium" is a communication imperative.[30] Chen called harmony "not only the guidepost of regulating the never-ending process, but also the ultimate goal of human communication."[31] This imperative stems from the assumption of interactivity: "Since all action is in concert with others, or at the very least affects others, harmony in relationships becomes a chief goal of social life."[32] Because of the overarching influence of the relational structure in defining communication, one learns and participates in relational dynamics that mirror and uphold the universe. In short, diversity is a feature of the relational universe, and by learning and preserving diversity, one preserves the relational universe. Like the circular serpent Ouroboros, the relational structure defines communication for the individual, and in turn, the communication of the individual contributes to the integrity and continuity of the relational structure. These relational dynamics are discussed sequentially in the next section, but Boundary Spanners should be mindful that they are interwoven; to speak of one is to evoke and imply another.

Harmony of the Whole

As we turn to the communication dynamics of the Holistic logic, we note two important points. First, because the paired relation is the basis for the relational universe, the Holistic logic includes the communication dynamics (contact points, co-presence, emotional expression, perspective-taking, reciprocity, and symbolism) of the Relational logic.[33] Second, in the Holistic logic, communication dynamics are better understood as actions and interactions rather than static phenomena such as a communicator, message, or even emotion. Because *being in a relation is communication*, we can think of these communication dynamics as relational dynamics. Yaqing Qin, who developed a relational theory of world politics, suggested the term "relators" when speaking of actors.[34] To underscore the relational dynamics, we can adopt the term "relators" alongside "communicators." Relational dynamics or behaviors in the Holistic logic are actions and interactions that preserve the integrity and continuity of the whole.

To help illustrate the relational dynamics at play in the Holistic logic, we can return to some ancient cosmograms. These cosmograms adorned temples, informed medical and agricultural practices, and helped locate humankind's relations to others: fellow humans, plants and animals, mountains and rivers, wind and fire, the sun and stars—and, most importantly, the gods.

Expanding Relations

The first communication dynamic of the Holistic logic, tied to the assumptions of interconnectivity, is the continual expansion of an individual relator's relationships. One reason the all-encompassing universe is not static is because of this constant expansion, both outward and inward. Yaqing Qin suggests that relations represent a form of power, and thus relators seek to expand their relations.[35] Expanding or creating new relationships is a prime relational behavior of the Holistic logic. Relationship expansion may extend in multiple dimensions, such as physically or geographically (from closest to farthest), emotionally (intimate to estranged), or ideologically (like-minded to conflicted). Outward expansion represents the infinite reach of an all-encompassing universe.

We can refer to Fei's idea of relationships as concentric circles, or what he called "different association,"[36] to visualize the outward and inward expansion of relationships. Raindrops, as shown in Figure 5.3, illustrate this concept aptly. The Individual logic, with its focus on the individual entity, may focus on the outward, radiating nature of the circles as each individual raindrop hits the water. However, if we assume a wider Holistic perspective, as multiple raindrops hit the water, their circles overlap.

Relators are ever cognizant of the dual nature of outward as well as inward expansion of relations. The inward, overlapping expansions can create dense interconnections among one's relations. Acts of reciprocity may further solidify the relational bond. Scholar Shi-Xu spoke of this internal relational expansion as interpenetrating and mutually influencing.[37] Within the Holistic logic, any idea of one-way communication or influence is illogical; one cannot seek to influence another without being vulnerable to being influenced by the other.

To help illustrate the dual outward and inward expansion, we can turn to the 12,000-year-old Sri Yantra (Figure 5.4) used in meditation. If one looks closely, in the center of the middle triangle of the Sri Yantra is the *bindu* (meaning "dot" or "point" in Sanskrit). The *bindu* is the center point from which the cosmogram is created. In ancient texts, it is a microcosm of the larger cosmic universe.

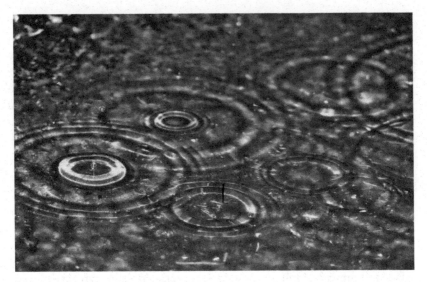

Figure 5.3 Concentric circles of raindrops.

Source: Image courtesy of National Oceanic and Atmospheric Administration, U.S. Department of Commerce (http://www.crh.noaa.gov).

The Sri Yantra illustrates the duality of expansion: as the triangles expand outward from the central *bindu*, they cross and overlap other triangles, and are interpenetrating. Like the raindrops, each outward expansion carries with it a corresponding inward expansion.

The communication dynamic of outward and inward expansion of connectivity was echoed in ancient India's mandala geopolitics—described in Kautilya's treatise on statecraft, *Arthashastra* (ca. 150 BCE), which defined a polity by its charismatic center rather than its boundaries. As Dellios explains, in ancient times, land was plentiful; people were the scarce and valued resource.[38] Power was based on solidifying human loyalties rather than conquering territory.

In contemporary public diplomacy, the dual direction of expansion would suggest that "public" in public diplomacy includes both external or foreign publics and internal or domestic publics. Internal publics—both the domestic as well as diaspora publics—may be the more important publics because they are closest physically or emotionally to the charismatic center of a political entity. Not only are publics interconnected with a political entity, but publics and other actors are all interconnected with each other. Boundary Spanners need a wide-angle lens for viewing both the expansive and the interpenetrating nature of relations between and among states and publics.

Figure 5.4 Sri Yantra with center *bindu* dot.
Source: Artwork by Daniel Conrad under direction of Harish Johari. Released to public domain by Daniel Conrad. https://commons.wikimedia.org/wiki/File:Sri_Yantra_Correct_Colors_Johari_1 974.jpg.

Identifying Commonality, Preserving Diversity

A second relational dynamic of the Holistic logic lies in identifying and creating commonality while simultaneously preserving diversity. These two seemingly opposite relational behaviors in fact go together. First, interconnectivity and shared humanity suggest an assumption of similarity or affinity. Relators seek to actively find or create areas of commonality. In the Individual logic, the search for commonality is often through dialogue. The Relational logic creates commonality through reciprocal gestures such as exchanges of visits or gifts. In the Holistic logic, as we will see, commonality can develop through the binding power of synchronous activities, such as chanting, singing, or dancing.

Figure 5.5 Female triangles. Author-supplied line art.

Figure 5.6 Male triangles. Author-supplied line art.

Perhaps counter-intuitive, an all-encompassing relational universe assumes both shared similarities and profound differences. Because diversity is another inherent assumption of a relational universe, preserving diversity is critical for maintaining the integrity of the relational universe. Diversity is important at the level of the paired relation because it helps retain the uniqueness and individuality of each entity, and thus the vitality of their relationship. For similar reasons, preserving diversity is equally critical at the level of the relational universe. Diversity is fundamental to the regenerative, synergistic capacity of the cosmos. As different elements combine, they create something new and different from their individual original essence. The whole becomes greater than the sum of the individual parts. This synergy, as a creative and interactive process, serves to maintain the integrity and continuity of the whole.

We can see how preserving and then combining diversity can create synergy again by turning to the Sri Yantra again and focusing on the interactivity of the triangles. Similar to the yin-yang symbol, the Sri Yantra has female elements, represented by the five downward-facing triangles (Figure 5.5), and male elements, represented by the four upward-facing triangles (Figure 5.6).

Consider the implications of the Sri Yantra's five female downward-facing triangles as the dominant orientation. If the four upward-facing male basic triangles were changed to conform to the dominant downward orientation, the result would be a loss of diversity and duplication of the original. We have nine triangles, all facing downward.

However, when the diversity of the downward-facing female orientation is preserved and combined with upward-facing male orientation, their combined diversity produces more than simple addition. Instead of only nine triangles, forty-three new triangles are created (Figure 5.7). This illustrates the phenomenon of synergy. By preserving and combining diversity, the whole becomes greater than the sum of its parts.

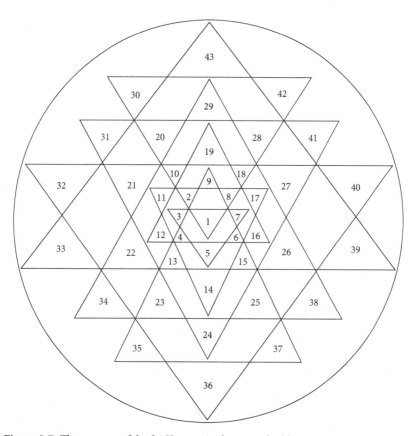

Figure 5.7 The synergy of the Sri Yantra. Author-supplied line art.

Many of the ancient cosmologies and pre-state polities assumed diversity. In the Central Asian steppes, for example, linguistic unity was not a defining feature of political allegiance, and polities and leaders assumed a diversity of languages, according to Neumann and Wigen.[39] Public diplomacy, by its global nature, is grounded in diversity. International conferences, which bring together participants from diverse geographic regions and cultural backgrounds, are a ready example. The give-and-take among conference participants, each retaining their different perspective, yields synergistic results. In such situations, friction is inevitable. But by leveraging diverse perspectives during problem-solving, participants can produce synergistic options that neither side would have been able to envision alone.

Learning and Practicing Contextual Sensitivity

Another key relational dynamic is practicing contextual sensitivity. This entails developing an awareness of the subtle nuances that distinguish different relational and situational contexts in which communication occurs and relations form. The importance of context is tied to connectivity. As Dissanayake noted, "The notion of context of communication becomes important only in a world where everything is interconnected and does not exist in isolation from others."[40] A separate or isolated entity might not be aware of or concerned with context or how its actions affect others. However, when one assumes connections, it follows that one's actions may affect others and vice versa.

Contextual sensitivity is the ability to detect and interpret subtle shifts in relational cues and dynamics of the situational context. Akira Miyahara likens contextual sensitivity to being able to "*feel the mood or air* of each interpersonal situation, and improvise appropriate social behaviors depending upon the reading of the contextual features" (emphasis added).[41] Jai B. P. Sinha and his colleagues delineated contexts in terms of place (*desh*), time (*kaal*), and person (*paatra*); a person would attune to the specificities of a situation and the long-range implications of a response to it.[42]

Contextual sensitivity and knowledge imply awareness of how one's actions may affect others or the relationship in both the immediate and long term. As Chen advised, in an interconnected web of relationships, one must know "how to trace the possible consequences of an interaction."[43] Sensitivity also relates to not only immediate relations but also distant relations. One may opt to compromise in the immediate run if doing so strengthens relations in the long term. Maddux and Yuki also speak of the complex distribution

Figure 5.8 Uzbek mandala. Author-supplied line art, adapted from design by
Shamsiddin Kamoliddin 2006.

of consequences, including indirect and distant consequences.[44] Unlike
network analysis, which measures observable relational links between
identifiable nodes, relational configuration in the cosmos may include un-
identifiable and even unseen entities. And although all are linked in a relational cosmos, they are not necessarily directly linked to each other, as in a
network. The interwoven relations may be so complex, as we see in the Uzbek
mandala (Figure 5.8), that one cannot fully trace the connections—even
though at first glance they seem obvious.[45] Such is the nature of indirect or
invisible relations bound by spirits, forces, or serendipity; one cannot trace
their connections directly.

In traditional diplomacy, contextual sensitivity has long been part of the diplomatic focus on symbolism and protocol. Public diplomacy has tended to focus
more on advocating the interests and goals of the state, sometimes with little
concern for context. Sometimes contextual norms are deliberately violated to
make a statement. In human-centered diplomacies, an initiative's effectiveness
may well be gauged by how well it blends into the context and expected norms
held by the people.

Synchrony: Mutual Adaption and Alignment

The Holistic logic also demands a continual process of mutually adapting and aligning to others, which is related to diversity and connectivity. Miike called mutual adaptation key to harmonious communication and relationships.[46] Individuals are not simply acting on their own within a context; they interact with others in a way that aligns with the actions of others. Gou-Ming Chen described communication as "a process in which communicators continuously adapt and relocate themselves toward interdependence and cooperation."[47]

This process of mutual alignment and adaptation highlights what scientists call "interaction synchrony." Interaction synchrony occurs when individuals match the tempo and tone of each other's verbal and nonverbal behaviors. Young Yun Kim, who conducted an extensive review of synchrony, highlighted how matching our behaviors to another can facilitate bonding and reciprocity of feeling.[48]

When paired interaction synchrony extends to the group level, we can have collective synchrony. Examples of synchrony abound in everyday life: teaching infants to clap or wave their hands, precision drills in military units, reciting hymns or prayers in religious services, sports fans rallying their teams, political protesters chanting slogans. Synchrony is an important aspect of the Holistic logic that illustrates how people can bond and connect when they act or speak in concert with others.[49] Because of its importance as a form of pan-human communication, we will return to synchrony later in this chapter and in the next chapter.

The assumption of constant mutual alignment and adaptation to the other is seen in the yin-yang symbol. Consider if the line between the black and white elements in the yin-yang symbol were straight instead of curved. Visually, the change speaks volumes. A static, straight line separating black and white would suggest a fixed partition between two starkly divided, equally fixed elements (Figure 5.9). A curve, or wavy line, conveys significantly different ideas about the relationship between the two elements of black and white. The arcs of the curve in the yin-yang symbol (Figure 5.10) suggest a constant state of flux, a wave of motion as elements adapt and align to the other.[50]

In public diplomacy, we see a hint of the idea of synchrony in Cowan and Arsenault's often-cited piece on the layers of public diplomacy that move from monologue (speech) to dialogue (speech) to collaboration (doing).[51] Their definition of collaboration as "initiatives in which people work together on a joint venture or project" implies action, face-to-face interaction, and coordinated efforts.[52] Synchrony is most evident in cultural diplomacy that engages the public in shared synchronous activities such as learning dance steps, playing music, or singing together.

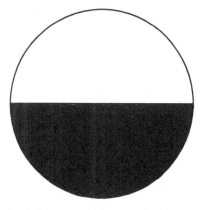

Figure 5.9 Static line, fixed elements. Author-supplied line art.

Figure 5.10 Wavy line, dynamic continuity and change. Author-supplied line art.

Synergy: Change and Continuity

Individual adaptation or alignment with others is not a one-time occurrence. The process of continual and mutual adaption and alignment at the individual level has ramifications for the whole of the relational universe. Again, because of connectivity *with diversity*, as each individual comes into contact with another and encounters different elements in the other, both individuals adapt or realign in order to sustain their connection. As the individual changes, so too does the relational pair. And, as each relational pair changes, so do the extended pairs. In a chain of continual change, so too the whole of the relational universe is also in constant motion. In an inter-connected universe, every individual action is, by definition, interaction.

Xu Wu and his colleagues likened the individual effect on the whole as "knots in a well-weaved net."[53] If you pull on one knot, all other knots connected with it, and sometimes even the whole net, will respond.

The constant change is what gives the cosmos or relational universe its synergistic quality, which is key to its sustainability. Synergy is a unique aspect of the Holistic logic that is both a product and process. As a process, synergy is the type of created energy that emerges through the constant adaptation of the diverse elements as they connect and bond to each other and integrate into the whole. As we saw earlier, many ancient cosmologies spoke of "a life force" of the universe. Synergy is this force. Without the diversity of the elements and the constant regenerative process of adapting, the relational universe, as an organic entity, might become static and atrophy. This synergistic process of connecting and realigning diverse elements is what gives the whole its sustainability—what Qin called "continuity through change."[54] Some scholars attribute the longevity of ancient heritages such as India to their constant integration of diversity.[55]

This aspect of synergy and dynamic change is again aptly captured in the wavy—not straight—line of the yin-yang symbol. Its curves reflect movement and change as the diverse elements interact and mutually influence each other. Although synergy is difficult to quantify, social capital derived from relational connections[56] may be a close proxy. Scholars have documented the emergence of social capital in NGO media networks in public diplomacy initiatives in Croatia and China.[57]

Cooperative Orientation

The interconnectivity and interactivity of the Holistic logic further imply that relators within this logic have intertwined fates and, by extension, a cooperative orientation. From the Individual logic, conflict may be the presumed norm and cooperation suspect. Why would an individual choose to cooperate unless there was some obvious benefit? This search for a plausible justification for cooperation has stymied contemporary (Western) scholarship. However, from a Holistic perspective, if each element is connected, then a cooperative orientation of co-existence with others becomes an imperative for the self. Perpetual conflict would not be sustainable for an individual entity. Additionally, from a holistic vantage point, perpetual conflict among individual entities could cause the larger relational whole to fracture, possibly lose its integrity, or cease to function productively. A cooperative orientation is critical to maintaining the integrity and the continuity of the whole. Within an interconnected whole, the "logic of relationality" makes cooperative rather than conflictual state the norm.[58]

In the ancient cosmologies we see the cooperative orientation and sense of connection in the idea of intertwined fates. In the interconnected realms of the human, the spiritual, and nature, the actions of one individual can affect all. An evil act can incite the wrath of the gods, bringing torrential rains that wash away the village. Emotional connections also serve to promote intertwined fates. The African concept of *ubuntu* echoes this assumption: "Whatever happens to the individual happens to the whole group, and whatever happens to the whole group happens to the individual."[59] The *Analects* (VI:30) of Confucius likewise assume shared fates: "If you wish to establish yourself, you have to help others to establish themselves; if you wish to complete yourself, you have to help others to complete themselves."[60]

We see the intertwined or shared fates in ancient medical diagrams that divides the yin-yang symbol into quarters (Figure 5.11). When the familiar yin-yang symbol is cut in quadrants, each quadrant shows yin contained in yang, and yang contained in yin. The Holistic logic's assumption of connectivity and mutuality suggests cooperation as a natural orientation as apparent opposites change and realign to the other.[61]

In the Holistic logic, most public diplomacy initiatives would *logically and by necessity* be predicated on a win-win approach. The notion of win-lose assumes that the two parties are independent, autonomous entities and can freely decide to enter or exit a relationship. The decision to adopt a win-lose approach is only logical if one assumes that the fates of the two parties are separate. However, if the fates of the parties are intertwined, as is the case in the Holistic logic, the fate of one party is that of the other. One party cannot win if the other loses. Even if

Figure 5.11 Quadrants of yin-yang. Author-supplied line art.

one party tries to sever the relation or cause the other party to lose, such a decision would come at a cost for both parties. The Individual logic may view conflict as natural and inevitable because of inherent but separate diversity. The Holistic logic also assumes inherent diversity as natural; however, because of complete connectivity, avoiding conflict and confrontation becomes the more logical predisposition. For all the individual interlocking elements to be in perpetual conflict with each other would drain valuable resources and energy—and inevitably destabilize the whole relational universe. Because the parties are interlinked, win-win is not simply ideal, but is instead a pragmatic necessary. Either both win or both lose.

The Holistic communication dynamics—expanding and interpenetrating relations, preserving diversity, being sensitive to context, mutually adapting and aligning, and leaning toward cooperation—help maintain the stability and continuity of the relational universe. For Boundary Spanners, we can move to a bird's-eye view of these dynamics to see how they further distinguish the Holistic logic.

For the Boundary Spanners

The Holistic logic, like the Individual and Relational logics, shifts our focus to different aspects of the human experience of communication. If we look closely at this logic's communication dynamics, we see an underlying thread of action. Whereas the verbal component or speech is privileged in the Individual logic and emotion was pivotal to the Relational logic, the Holistic logic highlights the dimension of action, or more specifically, interaction. It allows us to look at how action and interaction help shape identities and build and sustain relations.

Complex and Hierarchical Identities

The Holistic logic, like the other logics, provides an added third dimension to a person's constellation of identities, which surfaces and submerges in our interaction with others. As we saw previously, the Individual logic reflects our unique attributes that make each of us a one-of-a kind entity. The Relational logic reflects how relational bonds further layer our identities with relational identities derived from our emotional connections, such as brother, sister, or parent. The Holistic logic helps illustrate how truly multifaceted our identities are as we navigate the interconnected complexities of our social universe. When we wake up in the morning, our relational identities and duties may come to the fore as we go about fixing breakfast or having coffee with family members. Once we leave the house, other identities and roles surface and submerge as we move through the day. We may hop on a bus and become a commuter, interacting with others based on expected protocols such as how close to stand or sit next to someone. We may stop for coffee and engage in the identity of a "customer." Or we may meet up with others at a café before work, switching from the formality and briskness of coffee customer to a leisurely, informal coffee companion to our friends. When we enter our place of work, we take on yet another identity, employee.

Again, without realizing it, our behaviors may shift as we enter our workplace (even on Zoom) and find our identities shaped by hierarchies. From ancient religious orders to modern militaries, we see how hierarchies order and help define identities. These hierarchies may be formal, such as those found on an organizational chart hanging in an office's lobby or in the titles printed on employee name badges. Hierarchies may also be informal, expressed in subtle cues such as who leads a meeting or gets to talk the most without interruption on video conferences.

In the Holistic logic, hierarchies are part of the ordering mechanisms that help maintain the integrity and continuity of the whole. The Individual logic, which rests upon the ideal of the separate entity, tends to favor peer relations and shun hierarchy. Some researchers argue that hierarchy is detrimental to cooperation, as it sets up power differentials between individuals.[62] Ironically, however, one often finds intense competition among individuals in the absence of an acknowledged hierarchy.

In the Holistic logic, which assumes interconnectivity, hierarchy implies indivisible relational responsibilities rather than separate individual power. This assumption of relational responsibility is key to both identity and cooperation. As several scholars have argued, hierarchy is an aspect of evolution shared across human societies because it is instrumental for cooperation.[63] Shuang Liu traced the respect for hierarchy (*dengji*), or pyramid of interconnected relationships, in traditional Chinese society back to Confucianism and the five cardinal relationships (ruler-ruled, father-son, husband-wife, elder brother-younger brother, friend-friend).[64] Identity and order are implicit in this social matrix.

In Western societies, argued Harold J. Leavitt of Stanford University, hierarchies not only survive but thrive because they provide a multitude of practical and psychological benefits.[65] He pointed out that hierarchies are endemic to complex systems in the natural world as they help manage complexity, especially in performing complicated tasks. Hierarchies help meet the need for structure, providing regular routines, duties, and responsibilities. The social ordering of hierarchies is key to providing a sense of place and identity. Leavitt found that people, if asked to answer the question "Who am I?" in three ways, respond with at least one identity positioned in a hierarchy, such as parent. Leavitt also found that successful executives were constantly asking themselves: "'Am I, right now, in the presence of my superiors, my peers, or my subordinates? Have I calibrated my words, posture, and tone of voice accordingly?' "[66] Coincidentally, this sensitivity to nuanced hierarchy-attuned behaviors that Leavitt noted in successful Western executives is mirrored in studies by scholars studying successful communicators in Eastern contexts.[67]

For Boundary Spanners, a critical element of better understanding communication is identifying these hierarchies, identities, and behaviors and how they contribute to establishing order and preserving the relational universe. When looking at human-centered public diplomacy, Boundary Spanners need to be alert to the critical function hierarchies play in defining human identities and reciprocal behaviors. Such sensitivity appears to be a hallmark of success in navigating social complexities.

Embodied Communication

All three communication logics suggest a preference for in-person or face-to-face communication among the participants. Even in the Individual logic, which does not necessarily require an audience, the presence of an audience or listeners can help the communicator enhance their message and delivery. Public speakers rely on cues from a live audience to pace the timing and tone of their words. In the Relational logic, contact and co-presence are the first and second dynamics because of the role they play in anchoring the relationship. Even in the age of virtual meetings, people often insist on meeting the other in person before making a serious commitment to or investment in a relationship.

When we turn to the Holistic logic, *in-person* human communication—a recognition of actual physical presence of another entity—is an underlying and critical assumption.[68] All of the dynamics—connectivity, diversity, contextual sensitivity, alignment (synchrony), and change (synergy)—imply two or more individuals physically present and interacting with another person. This focus on the actual physical presence and interaction in the Holistic logic puts a spotlight on "embodied communication," or how the body is used in human communication. Embodied communication includes gestures, postures, facial expressions, and eye behaviors, as well as paralinguistic aspects such as vocal tone, pitch, or rate.

Given the dominance of the Individual logic in contemporary communication, the verbal dimension (rhetoric, speech, discourse, dialogue, etc.) has overshadowed the "non-verbal" embodied communication. However, a growing chorus of researchers argues that embodied communication is the most basic form of human communication, as it precedes speech.[69] Consider newborns: Infants cry spontaneously at birth, which triggers the attention of adults. The vocalization of crying also tends to be accompanied by wrinkled forehead, squinting eyes, and downturned or quivering lips. All of these facial expressions signaling the emotion of distress are embodied communication. Infants later learn that crying, even spontaneous crying, can get the attention of adults. In addition to learning the communicative value of crying, infants also learn that particular gestures have meaning for adults. By raising their arms, children can communicate that they want to be picked up.

Embodied communication is particularly significant when we turn to emotional expression. As we saw in Chapter 4, feelings and emotional bonds have a biological basis. We often feel even before we are able to "communicate" via words. Spontaneous laughter, yawning, or raising our voice might reflect states of joy, boredom, or anger. Tearing up or uncontrollable sobbing are often unregulated responses to grief and sadness. The body may suddenly stiffen, our posture going from relaxed to erect, in the face of a perceived threat. If a person is angered, their skin may also change color. We may also flush with embarrassment or shame. These embodied expressions of emotion may even be perceived to be more credible than words, because bodily reactions can be more difficult to control than words.

The phenomenon of mirror neurons is another instance of how communication relies on the corporal being for not only emotional expression but perception. As Marcus Holmes pointed out in what he called "the force of face-to-face diplomacy," the constant firing of mirror neurons enables a person to simulate the feelings and intentions of others, which, researchers found only occurs during face-to-face interaction.[70] Paying attention to embodied emotional cues has long been the hallmark of seasoned diplomats working behind closed doors with their counterparts.[71]

Synchrony and Entrainment

Another important aspect of embodied communication is found in the phenomena of synchrony and entrainment. While the Holistic logic views all action as interaction, not all interaction is necessarily attuned or in sync with others, at least initially. However, as people interact, they tend to mirror each other's behavior in form and tempo. For example, two people conversing may mirror their gestures, postures, gait, verbal tone, pace, or volume as they talk. Synchrony, as discussed earlier in the chapter, can involve both verbal and nonverbal behaviors.[72] We tend to sync without thinking and are unaware of this habit's power—unless we find ourselves out of sync. A moment of awkwardness takes hold as we try to recalibrate and get back in sync. Synchrony of behavior is vital in that it enables the coordination of action among individuals within complex social organizations.[73]

While synchrony is an observed phenomenon, entrainment is the internal process of aligning and synchronizing one's behavior with others. William Condon coined the term "entrainment" to describe the micromovements of humans as they pattern their movements to each other.[74] He and his colleagues found that human infants as young as two days old have demonstrated this innate ability to match movement to the language of adults, regardless of the language being spoken.[75] This ability is not only inborn, but it is also key to our survival. "Without the ability to entrain to others, as is the case in some forms of aphasia, life becomes almost unmanageable," wrote Hall in *The Dance of Life*.[76]

While synchrony appears innate in humans, it is among the most challenging traits to duplicate in machine and mediated communication as well as "post-human communication," in which human and machine communication transcend the body in virtual reality.[77] Even with the prospects of the "emotional avatar," cutting-edge embodied AI (artificial intelligence), robotic sciences, and virtual humans, researchers are struggling to duplicate the nuanced finesse of embodied human communication.[78] Synchronized timing of gestures, motor control, facial muscles, or emotion in conversational turn-taking is daunting. Silences between turns last less than 300 milliseconds.[79]

Some scholars have argued that human communication is limited because we are embodied entities. In *Speaking into the Air: A History of the Idea of Communication*, John Durham Peters focuses on words, and in doing so, shares Plato's lament of the impossibility of uniting two souls through dialogue because, alas they inhabit different bodies.[80] However, if we pause to consider evolutionary studies in biology and emerging research from neuroscience, it might be that it is *precisely because we are embodied entities* that we have enhanced communication abilities that go well beyond our words in dialogue. Our bodies communicate.

Reconnecting Diplomacy to the Spiritual Realm

Before leaving the Holistic logic, it is important to note from the ancients the wholistic nature of diplomacy and communication that involved not only the visible physical and social realms but also the unseen spiritual realm. For the ancients, the gods were a critical part of their world. Their presence was real. The ancients often created physical representations. We saw in Amarna diplomacy that the gods, in the form of statutes, accompanied the envoys on their missions. Religious rituals serve to powerfully intertwine the aesthetic realm with the social and spiritual realms through synchronous chanting, singing, and dancing.

The Iroquois nation in pre-colonial North America provides a vivid illustration of blending the spiritual with the emotional dimension in diplomatic practice.[81] According to tradition, their cosmic creator deliberately split the people into two tribes so that when a death occurred in one tribe, the other tribe would help the other through the grieving process through an extended mourning ceremony.

In contrast to the prominent role of the spiritual realm in ancient diplomacy, discussions of the spiritual dimensions in both contemporary communication and diplomacy have been absent or deliberately shunned—until fairly recently. The Holistic logic underscores the multiple realms of diplomacy in meeting the needs of human societies.

Summary

In this chapter, we turned to creation stories and cosmograms from across the ancient world to explore the underlying assumptions and dynamics of a relational universe in the Holistic logic. As mentioned in previous chapters, many of the insights into the communication dynamics in the Holistic logic are drawn from the seminal foundation laid by prominent Asian intercultural scholars, including most notably Wimal Dissanayake,[82] Satoshi Ishii,[83] Yoshitaka Miike,[84] and Guo-Ming Chen.[85]

The Holistic logic extends our vision of communication from the immediacy of paired relations bound together by emotion to an ever-expanding relational universe of sustained interactivity. As with the Individual and the Relational logics, the Holistic logic has its own set of relational premises and dynamics. The Holistic logic rests on the assumption that individuals are embedded in a pre-existing relational universe that shapes communication. Preserving the integrity and continuity of the relational universe is foundational to communication. In the Holistic logic, the communication or relational dynamics that help maintain the integrity and continuity of the relational universe include expanding and interpenetrating relations, preserving diversity, being sensitive to context, mutually adapting and aligning, and leaning toward cooperation.

Boundary Spanners need to be alert to how the relational universe is a communication and relational structure that one navigates rather than creates. The Individual logic's assumption of autonomy means that communicators need skill in learning how to "create" or "build" relations. The Holistic logic's assumption that individuals are already embedded in a pre-existing relational structure means that they—as relators—need to shift focus from trying to create relations to learning and mastering the social grammar of existing relations in order to navigate the complexity of the larger relational universe. Finally, given the importance of embodied communication, Boundary Spanners and scholars need to develop their awareness and skills in monitoring this area of uniquely human communication.

6

Enhancing Collaboration

Speech, Emotion, and Synchrony

As we globalize our vision of communication and diplomacy, we draw upon the different fortes of the three logics, each reflecting the strengths of the others to expand our evolutionary capacity to collaborate in a world of diversity and connectivity.

As the story goes, once there was a sultan who sought to settle a dispute be-tween the Greeks and the Chinese as to who were the better artisans. [1] He gave each group a palace room within which to work their artistry. The two rooms faced each other and were divided by a curtain so that neither side could see the endeavors of the other. The Chinese artisans painted the walls of their room with a splendid array of colors. The Greeks cleaned and polished the walls of their room to a brilliant shiny surface. At the competition's end, the sultan pulled back the curtain. To the wonder of all, the dazzling painted walls of the Chinese artisans appeared to come to life as the colors reflected off the mirror surface of the Greeks' polished walls.

This story embodies this chapter's goal: to show how the distinctive strengths of the three logics can reflect each other to create a pan-human vision of communication and public diplomacy. One critical takeaway from the Sultan's story is the reflection. Without the intricate painting, the polished walls would still shine, but their surface would be blank. Without the polished surface, the painting would still be splendid, yet it would lack the colors that danced in the light. The reflection amplifies the strengths of each, allowing them to transcend their individual limitations.

Similarly, globalizing our vision of the communication experience entails viewing the three logics operating in unison, allowing them to reflect each other's strengths. Under the previous mindset of separateness, the three logics would be viewed as separate, mutually exclusive categories for comparison. In this chapter, however, we deliberately and mindfully view the logics through the twin forces of diversity and connectivity. First, we provide an overview of the three logics. Next, we focus on the unique strengths of each logic and then use the technique of blending to layer on aspects of the other logics. We begin with the Individual logic, and the power of speech, and blend in elements from the Relational and Holistic logics. We then move to the power of emotion in the Relational logic, followed by the power of synchrony in the Holistic logic.

The aim of blending the logics is to help create an expansive, pan-human view of the communication experience. The process of blending the logics also helps move us beyond simply learning *about* different perspectives (or, learning how to cooperate individually) to learning *from* different perspectives (or, learning how to collaborate with others). It is through the collaborative process of incorporating different perspectives that innovation can occur. Collaboration allows the three logics to reflect and mutually enhance each other, much like the artisans' complementary works.

Globalizing through Blending

We opened this book with a call to the Boundary Spanners to rethink communication and public diplomacy with the intent of moving beyond a mindset of separateness to one that can navigate connectivity and diversity. Outlining the three logics was a first step in that direction. Our guiding question now is: How can we apply a mindset of connectivity and diversity to the three logics so as to enhance our evolutionary capacity for cooperation?

The previous three chapters sketched out the premises, assumptions, and dynamics of the three communication logics and highlighted their distinctive

Table 6.1 Overview of the Three Logics

	Individual logic	Relational logic	Holistic logic
Visual representation	linear arrow (→)	infinity sign (∞)	cosmic circle (O)
Communication defined by	Communicator	Relational Bond	Relational Universe
Communication imperative	Winning hearts and minds	Strengthening ties that bind	Preserving harmony of the whole
Communication dynamics	Communicator Message Medium Audience Goal-orientation Measurability	Contact points Nonverbal behaviors Emotional expression Perspective-taking Reciprocity Symbolism	Expanding relations Preserving diversity Contextual sensitivity Mutual adaptation Change and continuity Cooperative orientation

strengths. The Individual logic showcases the power of speech as a distinguishing feature of self-expression and persuasion in human communication. The Relational logic highlights the power of emotion and bonding in human communication. The Holistic logic features the power of synchrony of interaction in harmonizing diversity in human communication. By way of summary, Table 6.1 provides an overview of the three logics.

In one sense, the chart is helpful in highlighting the dynamics of each of the three logics. However, the very structure of the chart is segmented and linear, emphasizing divisions of humanity. Conceptual categories, as noted in the Introduction, are defined by their differences, which help delineate boundaries. As we have seen throughout this book, the concepts in the intercultural communication models are built on a mindset of separateness. Communication scholars have long focused on identifying distinctive behaviors and patterns (such as individualistic or collectivist tendencies) tied to geo-specific cultures, such as "Chinese communication" or "American communication." These different cultural and national patterns of communication are then laid out along a linear spectrum to suggest a global view of communication, such as Hofstede did in his models.[2] Creating and comparing categories is where intercultural communication tends to stop.

It is tempting to follow this practice and place the three logics into separate categories. Each logic appears to be distinctive—and they are. The communication dynamics of the Individual logic (communicator, message, medium, audience, effect) differ from those of the Relational logic (contact points, nonverbal behaviors, emotional expression, reciprocity, perspective taking, symbolism) and from the Holistic (see table). Further, the logics appear to align to different cultures. The Individual logic might resonate strongly with U.S. and U.K. perspectives; the Relational logic might resonate with continental Europe, the Middle East, and Latin American cultures; and the Holistic logic might align with Asian and African cultures.

However, to place the three logics into separate categories is to perpetuate the mindset of separateness. Instead of an expansive perspective, we once again have geo-cultural variations of a communication template. Instead of a pan-human dynamic of communication between people, we again have static categories for placing people in. We become vulnerable to casting and stereotyping interactions.

Additionally, if we look closely, the communication dynamics of the logics—while distinctive—are not mutually exclusive to any one culture or country or even logic. Messages, for example, may be prominent in the Individual logic. However, messages are not exclusive to the Individual logic any more than emotion is to the Relational logic. Shared or overlapping features are often portrayed through Venn diagrams. While the Venn diagram suggests connectivity, the separate regions preserve the mindset of separateness.

In theory, the categories overlap. But people are more than their categories. In reality, when people communicate, they do not overlap but rather interact with each other. And when people interact, they do not interact as static cultural categories of behaviors but rather blend and adapt to each other to co-create a communication experience. We need to look at the logics in the same way—not as separate categories but as interactive dynamics.

In practical terms for Boundary Spanners, globalizing communication means consciously and perhaps creatively layering or blending the dynamics of the three communication logics. For example, messages from the Individual logic might be blended with perspective-taking and reciprocity of the Relational logic, and then mutual adaptation from the Holistic logic. Figure 6.1 visually depicts all three logics blended together. The linear arrow ($\rightarrow$) represents the Individual logic, the infinity sign (∞) signifies the bond central to the Relational logic, and the cosmic circle (O) reflects the Holistic logic.

Blending these symbols helps highlight the need to shift from "learning about" to "learning from" others, as Miike advocated, in order to create a global vision of the dynamics of the communication experience. When we blend the three logics of communication, we are actively learning from different perspectives and intellectual heritages to develop an integrated, pan-human vision of communication.

As we see in the discussion that follows, the more communication dynamics we can add from across the three logics and blend them into the communication experience, the more likely the experience is to resonate across a broad spectrum of humanity. The next three sections highlight strengths from each logic

Figure 6.1 Blending the three logics. Author-supplied line art.

and then blend in communication dynamics from the other two logics. We begin with the Individual logic.

Individual Logic: Power of Speech

In August 2018, a Swedish teenager named Greta took a day off from school to protest and speak out against climate change, or what she called a climate crisis. A few months later, she would deliver a brief but powerful speech at the UN Climate Change COP24 Conference. She would go on to give impassioned speeches that went viral on social media and rallied millions around the world. In little more than a year, in December 2019, *TIME* magazine would choose Greta Thunberg as its Person of the Year, describing her rise as "one of the swiftest ascents to global influence in history" and likening her to other global change makers, such as Nelson Mandela and the Mahatma Gandhi.[3]

TIME attributed the phenomenon of Greta Thunberg to "The Power of Youth." Yet, we know there are many young environmental activists in the world today. What made Greta stand out was her remarkable speaking ability—an unexpected power in a teenage girl, unafraid to go it alone and speak up. That her speech captured global attention underscores the wide applicability and importance of the Individual logic in human communication. Whereas the individualism as a cultural trait may be tied to a particular culture or even country, the power of speech is a defining human trait.

The major strength of the Individual logic is the pan-human power of speech: the ability to galvanize the attention and imagination of others by the force of the spoken or written word. I have used the arrow sign (→) to signify the directness of the power of speech. In his treatise *Antidosis*, the Greek rhetorician Isocrates claimed that persuasive speech is what separated human civilization from the animal kingdom:

> Because there has been implanted in us the power to persuade each other and to make clear to each other whatever we desire, not only have we escaped the life of wild beasts, but we have come together and founded cities and made laws and invented arts; and generally speaking there is no institution devised by man which the power of speech has not helped us to establish."[4]

Public speaking and other oratory arts are prized worldwide. Throughout the ages in the public squares, plazas, and marketplaces where people have gathered, storytellers and poets have gathered as well to lift and delight human spirits. Eloquence in public speaking has been a particular trait of diplomats and political leaders throughout human history. In the ancient world, Greek city-states sent their finest orators as ambassadors or representatives. [5] In ancient India, *Arthashastra* (Treatise on Polity), attributed to Kautilya (322–298 BCE), posited that the duties of diplomacy relied on the diplomats' verbal skills as representatives, informers, communicators, and negotiators. [6] Similarly, in Asia at the time, as Van Dinh notes, all Vietnamese envoys to Peking were top poets and writers— "especially those endowed with a wit, a gift for quick repartee."[7] He relates several humorous tales of their verbal adeptness that have become part of Vietnamese folklore.

The power of speech is undeniably connected to the evolutionary development of the human species.[8] If we extend the power of speech from the individual level to the interpersonal paired level, we encounter the world's various speech traditions of debate, dialogue, and dialectics. When we move into the social level, we encounter another pan-human phenomenon, that of storytelling. Storytelling appears closely linked to our evolutionary capacity to collaborate.[9]

Our love of stories—from a fondness for childhood bedtime stories to a fascination with creation stories that explain our existence and place in the world— has earned us the title of *homo narrative*.[10] According to Jonathan Gottschall, author of *The Storytelling Animal, How Stories Make Us Human*, the enduring appeal of stories is reflected in our many forms of storytelling, from cave drawing to oral chanting, from elaborate operas to Facebook story posts.[11]

Stories do more than entertain us. Stories help us make sense of our social world. According to researchers, stories reflect how the human brain structures information: "Just as the brain detects patterns in the visual forms of nature—a face, a figure, a flower—and in sound, so too it detects patterns in information. Stories are recognizable patterns, and in those patterns, we find meaning."[12] A capacity for storytelling emerges at about twenty-four months in typically developing children—an age that coincides with the end of the weaning period and the child's expanding social sphere. Whereas speech or language can label our world, storytelling imbues the world with meaning and our place in the world, like the cosmos stories. Storyline organization of information is useful in instruction.

Stories instruct us in norms of behavior that lay a foundation for social cohesion and cooperation. Coe and her colleagues draw attention to the evolutionary function of stories that are passed down from generation to generation.[13] As they note, "stories that encourage generosity, cooperation, restraint and sacrifice . . . are directly related to the formation of the social relationships so crucial to our species."[14] We see the reliance on storytelling as a means of social instruction in the ancient texts such as Aesop's Fables, the Bhagavad Gita, or the Holy Bible, which lay out moral codes.

Thus, storytelling provides not only meaning but a way of being in the world with others—a blending of the Individual logic, in the message of the story, with the Holistic logic, as the story enhances social cohesion.

Finally, storytelling provides an understanding of the larger social context beyond our own immediate perception. Smith and his colleagues draw attention to the link between this aspect of storytelling and the evolutionary capacity for collaboration. [15] The researchers found that people are often hesitant to cooperate because they are unsure of how others may act. It is not enough to have instructions on how to behave; coordination requires knowing that others also know how to act as well. Stories address the problem of coordination with others by providing "meta-knowledge" for guiding behaviors. The researchers concluded that "storytelling may have played an essential role in the evolution of human cooperation by broadcasting social and cooperative norms to coordinate group behavior."[16]

Many of us may have intuitively sensed the pan-human appeal of storytelling. What is perhaps novel are the connections between speech, storytelling, and the capacity for collaboration. The power of speech represents the individual-level view of communication; the appeal of storytelling represents the social, or humanity-level of communication.

Enhancing Collaboration through Storytelling

How can Boundary Spanners tap into the power of speech and storytelling to enhance our capacity for collaboration in humanity-centered diplomacies? The

Individual logic lays a foundation for one dimension or logic of communication. What we need is to deliberately blend in the other two logics. Let us start with the forte of the Individual logic, and then, like the reflection of the artisans, layer in reflections of the Relational and Holistic logics.

Network Vision

While the power of speech is the forte of the Individual logic, at its most basic level the logic is about expressing and sharing information. Modes and means that enhance the sharing of ideas across time and space are most valued. As we saw in Chapter 1, early Greek diplomats used rhetorical devices in public speaking as a technical innovation to enhance information sharing from interpersonal to public forums. For contemporary state-centric public diplomacy, the mass media extends information sharing from public forums to a mediated national and international level. With the advent of social media tools, we see a parallel rise in public diplomacy of network communication for sharing information globally and instantaneously.[17]

While networks offer strategic advantages for information sharing, the very idea of being connected to others can be perceived as a constraint. Anne-Marie Slaughter was an early proponent of outlining a network approach for U.S. diplomacy. In her recent book, *The Chessboard and the Web*, she calls for "strategies of connection" to enable states to address global problems.[18] Against a backdrop of rising nationalism and regionalism that favor the go-it-alone primacy of the individual, some of her readers raised questions.[19] Network connections may yield benefits, but they are fraught with risks, including constraints on agency. Competing individual needs within an alliance, for example, may restrict agency.[20]

To expand our vision of networks to appreciate their potential benefits, we need an augmented view that includes elements of the other two logics. The Holistic logic begs us to shift our perspective from the individual to the whole. Most of the studies are egocentric network analysis. The field of international studies, in fact, is awash in egocentric network analyses, while whole-network analyses are comparatively rare.[21] A whole-network perspective gives a bird's-eye view of all of the actors. From this Holistic perspective, or whole-network vantage point, it becomes clear that whether states and other actors appreciate it or not, they are already connected. It is no longer a matter of choosing whether to be connected but rather how one might strategically shape those connections.

The Relational logic brings another dimension to our understanding of networks by highlighting emotion. Sharing information and interacting with others are about more than network density of connected nodes. Repeated sharing and interacting with other people can strengthen emotional bonds, creating a sense of belonging to others and a community, and, most importantly, lay a foundation for trust. Significantly, although researchers often speak of networks, people within the network, especially social media networks, often refer to themselves as a community. [22] Feelings of individual agency are often augmented by the feeling of being part of a larger whole. Fundraising initiatives, for example, operate on this feeling of being connected to a cause greater than oneself.

When we add aspects of the Holistic and Relational logics to our thinking about networks, we can see an expanded range of networks with different purposes in public diplomacy.[23] Rather than just using networks to disseminate information to create awareness or advocate, we can create networks of collaboration in which information sharing generates new thinking, knowledge, problem-solving and even inspire a sense of community.

Collaborative Story-Building and Resonant Narratives

In state-centric public diplomacy, one of the most innovative areas of research has been in the development of strategic narratives advanced by Miskimmon, O'Loughlin, and Roselle.[24] Political actors use strategic narratives "to extend their influence, manage expectations, and change the discursive environment in which they operate," say the scholars.[25]

Strategic narratives tap into the appeal of storytelling and make information readily digestible, adding a cognitive advantage. Strategic narratives readily glide over networks and digital and social media. This natural link between narratives and networks in diplomacy was advanced by Arquilla and Ronfeldt, who in the late 20th century predicted that future information battles would be about "whose story wins." [26]

While storytelling may be ideal, the strategic nature of storytelling reflects the limitations of employing one communication logic. Several aspects of the strategic narrative may make it less desirable and even counter-productive for enhancing the capacity for collaboration and humanity-centered diplomacies. First, strategic narratives, by definition, are strategic in that they have a pre-determined goal and are designed to influence. Moreover, that goal is driven primarily by the needs, interests, or image of an individual actor. Achieving those goals may even come at the expense of the needs or interests of others—showing a weakness of the Individual logic. The strategy of competing—that is, the question of "whose story wins"—is about maintaining the advantage of one's own strategic narrative. Finally, strategic narratives are intended as a pre-designed product, rather than a co-created organic process.

While strategic narratives may be limited by relying on only one logic, we can enhance the global traction of narratives, or storytelling, by adding elements of the Relational and Holistic logics to create what might be called a "resonant narrative." Resonant narratives are imbued with human emotions that are co-created by the diverse members of the network of humanity. Resonant narratives that bring in the emotional element from the Relational logic and synergy from the Holistic logic have a very different dynamic and character from a strategic narrative that relies only on the Individual logic.

I first noticed this dynamic during my early research after 9/11. Whereas states focused on wielding soft power using mass communication, non-governmental organizations appeared to be creating a soft power differential using network communication to influence global policy agendas. [27] In looking at the state public diplomacy at the time, government-run mass media appeared to be the tools of choice given the goal of disseminating persuasive information to publics. Strategically, states were trying to control the message. Interestingly, NGOs such as the Campaign to Ban Landmines, which I used as the case study, lacked the powerful mass media tools. Instead, the Campaign was relying on in-person meetings and simple facsimile machines to connect with each other. In the process, one could see how they were not just creating a network but a form of networked communication strategy.

A big part of that network communication strategy was story building. The network structure provided the means for circulating information. As the members of the anti-landmine coalition interacted with each other, they began to co-create their own narrative. Together, they were story-building an expanding narrative of who they were as a community (their identity) as well as what they wanted and could achieve together (their purpose). The narrative was not pre-determined or disseminated by any one actor, as in the Individual logic—it was co-created by the relational universe as envisioned by the Holistic logic. Beyond the co-creational aspect of narrative identity and purpose, there was also an emotional dimension. The storytelling and story-building created a sense of shared identity as well as belonging. In the process of participating in story-building, they defined themselves as a community.

As we see, by layering the dynamics of the Relational and Holistic logics rather than strategic narratives created by individual actors, we have resonant narratives that are co-created within a relational universe and strengthened by emotional ties that bind. Resonant narratives are not a pre-determined product but an organic process of people interacting intellectually, emotionally, and perhaps physically to co-create the narrative.

While resonant narratives abound, a vivid example comes from the Arab Spring of 2011. The public uprisings that swept through Tunisia, Egypt, Yemen, Bahrain, Libya, and Syria were originally heralded as a "social media revolution."[28] Commentators and researchers focused on the novel power of the new digital technology—social media—which enabled people to rapidly share information and organize protests. Papacharissi and de Fatima Oliveira, however, shifted their gaze from the media tools to the content people were sharing.[29] Emotions stood out. People were sharing personal stories, "blending emotion with opinion, and drama with fact," creating what the scholars termed "affective news."[30] These affective aspects, they said, nurtured and sustained involvement, connection, and cohesion. In a later study, Papacharissi went further to suggest that it was not just the *news* that provoked emotional response, but that the *publics* were emotional. In *Affective Publics*, Papacharissi highlighted the power of personal stories to create emotional connections: "The digital technologies network us but it is our stories that connect us to each other."[31] We can see the synergistic effect of a resonant narrative planted on Facebook during the Egyptian uprising. Former Google executive Wael Ghonim clandestinely posted pictures of a young protester named Khaled Said, who had been brutally beaten by Egyptian police, on a Facebook page titled, "We Are All Khaled Said."[32] Ghonim kept his identity hidden. Rather than managing the story posts alone, he encouraged others who saw the pictures to join and enlarge the story of the slain protester and add their stories to his. Within weeks, the resonant narrative that grew organically out of this collaborative power led to the ousting of the authoritarian leader who had ruled Egypt for four decades.

In public diplomacy, resonant storytelling might emerge as a natural and organic outgrowth of people working and collaborating together. In other cases, the seeds of a resonant narrative can be planted, as in the case of Khalid Said. Either way, the critical difference between resonant narratives and strategic narratives is the collaborative, story-building aspect.

Relational Logic—Power of Emotion

Greta Thunberg's dramatic rise is not merely a function of the power of speech; it also illustrates the power of emotion to connect with others and move them to action. Emotion is the central and pivotal strength of the Relational logic. Thunberg's speeches have been described as "emotional" and "impassioned," as well as in emotional terms such as "scathing." She herself has also been described in emotional terms. When U.S. President Trump described her as an "angry little girl," she appropriated the emotional descriptor for her Twitter profile. She also amplified her emotionally powerful words with heightened emotional delivery.

The Relational logic shines a spotlight on the power of human feeling—love, hate, guilt, humiliation, and triumph—running through the human experience and communication. The stress on the emotional bond between the parties is symbolized by the infinity sign (∞). Like speech, emotion is pan-human or global in scope. However, unlike speech, emotions flourish in the largely wordless realm of feeling (neurochemical impulses) and rely on embodied expression. As discussed in Chapter 4, what we call emotions are actually surges of neurochemicals that correlate with good feeling (approach) or bad feeling (avoid). Whereas speech relies on the capacity for language and abstraction that are part of the brain's neocortex structure; emotions reside in the limbic system and it has no capacity for language. [33] Translating felt experiences into words, is a learned communication skill or gift. Just ask the poets.

Because emotional expression does not rely solely on verbal expression, it can jump across language barriers to facilitate bonding with others, shape individual and collective identities, and provide intuitive ways of knowing. These multiple communicative roles of emotion are a distinctive contribution of the Relational logic.

The power of emotions for bonding and knowing undergirds each of the dynamics in the Relational logic. If we look at contact points, for example, people can often gather a "first impression" in as little as four seconds, based on their emotional reaction. [34] We may connect to others cognitively, agreeing with what they say—but we may ultimately trust or bond based on how we feel. Those feelings of initial contact may be further nurtured by the other dynamics of the Relational logic, including perspective-taking, reciprocity, and symbolism.

The turbulent period of 2020 amply displayed emotions as a pan-human phenomenon, particularly in examples related to the Covid-19 pandemic. First, almost immediately upon the outbreak of the pandemic, we saw widespread and spontaneous expressions of emotion on social media. An early powerful example of the emotional toll of "social distancing" was captured in a photo of a doctor, still dressed in his hospital scrubs, connecting with his young son through a glass pane.[35] The touching father-son photo of the two reaching out to each other and matching their hands on the glass (Figure 6.2) immediately went viral—first on Facebook and then in mainstream media. The spontaneous sharing of emotional photos and videos with others reflects the profound need of our mammalian brain to remain connected to others, especially in the face of a perceived threat.

Second—as the lethal virus spread, so too did images that were laden with emotions of fear, sadness, and grief as families around the world shared the loss of their mothers, fathers, sons, daughters, grandparents, and other loved ones. The element of emotion was one of the distinguishing features that early researchers found when they were trying to understand what made content go viral on social media.[36] The emotional milieu of social media may heighten emotional expression over the internet. [37] But there is a fine distinction to draw here: it's not that content goes viral because the material is emotional, but rather that humans are emotional beings who are attracted to emotional content. Human emotions are a

Figure 6.2 Viral photo of doctor separated from son during pandemic posted on Facebook, March 25, 2020. Reprinted with the permission of Alyssa Burks. All rights reserved.

magnet for users of social media, a maxim that proved especially relevant during a stressful time such as the pandemic.

Third, during the pandemic people engaged with emotional content on a global rather than national or even regional level. People commented, reposted, and shared based on the power of emotions such as those portrayed in the image of the two Chinese health care workers embracing after fighting the unknown virus's outbreak (Figure 6.3). Significantly, the very act of sharing emotional content globally means that people from different ethnic regions and cultures

Figure 6.3 Health care workers departing Wuhan.

were able to recognize the expression of emotions in others vastly different from themselves.

These observations about people readily recognizing and responding to emotional expressions of others, including those who are different, may seem obvious when we look at the flurry of images on social media. Yet what is remarkable is that it has taken 21st-century technology and our spontaneous behaviors during a global pandemic to demonstrate the innate, pan-human nature of human emotion and emotional expression. Ancient Sanskrit and Chinese texts expressed their belief in pan-human emotions thousands of years ago. [38]

The evolutionary biologist Charles Darwin made a similar observation in the late 19th century. He studiously documented global similarities of emotional expression in human societies in his little-known book, *The Expression of Emotions in Humans and Animals.*[39] In *Expression*, he persuasively argued for the innate nature of human emotional expressions, documenting how blind children produced similar facial expressions as sighted children.

While Darwin's book was widely popular with the public, cultural anthropologists would challenge the universality of emotional expressions, arguing that emotions were not innate but a product of cultural learning.[40] Cultural relativism held that just as each culture had its own spoken language, each had its own unique language of emotional expression. For much of the 20th century, emotions were seen as culture-specific and the product of nurture rather than human nature.[41]

In the 1960s, Paul Ekman and his colleagues began studying emotional expressions in different cultures. [42] In study after study, they found that people from different regions and cultures could recognize several basic emotions. However, the rules about displaying emotions vary greatly, such as when, where, and who might show anger. Today, controversy has resurfaced, but the prevailing sentiment is that emotional expressions are a combination of both nature and nurture.[43]

Noteworthy about Darwin's treatise was his observation about how emotional expression is linked to our evolution as a species. Compared to verbal expression, the spontaneity and immediacy of emotional expression make it a highly efficient form of communication, especially in life-threatening moments. Emotion also has the power to bind group members, providing comfort and facilitating mutual aid. For Darwin, the emotion of sympathy or fellow feeling was the impetus for moral behaviors that guided humans as "social animals."[44]

Many traditions single out fellow feeling as a defining feature of humanity. The writings of Chinese sage Mencius (Mengzi) on human nature provide a poignant example. Mencius gives the parable of the child in peril about to fall into a well.[45] Seeing a child in danger would fill the mind with alarm, distress, pity, and compassion, says Mencius, adding that "one who lacks a mind that feels pity and compassion would not be human." Mencius called "feelings of pity and compassion . . . the beginning of humanness (*ren*)."[46]

This observation made centuries ago still resonates today. Here we can turn to one last image from a widely shared video that surfaced during the summer of 2020: that of a Minneapolis police officer kneeling with his knee on the neck of a Black man in his custody named George Floyd. In the nine-minute video, we see the life pass from Floyd's body. What makes the video jarring is hearing the deeply emotional pleas of the dying man and calls of on-lookers desperate to help, yet seeing the steely, emotionless face of the officer. The officer's lack of emotional empathy for the suffering of another called into question his humanity. The common emotional chord of a dying man's pleas galvanized people worldwide to take to the streets in protest.

In the Relational logic we see the power of emotion as a pivotal element in human bonding, individual and group identity, as well as intuitive ways of knowing. Not only do people recognize basic emotional expressions, but they also respond powerfully when others violate expected norms that define our shared sense of humanity. For Boundary Spanners, gaining competencies with emotions in the public realm are vital in humanity-centered public diplomacies.

Enhancing Collaboration through Empathy

How can Boundary Spanners build on the innate, pan-human ability to express, interpret, and act on emotional expression to strengthen their capacity for collaboration in humanity-centered diplomacies? For some individuals, the emotional realm of the Relational logic may be their forte. The Relational logic may validate what they have always believed about human communication and diplomacy. In the subsections that follow, we see how the forte of emotions is enhanced by the power of speech from the Individual logic and the dynamic of interactivity from the Holistic logic.

Emotional Expression and Emotional Intelligence

Former Ambassador Harold Saunders argued that diplomacy has always been about relationships and that successful diplomats were particularly adept at "reading" the emotional tenor of their counterpart and situation.[47] He would likely admonish ambassadors of humanity to enhance their effectiveness by increasing their ability to assess, monitor, and respond to emotional expression, both verbally and nonverbally. David Matsumoto and his colleagues, who worked on documenting universal facial expressions around the globe, believe that people can be trained to expand their ability to assess emotional expressions and even micro-expressions.[48] Their research supports Ambassador Saunders's observation that people who do develop their perception skills are more effective in working with others.

Boundary Spanners can further enhance their effectiveness by developing their skills of emotional expression. Here we see how blending speech—the Individual logic's forte—with the strong emotional expression of the Relational logic can enhance the latter. While emotional expression is innate and spontaneous, effective emotional control, management, and verbal expression are learned skills. In Western scholarship, these skills would fall under the rubric of "emotional intelligence."[49] Emotional intelligence begins by building emotional literacy for identifying and labeling emotions. Competencies in emotional intelligence include self-awareness, self-regulation, and other awareness. Boundary Spanners may also turn to the ancient traditions that are rich in emotional insights. The Confucian focus on self-cultivation, for instance, appears similar to the preliminary steps of self-awareness and self-management in emotional intelligence. Because different social, political, or diplomatic settings may have their own display rules, Boundary Spanners would need to develop a sensitivity to and flexibility regarding differing emotional expression.

Emotional Expression and Bonding

Public diplomacy initiatives involving the arts tend to enjoy success, in part because the arts can tap into the power of emotions to facilitate bonding. Tours of national symphonies, dance troops, or artworks are not only about sharing heritages but also about sharing emotions—which music, visual art, and dance both express and elicit. In humanity-centered diplomacies, emotions play a key role in bonding and knowing, and are thus pivotal to effective physical or online collaboration. As we saw in the Covid-19 examples, emotions can spur people to action and engagement with others. Furthermore, synchronized interaction with others (a feature of the Holistic logic) acts as an emotional bonding element across differences.[50]

Emotional bonding through shared activity can provide the incentive for remaining engaged long after the initial reasons for connecting have waned. In his study of citizen diplomacy between the EU and China, Andreas Fulda tells the story of a German climate activist who was initially motivated by a passion to reduce carbon emissions.[51] That passion spurred him to travel to China to work with climate activists there. Although initially the German activist had little emotional affinity for his Chinese counterparts or the affected population, after living and working with them intensively, relationships formed. The incentive for solving the problem was no longer just a passion for the environment but also a felt personal connection to the people. Boundary Spanners may similarly seek to enhance the capacity for collaboration by looking for shared interests and activities that can bring people together.

Empathetic Public Diplomacy

Third, because emotion is becoming increasingly prominent and accepted in the public arena, public diplomats need to be able to respond to emotion in that realm. Empathy takes the importance of listening, for which Nicholas Cull has argued so compellingly, to the next level.[52] In the past, talk of emotion during a crisis may have been seen as sign of weakness. However, research on effective crisis response has shown that empathetic communication is a core skill in managing public sentiment and gaining compliance.[53] Practitioners distinguish between cognitive, emotional, and compassionate empathy. Of the three, compassionate empathy—which demonstrates compassion for the other's emotions and circumstances while nonverbally modeling assurance by maintaining composure and self-control—may be the most effective for public leadership during a crisis.[54]

We witnessed the value of empathy firsthand during the pandemic. During the height of the initial outbreak of the virus in Britain, Queen Elizabeth II made a rare, televised speech to the Commonwealth. As several commentators noted, unlike other national leaders, who amorphized the virus into an enemy waging war, she focused on the feelings of the people.[55] The pandemic was still in the early stages and people were fearful, anxious, and uncertain of what lay ahead. Already people had lost loved ones. The British monarch opened her brief speech with empathy, acknowledging the "challenging time for all," and the emotion of grief. The national traits she mentioned echo of emotional intelligence: "self-discipline, quiet, good-humoured resolve and fellow-feeling." She gave voice to the pain of separation: "Many will feel a painful sense of separation from their loved ones." And then she ended with reassurance of physically reuniting: "we will be with our friends again; we will be with our families again; we will meet again."

The Queen's speech resonated with many around the globe. Coincidentally, media reports began drawing attention to gender differences in how countries with female leaders (New Zealand, Germany, and Finland) were having more success in managing the virus spread by empathetically responding to and managing public emotions.[56] Scholars also noted the trend, as well as the role of empathy, particularly during crisis situations such as the pandemic.[57] Carolyn Childers, co-founder of the Milken Institute, highlighted the connection between empathy and reaching across boundaries during the pandemic crisis:

> In this highly uncertain time, empathy is one of the few things leaders can control. When we feel for others, our blinders fade, we welcome diverse perspectives, and we are able to make informed decisions rather than operating in silos.[58]

Given the likelihood of future crises, Boundary Spanners would do well to expand their comfort level and skills in dealing with emotions in the public realm.

Holistic Logic—Power of Synchrony

Again, we return to Greta Thunberg to see the major strength of the Holistic logic: the power of synchrony (matching behaviors in manner and tempo). When Thunberg marches in protests, and twenty other students join her, chanting slogans in unison, that is synchrony. When thousands join her, capturing news headlines and going viral, that is again the power of synchrony.

The Holistic logic highlights synchrony's role in communication—though synchrony is not even on the radar for many in communication studies or public diplomacy. Synchrony is understudied and its presence in daily communication overlooked, but that does not deflate its significance. Like speech and emotion, synchrony can both persuade and bond. And, like speech and emotion, the phenomenon of synchrony is found in ancient texts and traditions (especially spiritual rituals) that produce a visceral feeling of bonding. Emerging scientific research reveals that our bodies respond physically and neurobiologically to synchrony.

Notably, one cannot discern synchrony in isolation; one must observe individuals in relation to others and the whole. As soon as we try to separate one element from another, disassembling the whole, the phenomenon loses meaning. One also cannot observe synchrony—dynamic action, movement, and interaction—in a static or inactive state. The Individual logic assumes a process that can be frozen, allowing researchers to view and analyze discrete elements—a snapshot. The Holistic logic, by contrast, assumes constant interaction and continuity; a dynamic captured by the cosmic circle. To arrest the process is to distort it.

Edward T. Hall was among the first to draw attention to the importance of synchrony in contemporary communication. He suggested that rhythm ties people together and serves as the ultimate building block of communication. As he wrote in *The Dance of Life*:

> People in interactions move together in a kind of dance, but they are not aware of their synchronous movement and they do it without music of conscious orchestration. Being "in sync" is itself a form of communication.[59]

Hall, an anthropologist by training, called synchrony pan-human. Synchrony is linked to human survival, promoting bonding and cooperation within our complex social organizations. Without the ability to sync with or entrain to others, as in some forms of aphasia or autism, life becomes almost unmanageable, according to Hall.[60] We must act in concert with others to hunt, harvest crops, maintain territorial boundaries, and raise offspring. The ability to synchronize speech and movement also distinguishes humans from our closest primate relatives. Chimpanzees can coordinate movement but cannot keep time together.[61]

Examples of synchrony abound. Chanting, clapping, and swaying are prominent in religious rituals dating back to ancient times. In any house of worship, one can witness multiple layers of synchrony as worshipers stand, kneel, or recite verses together. Civic training also includes synchronic vocalization, such as singing the national anthem or pledging allegiance to the flag. Political events, including protests, rally supporters in chanting slogans, waving fists or signs, or marching together in silence. Military drills and "war dances"—such as the

Maori haka, which prepares warriors for battle—involve synchronous movement and chants.

In these examples of synchrony, many of which you and I have experienced
personally, we can grasp synchrony's power in communication. First, synchronous movement and speech promotes bonding. Researchers and lay observers
are quick to point out that lovers, friends, and close associates tend to mirror each
other's movements.[62] This syncing and bonding also occurs even with strangers.
Researchers have found that groups of people who repeated even nonsensical
words in synchrony worked together more efficiently afterward.[63] Synchronous
movement has promoted bonding even when there are obvious physical, ideological, or other differences between divergent groups. The military drills introduced to the Dutch army in 1590, spread rapidly across Europe after military
strategists observed their effect in creating *esprit de corps*, according to historian
William McNeill.[64] He writes of his own military drills:

> Something very visceral was at work. . . . Words are inadequate to describe
> the emotion aroused by the prolonged movement in unison that drilling in-
> volved . . . a strange sense of personal enlargement; a sort of swelling out, be-
> coming bigger than life, thanks to participation in collective ritual.[65]

The visceral response of feeling both individually empowered and yet "as one"
with others shows how synchrony can amplify individual efforts into synergistic
teamwork. Surviving ancient monuments, such as the pyramids of Giza or the
moai of Easter Island, reveal how coordinated behaviors can produce the synergy necessary to move stones several times the weight of a human team.

We see synchrony and its synergic results wherever humans do, make, and
play together. Sports, as a ready example, exhibit multiple levels of synchrony.
Players huddle before the game starts and then anticipate and respond to each
other in play. Fans reflect on-field action with synergistic behavior in the stands
as they shout or chant in unison or jump to their feet to cheer a winning goal. The
appeal of this synchrony may help explain the appeal of sports and sports diplomacy, dating to the Olympics of antiquity and still thriving in the modern era.

The 2020 pandemic offered multiple examples of spontaneous synchrony to
counter isolation. Most prominent was the simple act of clapping in the evening,
which spread globally with the virus from Wuhan to Milan, to London, Paris,
Istanbul, and New York. Confined to their homes, people convened on individual balconies to provide collective encouragement. In China, clapping was
accompanied by the phrase "more oil," an idiom meaning "keep up the fight."
In hard-hit Italy, clapping provided a shared emotional release from the grip of
fear. In Madrid, people clapping together from their balconies created a sense of

community: "I was a ghost on my street until started going to the balcony and establishing a relationship with my neighbors," proclaim one person."[66]

Online performances also mushroomed.[67] Music and dance are both highly synchronic, with performers' coordination being part of the aesthetic appeal. Within days of finding live rehearsals and shows canceled, quarantine performers offered online virtual performances, creating individual performances and then syncing them via technology.

With schools closed, and social gathering prohibited, people started holding online gatherings for birthday parties, happy hours, and classes.[68] People adapted quickly to the platforms' limitations in order to synchronize behavior. For example, norms were developed to enable only one speaker at a time, as participants used interaction protocols such as muting and unmuting, using chat, raising hands, or reaction features to regulate turn-taking.

One of the most intriguing pandemic examples of synchrony was people coming together in the digital space to play. Online interactive gaming saw an exponential increase. "Games have a unique ability to unite people across cultural and geographical boundaries, enabling a feeling of togetherness," said Yodo1 CEO Henry Fong.[69] In late March 2020, leaders from the interactive gaming industry launched the #PlayApartTogether campaign with events and rewards to help spread the World Health Organization (WHO) guidelines on social distancing, hand hygiene, respiratory etiquette, and virus prevention, earning a tweet of thanks from the WHO—which just a year earlier had labeled gaming an addictive disorder. "COVID-19 may be the turning point when the world realises playing video games is potentially a form of empowerment that brings people together to solve real-world problems," remarked gaming scholar Andy Phelps.[70] By May 2020, an estimated 2.5 billion, or one-third of the world's population, had joined the ranks of gamers.

The Holistic logic highlights the power of synchrony and its byproduct, synergy. When individuals engage in synchronous behaviors, we see a synergistic effect—which may be physical, as in the building of ancient monuments, or abstract, as in team problem-solving. We can now turn to ways to enhance synchrony at the individual, paired, and group levels.

Enhancing Collaboration through Play

In globalizing public diplomacies, the Holistic logic invites vigorous attention to the phenomenon of synchrony. Given the power and prevalence of synchrony in human experience, it seems odd that it has been so understudied. Leveraging diversity may well rely on aligning to the rhythmic patterns of others. What behaviors or mental states can help achieve synchrony?

Interpersonal Synchrony: "I Dance the Other"

In his study of intercultural communication, Edward Hall opined: "Rhythm may prove to be the most binding of all the forces that hold human beings together."[71] Learning the rhythm of people and places, he said, was one of the first steps he took when his anthropological research took him to new venues. Writing relatively recently, noted intercultural scholar Young Yun Kim appears to have come to a similar conclusion about the importance of paying attention to synchrony. She called achieving synchrony "a foundational dimension of intercultural communication competence."[72] She says that people often do not even realize that the awkwardness or discomfort they feel with others stems from different patterns of synchrony; instead, they point to other, more obvious features such as manner of speaking, poor listening, or other behaviors.

For Boundary Spanners, learning to actively attend to the rhythms of others and synchronize is a critical aspect of working in a global environment. Within our own familiar relational circles, we become habituated to the interaction synchrony of those circles. In new social settings, we may suddenly find ourselves "out of sync" with others. We need at these times to suspend our familiar interaction rhythm and become attuned to the new rhythm. Syncing is different from deliberately mimicking or mirroring the other's behaviors. It requires deeply attuning to the other intuitively. Léopold Senghor, the West African philosopher, captured this attuning most beautifully when he said, "I feel the other, I dance the other, therefore I am."[73] Achieving synchrony, as Kim advised, should be at the top of the list of coveted global communication skills—especially, I would add, for global Boundary Spanners.

Collective Synchrony

In addition to developing their own ability to synchronize with others, Boundary Spanners can learn how to use synchrony to bridge differences and mitigate competition. We see this skill in iconic global leaders. Nelson Mandela, for example, tapped into the power of synchrony in sports, particularly the South African love of rugby, to help cross divisions as the country's first post-apartheid Black president.[74] His bold idea was the inspiration for the Hollywood film *Invictus*. While Boundary Spanners do not need to reach this magnitude, being able to organize and reach across divides is a key to effective global collaborations.

We can look, also, to practical models of training people in synchrony. Marshall Ganz, who worked with U.S. civil rights organizers, developed a training model for social activists that tapped into the power of synchrony to create the group cohesion and trust needed for political action.[75] Communication professor

Erin Rand documented her experience during one such training session that combined the use of storytelling and synchrony.[76] Trainers sought to forge bonds of connectivity among disparate individuals without relying on similarity of identity by focusing on developing commonalities. Rand documented three techniques, all of which rely heavily on synchrony. First, participants were coached in a specific style of narrating their stories in a group setting. The participants were then engaged in ritualized chanting and call-and-response techniques. This was followed by the participants using directed applause to guide and affirm their shared affective experience. Rand found her brief half-day experience transformative.

Play

Gaming represents a relatively unexplored area for enhancing the capacity for cooperation. The pan-human appeal of sports is about not only synchrony but also the power of play and games. Most people may think of games as highly competitive. Yet, as Bernard De Koven, author of *The Well-Played Game*, observes, the line between competition and cooperation in games is an artificial one.[77] Before players can compete, they must first cooperate by agreeing on the rules of the game. When people play together, they become deeply attuned to each other, a process De Koven calls "confluence." Confluence, he explains, means " 'flowing together.' Like two streams coming together to create a larger stream."[78] According to De Koven, confluence is at the very heart of what makes cooperative games fun.

For Boundary Spanners, tapping into the appeal of play through offline and online gaming represents one of the most innovative avenues for increasing the capacity for cooperation. Child psychologist Jean Piaget long ago noted the importance of play for learning and understanding the world. In professional settings, adult games such as icebreakers and team-building exercises can increase members' comfort levels in working with each other and result in higher levels of performance. Benjamin Stokes, author of *Locally Played*, demonstrated how community-building games have enabled city officials to advance their goals and create social cohesion among different publics.[79] Globally, online interactive gaming has shown it can engender and sustain participation across linguistic, cultural, and national differences. Perhaps most critically, as game designers will tell you, games are about getting people to constructively engage with challenges, feedback, uncertainty, and problem-solving. These features—along with working with others—are some of the same critical skills needed in tackling the complex wicked problems of humanity-centered public diplomacy. While gaming is still a relatively new research discipline, it offers Boundary Spanners the potential for creative and innovative problem-solving.

Summary

This chapter has focused on the forte of each logic and then sought to strengthen that aspect by blending in features of the other two logics. The Individual logic reflects the power of speech and expands collaboration through storytelling. The Relational logic reflects the power of emotion and expands collaboration through empathy. The Holistic logic reflects the power of synchrony and expands collaboration through synergy and play.

This chapter has shown that through blending—rather than substituting communication patterns into one template—we can expand our vision of the many elements of the communication experience and see how they enhance our evolutionary capacity for collaboration. Building this capacity is key to tackling complex global problems. I know that is a tall order. For this, I ask my readers to move from being Boundary Spanners across the separate logics, to becoming Boundary Spanners of humanity who are able to blend the three logics and enhance the capacity for cooperation in order to address the needs, interests, and goals of humanity.

Conclusion

Boundary Spanning Agenda for Global Collaboration

Iver Neumann suggested that "humanity shapes diplomacy and diplomacy is shaped by humanity."[1] This book began with a call to the Boundary Spanners, those who would bridge the boundaries that divide us as well as those that bring us together. In doing so, the goal was to expand our vision of communication and diplomacy.

In our journey together, I have sought to sketch out a pan-human vision of communication that enhances our evolutionary capacity to collaborate and leverages our diversity to tackle the many wicked problems we face. Leveraging diversity goes beyond simply learning about how others are different and placing them into categories for comparison. Rather than simply learning *about* the other, the quest was to learn *from* the other, as intercultural scholar Yoshitaka Miike has advised.[2] "Learning about" represents the mindset of separateness. "Learning from" implies connectedness and interaction.

Our focus has been on humanity-centered diplomacies. Unlike state-centric diplomacy—or even actor-centered diplomacy, which focus on the needs, interests, and goals of a single actor—humanity-centered diplomacies focus on the whole of humanity, including the planet, ecosystem, and biosphere. Without those, humankind will not flourish.

As we bring this work to a close, we can highlight several significant takeaways and spotlight points that invite further study.

Humanity-Level Perspective

Let me start with the most important takeaway: Globalizing communication and diplomacy rests on a shift in perspective from the individual-level to a humanity-level perspective. This shift lies at the heart of moving from a mindset of separateness to one of connectivity and diversity. It is the key to understanding the logics of communication and public diplomacy, which is in turn critical to building our capacity for collaboration.

Contemporary communication and public diplomacy appear to be rooted in the individual-level perspective. In communication studies, we see this individual-level perspective in the focus on communication actors, that is, the "communicator" and the "receiver." For public diplomacy, we see a corresponding focus on actorness, whether state or non-state actor. Traditional purposes of communication—namely, to inform, educate, persuade, or entertain—likewise highlight the individual level, as do communication theories and research. Uses and gratification theory, for example, explores how individuals use and obtain gratification from the media. Similarly, strategic communication is strategic in the sense of meeting the goals of an individual actor or entity. Research implicitly proceeds from assumptions of individual entities. Polling sampling methods, for instance, are based on individual entities, and results flow from aggregates of individual attitudes, behaviors, or beliefs. Even social network analysis, which presumes connectivity, has been dominated by egocentric network analysis of individual actors. Public diplomacy echoes these communication traditions. Public diplomacy functions such as advocacy, relationship building, nation branding, and even cultural diplomacy similarly privilege an individual-level perspective.

A humanity-level perspective assumes the vantage point of all of humanity, from which one can see the expansiveness of the purposes of both communication and public diplomacy. The purpose is not immediate but global in its reach and implications: It is the survival of all of humankind and the planet. The importance of the health of the planet for the survival of humankind is analogous to that of the health of the body for the individual.

A humanity-level perspective also assumes an expanded timeframe. The individual level assumes a timeframe tied to a particular entity: past, present, or future. Even the longer span of history is slotted within these three dimensions. When we turn to the level of humanity, we move into an evolutionary time frame. This evolutionary time horizon, as we saw in Chapter 6, represents another whole dimension of relations, communication, and public diplomacy. The chapter highlighted the intertwined nature of other areas such as play, storytelling, arts, or spirituality—all of which share a role in enhancing the human capacity for collaboration.

A humanity-level perspective helps demystify cooperation and collaboration. It is telling that many studies begin with the need for cooperation but wrestle with a rationale for explaining cooperation. Much of the research on cooperation has focused on trying to explain why the phenomenon exists, proposing theories of exchange, trust, altruism, even power coercion.[3] Perhaps because of the buried assumptions of individualism, the need to preserve autonomy—the bedrock of separateness—makes competition the norm. Cooperation becomes an ideal or aberration that must be explained, debated, and promoted. One text aptly captures this sentiment by calling cooperation "problematic":

As argued earlier, social capital theories expand the factors—such as trust, networks and norms—that we can use to *explain troublesome human behaviors such as cooperation*. . . . Although economists have already unraveled some of its assumptions, the model still treats cooperation—except under severely prescribed conditions—as a seemingly irrational endeavor. Yet, as one colleague pointed out, even economists cooperate.[4] (emphasis mine)

Viewed from an individual-level perspective, cooperation may make little sense. Why would someone willingly seek to cooperate? Moreover, if individuals struggle to cooperate, why would large entities do so globally? At both the individual and global level, cooperation appears lost in an explanatory void.

However when viewed from a humanity-level perspective, cooperation makes evolutionary sense. Cooperation, as discussed earlier with reference to Darwin's research and that of neuroscience, is key to the evolutionary success and perpetuation of the human species.[5] Iver Neumann highlighted the capacity for cooperation for diplomacy in his analysis of tipping points from prehistoric times to the present.[6] An evolutionary perspective of human communication and its link to the capacity for collaboration has been missing in the field of communication. For Boundary Spanners, there is a need for much more research from across the world's many intellectual heritages that can help us develop a more expansive understanding of how communication contributed to human evolution.

Proficiency across the Logics

An interconnected, diverse global arena demands a view of the communication experience that recognizes the validity and necessity of all three logics. This means developing a proficiency across the logics. Because each logic highlights different assumptions and dynamics of the communication experience, one logic is not sufficient for communicating globally. We saw this plainly in Chapter 1. Despite its seeming mastery of strategic communication, post-9/11 U.S. public diplomacy struggled in connecting with global publics.

In reality, strategic communication, which is a cornerstone of public diplomacy, is a template of the Individual logic and includes the primary elements of separate autonomous entities sending messages through various media. Strategic communication in the international area involves identifying a target audience, matching an intercultural model to the target audience, and using that model of patterned cultural behavior to tailor a culturally appropriate approach in designing a message and delivering it to the target audience. Strategic communication is built on the belief that it is possible to identify, isolate, and target audiences. It also puts faith in the validity of intercultural models, including the idea that societies could be purely "individualistic" or "collectivist." Strategic communication misses the valued dynamics of the other two logics, such as reciprocity, emotion, or synchrony, as well as the idea of connectivity.

The strategic communication approach and intercultural models (discussed in Chapter 2) also reflect the mindset of separateness. As I have sought to demonstrate in this book, intercultural communication is growing increasingly obsolete. It emerged and thrived during a period that spawned the idea of separate and distinct cultures and/or worldviews, which supposedly created unique culture-specific communication patterns. It is not just that individual cultural models (individualism/collectivism) are problematic and rife with inconsistencies; it is the whole idea of using separate and distinct cultural categories that is the problem.

These cultural observations were useful at one time in learning about others, but they are becoming increasingly problematic for several reasons. First, cultures are often portrayed as huge monolithic entities. The Arab culture, which I have written about, spans from the Northwest coast of Africa to the east coast and then to the Middle East. National cultures often have as much diversity within them as between them. Using such broad yet rigid cultural categories today makes one vulnerable to misunderstandings and stereotypes.

Second, cultures get nailed down to specific geographic territories: Chinese culture is tied to a country in Asia, for example. Divisions of humanity are reinforced, even as mobile diaspora transport and transform traditions. Third, observers often define cultural traits as opposites, making them mutually exclusive. Such thinking precludes the idea of opposites as co-existing or that cultural traits are not applicable to or understandable by others. The idea that cultural beliefs are not comprehensible to "outsiders" defies the logic of social customs as learned and passed from generation to generation.

Basing communication patterns on "culture," as intercultural communication models have done in the past, multiplies the problems of culture. In the future, as this book has argued, we must move from culture-based modes of communication to pan-human communication based on our shared relational patterns, intellectual heritages, and neuro-biological features.

Blending the Logics

To "communicate" in a global arena, we need all three logics working together. As this book has argued, we must shift from seeing communication as separate, mutually exclusive cultural categories to blending the three logics. Whereas categories represent separateness, blending reflects connectivity and diversity.

The strategy of blending recognizes that it is not helpful to think of isolating audiences, even though the technology may exist for micro-targeting. In an interconnected world, one can get more communication mileage by amplifying connections. Blending the three logics acknowledges the inherent links and diversity within societies. In the examples from the pandemic in Chapter 6, we saw three-fold blending of the dynamic of speech from Individual logic, with emotion and perspective of the Relational logic, with interaction and synchrony from the Holistic logic.

In face-to-face communication, people tend to blend naturally, almost instinctively. As we saw, human communication is a whole-body, or embodied, experience. Beyond the words (Individual logic), every aspect of a communicator's voice and body contain an emotional element that helps define the relational bond (Relational logic). During interactions, there is constant adaptation and alignment of one's behaviors to the other (Holistic logic).

With accelerating advancements in technology, we already see the tendency toward blending occurring in mediated environments. For example, what began as text-only email messages (Individual logic) quickly added emotional cues (Relational logic). Using ALL CAPITAL LETTERS, for instance, was equated with angry shouting. The use of emojis, imitations of embodied facial expression of emotion (Holistic logic), soon followed. Physical immediacy and interaction (Holistic logic) was captured by "instant" messages and sound notifications announcing one's presence. These technological enhancements, which emerged spontaneously in the virtual environment reflect the blending of the three logics that occurs naturally in in-person communication experience.

On a global level, iconic leaders—such as the Mahatma Gandhi, Nelson Mandela, or the Reverend Dr. Martin Luther King, Jr.—all had a proficiency across the three logics—and skillfully blended the logics. All were trained in public speaking, thus mastering the Individual logic. Both Gandhi and Mandela were trained as lawyers, while King was a pastor. Gandhi was initially too shy to argue in court and went to South Africa to hone his speaking skills.[7]

All three leaders were also masterful relationship builders, attending to relational bonds that typify the Relational logic. During his first venture abroad to England, Gandhi began networking with the Indian diaspora. While in South Africa, his drew on his extensive relations within the Indian diaspora to rally behind the idea of satyagraha, the principle of nonviolent protests against discriminatory practices. King focused on relationship building and organizing among African Americans in Southern U.S. churches.

All three leaders were able to inspire action, even across racial, social and religious divides, and bring different peoples together in common cause. This skill is emblematic of the Holistic logic. Mandela, passionate about sports, used the South African love of rugby to heal divisions as the country's first post-apartheid

Black president. Back in his native India, Gandhi focused on salt, a commodity precious to all Indians, to rally Indians against British rule. Hindus and Muslims joined him on his 241-mile (390 km) walk to the sea to protest British efforts to tax salt.

These leaders were masterful in organizing collective synchronous activities. They used the power of speech (Individual logic), combined with emotional bonding (Relational logic), to inspire others to take bold and risky action (Holistic logic). Learning to creatively blend the communication logics, whether in person or online, is a critical skill set for navigating connectivity and diversity. It is especially important for Boundary Spanners when they engage in sustained interaction during processes of identity mediation and problem-solving.

Moving from Cooperation to Collaboration

Blending is critical for transforming our evolutionary capacity for cooperation into a vision of a global capacity for collaboration. Throughout this work, I have used the phrase "capacity for cooperation," the term most commonly used in the specialist literature in this area. Cooperation in the evolutionary literature suggests helping behavior, such as coming to the aid of another in need. "Mutual aid" was the term used by Russian philosopher Peter Kropotkin (1842–1921).[8] Mutual aid may explain the survival of the human species. Yet, the wealth of human creativity and innovation from antiquity to the present suggests much more than mere cooperation.

As we saw from the examples during the pandemic (Chapter 6), people spontaneously seized social media tools to break through imposed isolation to connect with others. People not only provided mutual aid in the form of offering comfort and solace to each other; they were also collaborating. They were creatively innovating together. Such participatory creativity is found across humanity's rich and varied traditions and heritages. Cooperation, or providing aid, may have helped human species *to survive*. However, it appears that the capacity for collaboration—joining with others to create and innovate—has helped the species *to thrive*.

The distinction between "cooperation" and "collaboration" represents the difference between the previous mindset of separateness and that of connectivity. Whereas cooperation assumes and preserves the separate contributions of individuals to a group endeavor, collaboration rests on the interconnected synergy of a unified endeavor. Connectivity is implied. Roschelle and Teasley capture this distinction in their often-cited piece on problem-solving.[9] The scholars distinguish between cooperation as "a division of labour among participants" and collaboration as "a coordinated, synchronous activity that is the result of a continued

COOPERATION | COLLABORATION

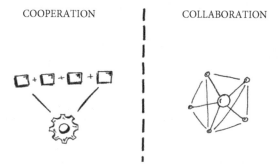

Figure C.1 Cooperation or Collaboration.

Source: The Difference between Cooperation and Collaboration, by John Spence, June 22, 2016. https://spencerauthor.com/can-you-force-collaboration/. Reprinted with the permission of John Spencer. All rights reserved.

attempt to construct and maintain a shared conception of a problem."[10] John Spencer visually captured the distinction of separation in cooperation and connectivity in collaboration (Figure C.1).[11]

The literature on cooperation resonates with the 19th- and 20th-century mindset of separateness. Separateness made competition the norm and cooperation aspirational, or ideal. Going forward in a 21st-century mindset of connectivity, cooperation should be the presumed norm and collaboration the aspirational ideal. For some, the mindset of a capacity for collaboration has already taken root. Lucian Hudson specifically explores many of the conceptual tools and skills needed for collaborative public diplomacy in his report for the British FCO, *The Enabling State.*[12] Ali Fisher extends this vision to non-state actors in his work on collaborative public diplomacy.[13] The success of humanity-centered diplomacies rests on a foundation of a capacity to collaborate.

Search for Commonality

Taking a cue from Charles Darwin, we can shift our research attention from a focus on differences to an exploration of commonality. What made Darwin's work so remarkable is that he looked for the commonalities across the species, and across humankind. This search for commonalities goes against the grain of research for most social sciences. As discussed in the Introduction, strong paradigms, such as Kuhn outlined, call for conceptual clarity, which in turn means drawing distinctive borders.[14] Such thinking privileged a search for differences over commonalities.

Donald E. Brown, professor emeritus of anthropology of the University of California, similar to Darwin, was intrigued by the possibility of human universals. He noted that his own field of anthropology, which is devoted to the study of man, "has been riveted more surely by differences between societies than by their commonalities. . . . Innate universals have tended to be neglected (in extreme cases, their existence was even denied)."[15] He documented more than four hundred commonalities among human societies, across several realms. In the social realm, for example, universals include division of labor, social groups, age grading, the family, play, exchange, cooperation, and reciprocity. He speculated that there are a great many universals still unidentified.

Communication, like anthropology, has followed the tendency in the social sciences to privilege differences over similarities. This focus is changing somewhat with the study of social media, though the field still tends to document differences in internet use across societies. As we saw from examples during the pandemic, there are remarkable similarities in how people gravitate to the online space to connect with others who are different. More remarkable still is how readily some practices are adopted and shared, emoji use being a ready example.

Finding commonality in communication and public diplomacy studies represents an exciting scholarly pursuit. The tendency has been to use that research to refine and reinforce the categories—again, what Miike calls the focus on *learning about* others, rather than *learning from* heritages. The three logics remind us of the pressing need to learn from other heritages. Both emotions and synchrony have been understudied in contemporary communication scholarship. Rather than isolating emotion in subgenres or academic schools—such as emotion in feminist scholarship, or synchrony and harmony for Asian studies—we can use these as models to find commonality across the human communication experience.

Shifting the focus from differences to commonalities is not reserved for scholarship; it applies to practices as well. We can see how blending the communication logics might play out in humanity-centered diplomacies that seek to find commonality in identity mediation. Blending is critical in leveraging diversity because it helps locate commonality. The Individual logic assumes we arrive at commonality primarily through speech, such as dialogue, speech, and words, or cognitively through shared understanding. The Relational logic assumes commonality based on pre-existing or cultivated bonds and intuitive ways of knowing the other. The Holistic logic strives to create a spirit of commonality through synchronized physical or vocal activity.

Blending is also important for communication and identity. Most works on communication in the global arena highlight culture as a dominant feature of communication. Culture as a macro-level of identity suggests a rigid category. Mutually exclusive cultural categories conceptually and theoretically clash.

However, as I tried to show in the "For the Boundary Spanners" section of each chapter, people have a multifaceted, diverse array of identities. The Individual logic highlights personal attributes and agency. Relational logic highlights emotional bonds and relational identities, such as brother, parent, colleague, or even Boundary Spanner. The Holistic logic spotlights how hierarchies provide another layer of identities in a complex relational universe.

In human interactions, different facets of identity—often signaled by verbal and nonverbal cues—continually emerge and recede. As they interact with others, people often seek to find commonality in shared aspects of their identities. Verbally, they may to look for commonality, asking questions of place, occupation, or preferences. Often people find commonality in the most mundane experiences. The homebound nature of work during the pandemic pulled back the curtain of professionalism, revealing a shared experience of toddlers roaming in the picture, dogs barking, or cats jumping onto the computer.

Humanity-centered diplomacies are particularly ripe for accentuating commonalities. "Everyday diplomacies," in which people build relations across boundaries, are often based on similarities.[16] A fascinating venture would be to identify practices of traditional diplomacy and indigenous diplomacy, and using this research not to place these practices into Western/non-Western categories, but to explore and identify commonalities across diplomatic traditions.

Public Diplomacy's Global Mandate

At the beginning of this book, I made a call to the Boundary Spanners, those who would bridge differences as well as find similarities. In this final chapter, I make a call to the Boundary Spanners to attend to a global mandate of humanity-centered public diplomacy.

In traditional diplomacy, diplomats as boundary spanners were representatives of the state and acted toward the needs, interests, and goals of the state. This mandate focused on fulfilling the functions of reporting (information gathering), representation, and negotiation on behalf of the state. Notably, diplomatic functions are tied to the actor. Public diplomacy has similar actor-based functions, such as informing, influencing, engaging, advocacy, relationship building, and so forth.

In humanity-centered diplomacies, the word "humanity" may prompt some to think of the general public and substitute it as the main actor of public diplomacy. However, humanity-centered is less about *who* (actorness, or who is conducting diplomacy) and more about *what*—addressing the needs of humanity. This shift in focus, from actorness to purpose or issue, suggests different diplomatic priorities than the functions of traditional or public diplomacy. Three interrelated diplomatic functions of humanity-centered diplomacies stand out as part of its global mandate.

A first and most immediate function of humanity-centered diplomacies is collaborative problem-solving. Addressing our many global wicked problems has become a top function in public diplomacy's global mandate. Many, such as climate crisis, water scarcity, and even the Covid-19 pandemic, are linked in some way to human action and thus require human action. We need more research on collaborative problem-solving. Here traditional diplomacy may offer insights. As Christer Jönsson noted, diplomatic studies on negotiations distinguish between bargaining, which involves manipulative tactics in order to secure relative advantages, and problem-solving is "associated with creativity and the search for new, inventive solutions" and "implies information sharing and a joint search for common interests."[17] Learning how to creatively leverage diversity is part of the quest to advance problem-solving strategies in humanity-centered diplomacies.

A second function in the global mandate of humanity-centered diplomacies, which is related to problem-solving, is mediating human diversity. Under the 19th- and 20th-century mindset of separateness, the traditional diplomatic function of representation and "mediating identities," was predicated on state recognition. As veteran Vietnamese diplomat Tran Van Dinh observed, "Recognition is at the heart of diplomacy, and it formally establishes communication between governments."[18] He also noted that until the late 19th and early 20th centuries, diplomatic recognition of political entities was not a matter of approval but an acknowledgment of a political reality. That practice, he noted, changed when recognition became conditional upon approval by other states.

Mediating identities had a rather big caveat. Stateless peoples—including many indigenous peoples of former colonial conquests by states—were dismissed from that state-based recognition of identity in diplomacy. Nomadic traditions, pre-colonial practices, and non-territorial entities such as diaspora populations fell through the cracks of the state-based actor model. In the 21st-century dynamic of interconnectivity, mediating human diversity and identity in all of its forms, including or especially political, is another priority function of humanity-centered diplomacy.

A third function, highlighted most vividly by the pandemic, is the need for public diplomacy to respond to the needs of humans, most prominently emotional and spiritual needs. When public diplomacy reappeared on the diplomatic stage in the aftermath of 9/11, scholars largely shaped its contours in the image of traditional diplomacy. The "rational actor" assumed prominence and focus was on observable interests, needs, and goals of the state. Emotions were not part of those visible or measurable goals.

Emotion has been receiving greater attention in international studies, thanks to the early works of Richard Ned Lebow[19] and other scholars.[20] Additionally, scholars have been notable in highlighting emotions specifically in diplomacy.[21] The study of emotion has also emerged in public diplomacy, beginning with the work of Sarah Ellen Graham and more recently by Constance Duncombe.[22]

In looking to the future, emotion is not just an element of study or scholarship but is critical for diplomatic practice. As the virus demonstrated, human societies have profound emotional needs. The practice of empathetic public diplomacy (Chapter 6) elevates public diplomacy practice from the *battle* for hearts and minds to the *care* of hearts and minds. Public diplomacy practices that attend to emotions represents a critical area for future research. Humans also have profound spiritual needs. Again, while we have the pioneering work by Johnston on faith-based diplomacy and Constantinou on spiritual diplomacy,[23] what we need is active translation and application of spiritual diplomacy in practice.

* * *

A final note to the Boundary Spanners is about looking ahead. This book has sought to sketch the outlines of a global collaboration by expanding our thinking about communication and public diplomacy from a mindset of separateness to one of connectivity. This connectivity is already evident in the steady proliferation of our digital and social media technologies. Research to understand the communication dynamics of new media technologies is growing. We desperately need a better understanding of the human dimension of connectivity and diversity—that is, the connected and yet diverse span of human users. Ironically, the ancient world assumed such connectivity and a diversity in the human communication experience. I have tried to share some of that literature from the world's intellectual heritages in this book as best I could. But to do so fully is beyond my reach. For that reason, I close this study with a call to the Boundary Spanners of humanity, who, both in scholarship and in practice, can carry on the task of explaining and expanding the logics so that we can better leverage our diversity to enhance our evolutionary capacity for collaboration—and, I hope, in the process, make our world a better place.

Notes

Introduction

1. Refugees International, "COVID-19 and the Displaced: Addressing the Threat of the Novel Coronavirus in Humanitarian Emergencies," March 30, 2020, p. 2, https://www.refugeesinternational.org/reports/2020/3/29/covid-19-and-the-displaced-addressing-the-threat-of-the-novel-coronavirus-in-humanitarian-emergencies.
2. Horst W. J. Rittel and Melvin M. Webber, "Dilemmas in a General Theory of Planning," *Policy Sciences* 4, no. 2 (1973): 155–69.
3. Ben Ziegler, "How to Accelerate the Development of New Collaborative Relationships," *Collaboration Strategies and Solutions* (blog), July 21, 2015, http://collaborativejourneys.com/how-to-accelerate-the-development-of-new-collaborative-relationships/.
4. Scott E. Page, *The Difference: How the Power of Diversity Creates Better Groups, Firms, Schools, and Societies* (Princeton, NJ: Princeton University Press, 2008).
5. Wilbur Lang Schramm, *The Science of Human Communication: New Directions and New Findings in Communication Research* (New York: Basic Books, 1963).
6. Christer Jönsson and Martin Hall, *Essence of Diplomacy* (New York: Springer, 2005).
7. Iver B. Neumann, "A Prehistorical Evolutionary View of Diplomacy," *Place Branding and Public Diplomacy* 14 (2018): 9.
8. Carolyn Burdett, "Post Darwin: Social Darwinism, Degeneration, Eugenics," *British Library, Discovering Literature: Romantics and Victorians* (blog), May 15, 2014, https://www.bl.uk/romantics-and-victorians/articles/post-darwin-social-darwinism-degeneration-eugenics#.
9. Dirk Messner and Silke Weinlich, *Global Cooperation and the Human Factor in International Relations* (New York: Routledge, 2015).
10. Charles Darwin, *The Descent of Man and Selection in Relation to Sex*, new rev. ed. (New York: D. Appleton, 1896), 131.
11. Darwin, 107.
12. Charles Darwin, *The Descent of Man, and Selection in Relation to Sex* (London: J. Murray, 1871); Charles Darwin, *The Expression of the Emotions in Man and Animals (with an Introduction by Paul Ekman)*, (New York: Oxford University Press, 1998).
13. See, for example, Samuel Bowles and Herbert Gintis, *A Cooperative Species: Human Reciprocity and Its Evolution*, reprint ed. (Princeton: Princeton University Press, 2013); Edward O. Wilson, *The Social Conquest of Earth* (New York: Liveright Publishing Corporation, 2012).
14. J. M. Burkart et al., "The Evolutionary Origin of Human Hyper-Cooperation," *Nature Communications* 5, no. 1 (August 27, 2014): 4747.

15. Bowles and Gintis, *A Cooperative Species*; Wilson, *The Social Conquest of Earth*.
16. Douglas Rushkoff, *Team Human* (New York: W. W. Norton & Company, 2019); see also, Nicholas A. Christakis, *Blueprint: The Evolutionary Origins of a Good Society* (New York: Little, Brown Spark, 2019); Yuval Noah Harari, *Sapiens: A Brief History of Humankind*, repr. ed. (New York: Harper Perennial, 2018).
17. Neumann, "A Prehistorical Evolutionary View of Diplomacy."
18. See, for example, the work at the lab of Stuart Anstis at the University of California, San Diego.
19. Arjun Appadurai, *Modernity at Large: Cultural Dimensions of Globalization*, Public Worlds, Vol. 1 (Minneapolis: University of Minnesota Press, 1996).
20. Bertrand Badie, "The European Challenge to Bismarckian Diplomacy," *International Politics (Hague, Netherlands)* 46, no. 5 (2009): 517–26; cited in Ole Jacob Sending, Vincent Pouliot, and Iver B. Neumann, "The Future of Diplomacy: Changing Practices, Evolving Relationships," *International Journal (Toronto)* 66, no. 3 (2011): 534.
21. Kuhn's book *The Structure of Scientific Revolution*, which advocated strong conceptual foundations for theory-building and methodology, was particularly for new fields such as communication, and even more so for emerging fields such as intercultural communication. The book came at a particularly poignant time as emerging fields such as communication were challenged by older disciplines such as anthropology and sociology. Turf battles in academia can be particularly vicious. Being able to delineate boundaries between the social sciences meant being able to establish distinctive academic departments, professional organizations, and journals. Thomas S. Kuhn, *The Structure of Scientific Revolutions* (Chicago, IL: University of Chicago Press, 1996).
22. John Gerring, "What Makes a Concept Good? A Criterial Framework for Understanding Concept Formation in the Social Sciences," *Polity* 31, no. 3 (1999): 381.
23. Samuel Grandados et al., "Raising Barriers: A New Age of Walls," *Washington Post*, October 12, 2016,https://www.washingtonpost.com/graphics/world/border-barriers/global-illegal-immigration-prevention/; Reece Jones, "Borders and Walls: Do Barriers Deter Unauthorized Migration?," migrationpolicy.org, 2016, https://www.migrationpolicy.org/article/borders-and-walls-do-barriers-deter-unauthorized-migration; Elisabeth Vallet, *Borders, Fences and Walls: State of Insecurity?* (Farnham, Surrey, UK: Routledge, 2016).
24. Yale Infant Lab, "The Infant Cognition Center | Yale University," 2021, https://campuspress.yale.edu/infantlab/; see profile: CBS News, "Babies Help Unlock the Origins of Morality," *60 Minutes*, November 18, 2012, https://www.cbsnews.com/news/babies-help-unlock-the-origins-of-morality/.
25. Mark W. Moffett, *The Human Swarm: How Our Societies Arise, Thrive, and Fall* (New York: Basic Books, 2019).
26. For an overview of this historical trend, see the collection of Harvard historian Akira Iriye and colleagues: Sebastian Conrad, Jürgen Osterhammel, and Akira Iriye, eds., *An Emerging Modern World: 1750–1870* (Cambridge, MA: Belknap Press, 2018); Emily S. Rosenberg et al., *A World Connecting: 1870–1945* (Cambridge, MA: Harvard

University Press, 2012); Akira Iriye et al., *Global Interdependence: The World after 1945* (Cambridge, MA: Harvard University Press, 2014).

27. James Der Derian, *On Diplomacy: A Genealogy of Western Estrangement* (Oxford: Blackwell, 1987).

28. Paul Sharp, *Diplomatic Theory of International Relations* (New York: Cambridge University Press, 2009), 2.

29. Ole Jacob Sending, Vincent Pouliot, and Iver B. Neumann, *Diplomacy and the Making of World Politics* (Cambridge: Cambridge University Press, 2015); G. R. Berridge, *Diplomacy: Theory and Practice* (New York: Springer, 2015); Adam Watson, *Diplomacy: The Dialogue between States* (New York: Routledge, 2013).

30. Geoffrey Allen Pigman, *Contemporary Diplomacy: Representation and Communication in a Globalized World* (Cambridge: Polity, 2010).

31. Nicholas J. Cull, "Public Diplomacy: Taxonomies and Histories," *The Annals of the American Academy of Political and Social Science* 616, no. 1 (2008): 31–54; Nancy Snow, "Rethinking Public Diplomacy," in *Routledge Handbook of Public Diplomacy*, ed. Nancy Snow and Nicholas J Cull, 2nd ed. (New York: Routledge, 2020), 3–12.

32. John Robert Kelley, *Agency Change: Diplomatic Action beyond the State* (Lanham: Rowman & Littlefield Publishers, 2014).

33. See, for example, the Palgrave Global Public Diplomacy series, which includes studies on Turkey, Sweden, China, India, and Canada. Efe Sevin, *Public Diplomacy and the Implementation of Foreign Policy in the US, Sweden and Turkey* (New York: Palgrave Macmillan, 2017); Jian Wang, ed., *Soft Power in China: Public Diplomacy through Communication*, Palgrave Macmillan Series in Global Public Diplomacy (New York: Palgrave Macmillan, 2010); Daya Kishan Thussu, *Communicating India's Soft Power: Buddha to Bollywood*, Palgrave Macmillan Series in Global Public Diplomacy (New York: Palgrave Macmillan, 2013), https://doi.org/10.1057/9781137027894; Nicholas J. Cull and Michael K. Hawes, eds., *Canada's Public Diplomacy*, Palgrave Macmillan Series in Global Public Diplomacy (New York: Palgrave Macmillan, 2021), https://doi.org/10.1007/978-3-319-62015-2.

34. Costas M. Constantinou, "Between Statecraft and Humanism: Diplomacy and Its Forms of Knowledge," *International Studies Review* 15, no. 2 (June 1, 2013): 142.

35. Douglas Johnston, ed., *Faith-Based Diplomacy: Trumping Realpolitik* (New York: Oxford University Press, 2003), https://oxford.universitypressscholarship.com/view/10.1093/acprof:oso/9780195367935.001.0001/acprof-9780195367935.

36. Tran Van Dinh, *Communication and Diplomacy in a Changing World* (Norwood, NJ: Ablex, 1987), 11.

37. R. S. Zaharna, "Culture, Cultural Diversity and Humanity-Centred Diplomacies," *The Hague Journal of Diplomacy* 14, no. 1–2 (April 22, 2019): 117–33.

38. Manuel Castells, "The New Public Sphere: Global Civil Society, Communication Networks, and Global Governance," *The Annals of the American Academy of Political and Social Science* 616, no. 1 (March 1, 2008): 78–93.

39. Juyan Zhang and Brecken Chinn Swartz, "Public Diplomacy to Promote Global Public Goods (GPG): Conceptual Expansion, Ethical Grounds, and Rhetoric," *Public Relations Review* 35, no. 4 (November 1, 2009): 382–87.

40. Kathy R. Fitzpatrick, "Public Diplomacy in the Public Interest," *Journal of Public Interest Communication* 1, no. 1 (2017): 78–93.

41. Simon Anholt, *The Good Country Equation: How We Can Repair the World in One Generation*, (New York: Berrett-Koehler, 2020); See also the Good Country Index website at https://www.goodcountry.org/.

42. Noé Cornago, *Plural Diplomacies: Normative Predicaments and Functional Imperatives*, (Leiden: Martinus Nijhoff Publishers, 2013).

43. Costas M. Constantinou and James Der Derian, "Introduction: Sustaining Global Hope: Sovereignty, Power and the Transformation of Diplomacy," in *Sustainable Diplomacies*, ed. Costas M. Constantinou and James Der Derian (London: Palgrave Macmillan UK, 2010), 1–22.

44. Seçkin Barış Gulmez, "Cosmopolitan Diplomacy," in *Routledge International Handbook of Cosmopolitanism Studies*, ed. Gerard Delanty (New York: Routledge, 2018); Cesar Villanueva Rivas, "Cosmopolitan Constructivism: Mapping a Road to the Future of Cultural and Public Diplomacy," *Public Diplomacy Magazine* Winter, no. 3 (2010): 45–56.

45. Magnus Marsden, Diana Ibañez-Tirado, and David Henig, "Everyday Diplomacy," *The Cambridge Journal of Anthropology* 34, no. 2 (September 1, 2016): 2–22.

46. Villanueva Rivas, "Cosmopolitan Constructivism."

47. Akira Iriye, *Global Community: The Role of International Organizations in the Making of the Contemporary World* (Berkeley: University of California Press, 2002), 8.

48. Donna Marie Oglesby, "*Spectacle in Copenhagen: Public Diplomacy on Parade*," *CPD Perspectives on Public Diplomacy*, Paper 4, December 2010, https://uscpublicdiplomacy.org/sites/uscpublicdiplomacy.org/files/useruploads/u35361/2010%20Paper%204.pdf.

49. Anna Naupa, "Indo-Pacific Diplomacy: A View from the Pacific Islands," *Politics and Policy* 45, no. 5 (October 1, 2017): 902–17.

50. Andrew F. Cooper, Brian Hocking, and William Maley, eds., *Global Governance and Diplomacy—Worlds Apart?* (Houndmills: Palgrave Macmillan, 2008).

51. Iriye, *Global Community*, documents the rise of international NGOs from five in 1850 to 135 in 1910 to more than 10,000 by 2000.

52. Walker Connor, "When Is a Nation?," in *Nationalism*, ed. John Hutchinson and Anthony D. Smith (Oxford: Oxford University Press, 1994), 154–59; John A. Armstrong, *Nations before Nationalism* (Chapel Hill: University of North Carolina Press, 2017), originally published 1982; Anthony D. Smith, *Nationalism: Theory, Ideology, History* (John Wiley & Sons, 2013); John Hutchinson and Anthony D. Smith, "Introduction," in *Nationalism*, ed. John Hutchinson and Anthony D. Smith (Oxford: Oxford University Press, 1994), 3–16.

53. Sebastian Conrad, Jürgen Osterhammel, and Akira Iriye, eds. *An Emerging Modern World: 1750–1870*, A History of the World, 4 (Cambridge, MA: Harvard University Press, 2018); Barry Buzan and George Lawson, *The Global Transformation: History, Modernity and the Making of International Relations* (Cambridge: Cambridge University Press, 2015), https://doi.org/10.1017/CBO9781139565073.

54. Hutchinson and Smith, "Introduction," 4.

55. Connor, "When Is a Nation?," 156.

56. Alisher Faizullaev, "Diplomacy and Symbolism," *The Hague Journal of Diplomacy* 8, no. 2 (January 1, 2013): 91–114.

57. Benedict R. Anderson, *Imagined Communities: Reflections on the Origin and Spread of Nationalism* (London: Version, 1983).

58. Anderson, *Imagined Communities*; Michael Billig, *Banal Nationalism* (London: SAGE Publications Ltd., 1995).

59. Edward B. Tylor, *Primitive Culture: Researches into the Development of Mythology, Philosophy, Religion, Art, and Custom* (London: John Murray, 1871).

60. Raymond Williams, *Culture and Society, 1780–1950* (New York: Columbia University Press, 1958).

61. Lila Abu-Lugod, "Writing against Culture," in *Recapturing Anthropology: Working in the Present*, ed. Richard G. Fox (Santa Fe, NM: School of American Research, 1991), 137–62.

62. Susan Wright, "The Politicization of 'Culture,'" *Anthropology Today* 14, no. 1 (February 1, 1998): 7–15, https://doi.org/10.2307/2783092; Barbara Adam and Stuart Allan, *Theorizing Culture: An Interdisciplinary Critique after Postmodernism* (New York: New York University Press, 1995); Homi K. Bhabha, *The Location of Culture*, 2nd ed. (London: Routledge, 2004).

63. Ingrid Piller, *Intercultural Communication: A Critical Introduction* (Edinburgh: Edinburgh University Press, 2017), https://books.google.com/books/about/Intercul tural_Communication.html?id=mC1WDwAAQBAJ.

64. Brian Street, "Culture Is a Verb: Anthropological Aspects of Language and Cultural Process," in *Language and Culture: Papers from the Annual Meeting of the British Association of Applied Linguistics Held at Trevelyan College, University of Durham, September 1991*, by British Association for Applied Linguistics Meeting (Multilingual Matters, 1993), 23–59; Roy Wagner, *The Invention of Culture* (Chicago: University of Chicago Press, 1975); Wright, "The Politicization of 'Culture'"; William H. Sewell, "The Concept(s) of Culture," in *Beyond the Cultural Turn: New Directions in the Study of Society and Culture*, ed. Victoria Bonnell and Lynn Hunt (Berkeley: University of California Press, 1999), 35–61.

65. Sewell, "The Concept(s) of Culture," 57.

66. Bhabha, *The Location of Culture*; Marwan M. Kraidy, *Hybridity: The Cultural Logic of Globalization* (Philadelphia: Temple University Press, 2005).

67. Isocrates, *Nicocles*, cited by Charles Marsh, "Converging on Harmony: Idealism, Evolution, and the Theory of Mutual Aid," *Public Relations Inquiry* 1, no. 3 (September 1, 2012), 317.

68. The Analects, Chapter 9/26, cited by Johnathan D. Spence, "What Confucius Said," China File, April 10, 1997, https://www.chinafile.com/library/nyrb-china-archive/what-confucius-said.

69. Joe Carmichael, "How the Theoretical Physics Finally Caught Up with Ancient Philosophy," *Inverse*, June 28, 2016, https://www.inverse.com/article/17276-how-theoretical-physics-finally-caught-up-with-ancient-philosophy; Catherine Offord, "Quantum Biology May Help Solve Some of Life's Greatest Mysteries," *The Scientist*,

June 1, 2019, https://www.scribd.com/book/351486816/Energy-Medicine-Techn ologies-Ozone-Healing-Microcrystals-Frequency-Therapy-and-the-Future-of-Health.

70. Marco Iacoboni, *Mirroring People: The Science of Empathy and How We Connect with Others* (New York: Picador, 2009); Loretta Graziano Breuning, *Habits of a Happy Brain: Retrain Your Brain to Boost Your Serotonin, Dopamine, Oxytocin, and Endorphin Levels* (Avon, MA: Adams Media, 2015); Michael Tomasello et al., "Two Key Steps in the Evolution of Human Cooperation: The Interdependence Hypothesis," *Current Anthropology* 53, no. 6 (2012): 673–92.

71. Keith Dinnie, *Nation Branding: Concepts, Issues, Practice* (London: Routledge, 2015); Michael Kunczik, *Images of Nations and International Public Relations* (Mahwah, NJ: Lawrence Erlbaum Associates, 1996); Alexander Buhmann and Diana Ingenhoff, "The 4D Model of the Country Image: An Integrative Approach from the Perspective of Communication Management," *International Communication Gazette* 77, no. 1 (February 1, 2015): 102–24.

72. Kwame Anthony Appiah, *The Ethics of Identity* (Princeton, NJ: Princeton University Press, 2010), https://doi.org/10.1515/9781400826193.

73. Brian L. Hocking, "Introduction: Gatekeepers and Boundary-Spanners: Thinking about Foreign Ministries in the European Union," in *Foreign Ministries in the European Union: Integrating Diplomats*, ed. Brian Hocking and David Spence (Basingstoke: Palgrave, 2005), 1–16.

74. Costas M. Constantinou, *Human Diplomacy and Spirituality* (report, *Netherlands Institute of International Relations "Clingendael,"* 2006), 21.

75. Philip Seib, *The Future of #Diplomacy* (Cambridge, UK: Polity, 2016).

76. Daryl Copeland, *Guerrilla Diplomacy: Rethinking International Relations* (New York: Lynne Rienner, 2009).

77. Kelley, *Agency Change*.

78. Leo E. Otoide, "Re-Thinking the Subject of Africa's International Relations," *Voice of History (Nepal)* 16, no. 2 (2001): 43–56.

79. Chris Rumford and Andrew Cooper, "Bordering and Connectivity: Thinking about Cosmopolitan Borders," in *Routledge International Handbook of Cosmopolitanism Studies*, 2nd ed. Gerard Delanty (New York: Routledge, 2018), 277–86.

Chapter 1

1. Richard Lugar, U.S. Senate Foreign Relations Committee, Opening Statement for Nomination Hearings for Margaret D. Tutwiler for Undersecretary of State for Public Diplomacy, October 29, 2003; Brian Knowlton, "Lugar Says U.S. is All Thumbs in Dealing with Muslims," The New York Times, October 29, 2003, https://www.nyti mes.com/2003/10/29/international/middleeast/lugar-says-us-is-all-thumbs-in-deal ing-with-muslims.html.

2. R. S. Zaharna, *Battles to Bridges: U.S. Strategic Communication and Public Diplomacy after 9/11* (Basingstoke: Palgrave Macmillan, 2010), http://dx.doi.org/10.1057/978023 0277922.

3. George W. Bush, "Press Conference," October 11, 2001, http://www.washingtonpost.com/wp-srv/nation/specials/attacked/transcripts/bush_text101101.html.

4. For campaign launch, see U.S. Department of State Archives 2001–2009: Charlotte Beers, Under Secretary for Public Diplomacy and Public Affairs, "Public Diplomacy after September 11," U.S. Department of State, ARCHIVE (Department of State, Office of Electronic Information, Bureau of Public Affairs, December 18, 2002), https://2001-2009.state.gov/r/us/16269.htm; U.S. State Department, "Muslim Life in America," n.d., http://usinfo.state.gov/products/pubs/muslimlife/homepage.htm.

5. See, Charlotte Beers, Under Secretary for Public Diplomacy and Public Affairs, "American Public Diplomacy and Islam" (U.S. Department of State, Office of Electronic Information, Bureau of Public Affairs, February 27, 2003), https://2001-2009.state.gov/r/us/18098.htm; Beers, Under Secretary for Public Diplomacy and Public Affairs, "U.S. Public Diplomacy in the Arab and Muslim Worlds" (Department of State, Office of Electronic Information, Bureau of Public Affairs, May 7, 2002), https://2001-2009.state.gov/r/us/10424.htm; Beers, Under Secretary for Public Diplomacy and Public Affairs, "Public Service and Public Diplomacy" (Department of State, Office of Electronic Information, Bureau of Public Affairs, October 17, 2002), https://2001-2009.state.gov/r/us/15912.htm.

6. Kenneth Y. Tomlinson, "Testimony of Kenneth Y. Tomlinson, Chairman, Broadcasting Board of Governors, before the Committee of Foreign Relations, United States Senate on American Public Diplomacy in the Islamic World," February 27, 2003, https://www.foreign.senate.gov/imo/media/doc/TomlinsonTestimony030227.pdf; Nancy Youssef, "Music, All-Arabic Format Thrive; Some Say News Is Slanted," *Detroit Free Press*, March 11, 2003.

7. Interestingly, The State Department's Washington File reported that "Alhurra aims to deliver 'accuracy' and 'free and open debate,'" adding, "The Alhurra project has been greeted with skepticism in much of the Middle Eastern press where many local pundits maintain that the station will be dismissed as government propaganda." David Shelby, "US Starts New Arabic-Language Satellite TV Broadcast," February 13, 2004, https://govinfo.library.unt.edu/cpa-iraq/pressreleases/20040214_satellite.html;   Ed Finn, "Unhip, Unhip Al Hurra, The Middle East Hates Its New TV Station," *Slate*, February 20, 2004, https://slate.com/news-and-politics/2004/02/the-middle-east-hates-its-new-tv-station.html; Marwan Al Kabalan, "Al Hurra's Chances of Success Are Remote," *Gulf News*, February 20, 2004, https://gulfnews.com/uae/dr-marwan-al-kaba lan-al-hurras-chances-of-success-are-remote-1.314218.

8. Teri Schultz, "State Department Magazine Courts Arab Youth," *Fox News*, September 1, 2003; Tim Cavanaugh, "Hi Times: Citizen Powell's State Department Publishing Adventure," Reason, September 30, 2003, https://reason.com/2003/09/30/hi-times/; Peter Carlson, "America's Glossy Envoy," *The Washington Post*, August 9, 2003, https://www.washingtonpost.com/archive/politics/2003/08/09/americas-glossy-envoy/94567794-380c-4aad-b007-e324fe596145/.

9. In addition to the sources already mentioned, see Marwan Bishara, "Washington's New Channel: Propaganda TV Won't Help the U.S.," *The New York Times*, February 23, 2004, sec. Opinion, https://www.nytimes.com/2004/02/23/opinion/washingt ons-new-channel-propaganda-tv-wont-help-the-us.html; Chris Toensing, "Hi and a Low at the State Department," *The Daily Star*, August 23, 2003, sec. Opinion, http://www.dailystar.com.lb/Opinion/Commentary/2003/Aug-23/103843-hi-and-a-low-at-the-state-department.ashx.

10. See, for example, Pew Research Center, "What the World Thinks in 2002," The Pew Global Attitudes Project, December 4, 2002, https://www.pewresearch.org/global/2002/12/04/what-the-world-thinks-in-2002/; Pew Research Center, "Views of a Changing World 2003: War with Iraq Further Divides Global Publics," June 3, 2003, https://www.pewresearch.org/politics/2003/06/03/views-of-a-changing-world-2003/; Pew Research Center, "America's Image Further Erodes, Europeans Want Weaker Ties: But Post-War Iraq Will Be Better Off, Most Say," March 18, 2003, https://www.pewresearch.org/politics/2003/03/18/americas-image-further-erodes-europe ans-want-weaker-ties/; Pew Research Center, "A Year after Iraq War: Mistrust of America in Europe Ever Higher, Muslim Anger Persists," The Pew Global Attitudes Project, March 16, 2004, https://www.pewresearch.org/global/2004/03/16/a-year-after-iraq-war/.

11. Pew Research Center, "Views of a Changing World 2003," 3.

12. See, for example, Makram Khoury-Machool, "Losing Iraqi Hearts and Minds," Iraqi Crisis Report (Global Vision News Network, June 11, 2003); Samer Shehata, "Why Bush's Middle East Propaganda Campaign Won't Work," Salon, July 13, 2002, https://www.salon.com/2002/07/12/propaganda_8/; Jihad Fakhreddine, "US Public Diplomacy in Broken Arabic: Evaluating the Shared Values Advertising Campaign Targeting Arab and Muslim Worlds," *Global Media Journal* 2, no. 4 (Spring 2004), https://www.globalmediajournal.com/open-access/us-public-diplomacy-in-broken-arabic.pdf.

13. Rami Khouri, "The US Public Diplomacy Hoax: Why Do They Keep Insulting Us?" (Commentary), *The Daily Star*, February 11, 2004, http://www.dailystar.com.lb//Opinion/Commentary/2004/Feb-11/92631-the-us-public-diplomacy-hoax-why-do-they-keep-insulting-us.ashx.

14. Mohan J. Dutta-Bergman, "U.S. Public Diplomacy in the Middle East," *Journal of Communication Inquiry* 30, no. 2 (April 1, 2006): 102–24, https://doi.org/10.1177/0196859905285286; Jian Wang, "Managing National Reputation and International Relations in the Global Era: Public Diplomacy Revisited," *Public Relations Review* 32, no. 2 (2006): 91–96.

15. Nancy Snow, *The Arrogance of American Power: What US Leaders Are Doing Wrong and Why It's Our Duty to Dissent* (Lanham: Rowman & Littlefield, 2007).

16. Peter G. Peterson, "Public Diplomacy and the War on Terrorism," *Foreign Affairs* 81, no. 5 (2002): 75, https://doi.org/10.2307/20033270.

17. Nicholas J. Cull, "Public Diplomacy: Taxonomies and Histories," *The Annals of the American Academy of Political and Social Science* 616, no. 1 (2008): 31–54; Council on Foreign Relations, "Public Diplomacy: A Strategy for Reform," Council on Foreign

Relations, July 30, 2002, http://www.cfr.org/diplomacy-and-statecraft/public-diplom acy-strategy-reform/p4697.

18. Geoffrey Cowan and Amelia Arsenault, "Moving from Monologue to Dialogue to Collaboration: The Three Layers of Public Diplomacy," *The Annals of the American Academy of Political and Social Science* 616, no. 1 (2008): 10–30.

19. E. Comor and H. Bean, "America's 'Engagement' Delusion: Critiquing a Public Diplomacy Consensus," *International Communication Gazette* 74, no. 3 (April 1, 2012): 203–20; Bruce Gregory, "American Public Diplomacy: Enduring Characteristics, Elusive Transformation," *The Hague Journal of Diplomacy* 6, no. 3 (2011): 351–72.

20. Edward P. Djerejian, "Changing Minds, Winning Peace: A New Strategic Direction for US Public Diplomacy in the Arab and Muslim World" (Washington, DC: Advisory Group on Public Diplomacy, U.S. Department of State, October 2003), 5.

21. Margaret Tutwiler, "Public Diplomacy: Reaching Beyond Traditional Audiences," § House Appropriations Subcommittee on Commerce, Justice, State and the Judiciary (2004), https://2001-2009.state.gov/r/us/2004/29111.htm.

22. Kathy Fitzpatrick, *The Future of U.S. Public Diplomacy: An Uncertain Fate* (Leiden: Martinus Nijhoff, 2010).

23. Shaun Riordan, "Dialogue-Based Public Diplomacy: A New Foreign Policy Paradigm?," Netherlands Institute of International Relations 'Clingendael,' Discussion Papers in Diplomacy No. 95, (November 2004): 1–17; Jan Melissen, "The New Public Diplomacy: Between Theory and Practice," in *The New Public Diplomacy: Soft Power in International Relations* (New York: Palgrave Macmillan, 2005), 3–27; R. S. Zaharna, Amelia Arsenault, and Ali Fisher, eds., *Relational, Networked and Collaborative Approaches to Public Diplomacy: The Connective Mindshift* (New York: Routledge, 2013).

24. Ronit Kampf, Ilan Manor, and Elad Segev, "Digital Diplomacy 2.0? A Cross-National Comparison of Public Engagement in Facebook and Twitter," *The Hague Journal of Diplomacy* 10, no. 4 (2015): 331–62.

25. Comor and Bean, "America's 'Engagement' Delusion," 204.

26. Molefi Asante, *Afrocentric Idea Revised* (Philadelphia: Temple University Press, 2011); Shelton A. Gunaratne, "De-Westernizing Communication/Social Science Research: Opportunities and Limitations," *Media, Culture & Society* 32, no. 3 (2010): 473–500, https://doi.org/10.1177/0163443709361159; Guo-Ming Chen, "A Model of Global Communication Competence," *China Media Research* 1, no. 1 (2005): 3–11; Chen, "Toward an I Ching Model of Communication," *China Media Research* 5, no. 3 (2009): 72–81; Yoshitaka Miike, "Theorizing Culture and Communication in the Asian Context: An Assumptive Foundation," *Intercultural Communication Studies* 11, no. 1 (2002): 1–22; Miike, "Non-Western Theory in Western Research? An Asiacentric Agenda for Asian Communication Studies," *The Review of Communication* 6, no. 1–2 (2006): 4–31; Miike, "Asian Contributions to Communication Theory: An Introduction," *China Media Research* 3, no. 4 (2007); Min-Sun Kim, *Non-Western Perspectives on Human Communication: Implications for Theory and Practice* (Thousand Oaks: Sage Publications, 2002); Silvio Waisbord

and Claudia Mellado, "De-Westernizing Communication Studies: A Reassessment," *Communication Theory* 24 (2014): 361–72; Georgette Wang, "Paradigm Shift and the Centrality of Communication Discipline," *International Journal of Communication* 5 (2011): 1458–66; Satoshi Ishii, "Complementing Contemporary Intercultural Communication Research with East Asian Sociocultural Perspectives and Practices," *China Media Research* 2, no. 1 (2006): 13–20; Youichi Ito, "Mass Communication Theories from a Japanese Perspective," *Media, Culture & Society* 12 (1990): 423–64; D. Lawrence Kincaid, *Communication Theory: Eastern and Western Perspectives* (San Diego: Academic Press, 2013); Hamid Mowlana and William B. Gudykunst, "Mass Media and Culture: Toward an Integrated Theory," in *Intercultural Communication Theory: Current Perspectives* (Beverly Hills, CA: Sage, 1983), 149–70.

27. Wilbur Lang Schramm, *The Science of Human Communication: New Directions and New Findings in Communication Research* (New York: Basic Books, 1963), 7.

28. Frank E. X. Dance, "The 'Concept' of Communication," *Journal of Communication* 20 (1970): 201–10.

29. UNESCO used the definition from the International Scientific Information (ISI): "Despite this rapid change, communication studies remains radically heterogeneous as an intellectual field, defined as study of the verbal and non-verbal exchange of ideas and information." International Social Science Council and UNESCO, Director-General, 2009–2017, *World Social Science Report, 2010: Knowledge Divides* (Paris: ISSC/UNESCO, 2010), 196, https://unesdoc.unesco.org/ark:/48223/pf000 0188333.

30. 2016 International Communication Association Conference "Call for Papers," Fukuoka, Japan.

31. Edwin McDaniel and Larry A. Samovar, "Understanding and Applying Intercultural Communication in the Global Community: The Fundamentals," in *Intercultural Communication: A Reader* (40th edition), ed. Larry A. Samovar et al. (Belmont, CA: Cengage Learning, 2014), 7.

32. Guo-Ming Chen and William J. Starosta, *Foundations of Intercultural Communication* (Boston: Allyn and Bacon, 1998), 29.

33. Satoshi Ishii, "Complementing Contemporary Intercultural Communication Research with East Asian Sociocultural Perspectives and Practices," 13.

34. See, for example, Geertz Hofstede, *Culture's Consequences: International Differences in Work-Related Values* (Beverly Hills: Sage, 1980); Harry Charalambos Triandis, *Individualism and Collectivism* (Boulder, CO: Westview Press, 1995).

35. Florence Rockwood Kluckhohn and Fred L. Strodtbeck, Variations in Value Orientations (Evanston, IL: Row, Peterson, 1961), 1–48.

36. David Levine, *The Flight from Ambiguity* (Chicago: University of Chicago Press, 1982); Dorothy Lee, "A Lineal and Nonlineal Codification of Reality," in *The Production of Reality*, ed. P. Kollock and J. O'Brien (Thousand Oaks, CA: Pine-Forge Press, 1977), 101–11; Carley Dodd, *Dynamics of Intercultural Communication* (Dubuque: Willian C. Brown, 1982), 162.

37. W. Ong, "Literacy and Orality in Our Times," *Journal of Communication* 30 (1980): 197–204.

38. Daphna Oyserman, Heather M. Coon, and Markus Kemmelmeier, "Rethinking Individualism and Collectivism: Evaluation of Theoretical Assumptions and Meta-Analyses," *Psychological Bulletin* 128, no. 1 (2002): 3–72; Triandis, *Individualism and Collectivism.*

39. P. Christopher Earley and Cristina B. Gibson, "Taking Stock in Our Progress on Individualism-Collectivism: 100 Years of Solidarity and Community," *Journal of Management* 24, no. 3 (1998): 265–304; Robert Hurteau, "Navigating the Limitations of Western Approaches to the Intercultural Encounter: The Works of Walter Ong and Harry Triandis," *Missiology* 34, no. 2 (2006): 201–17; Vas Taras et al., "Opposite Ends of the Same Stick? Multi-Method Test of the Dimensionality of Individualism and Collectivism," *Journal of Cross-Cultural Psychology* 45, no. 2 (2014): 213–45.

40. Marilynn B. Brewer and Ya-Ru Chen, "Where (Who) Are Collectives in Collectivism? Toward Conceptual Clarification of Individualism and Collectivism," *Psychological Review* 114, no. 1 (2007): 133–51, https://doi.org/10.1037/0033-295X.114.1.133; Dapha Oyserman, Heather M. Coon, and Markus Kemmelmeier, "Rethinking Individualism and Collectivism: Evaluation of Theoretical Assumptions and Meta-Analyses," *Psychological Bulletin* 128, no. 1 (2002): 3–72.

41. David Y. F. Ho et al., "Indigenization and Beyond: Methodological Relationalism in the Study of Personality across Cultural Traditions," *Journal of Personality* 69, no. 6 (2001): 925–53, https://doi.org/10.1111/1467-6494.696170; Kwang-Kuo Hwang, "Chinese Relationalism: Theoretical Construction and Methodological Considerations," *Journal for the Theory of Social Behaviour* 30, no. 2 (2000): 155–78; H. C. Triandis et al., "Individualism and Collectivism: Cross-Cultural Perspectives in Self-in-Group Relationships," *Journal of Personality and Social Psychology* 54 (1988): 323–38; Georgette Wang and Zhong-Bo Liu, "What Collective? Collectivism and Relationalism from a Chinese Perspective," *Chinese Journal of Communication* 3, no. 1 (2010): 42–63; Kuang-Hui Yeh, "Relationalism: The Essence and Evolving Process of Chinese Interactive Relationships," *Chinese Journal of Communication* 3, no. 1 (2010): 76–94.

42. Brewer and Chen, "Where (Who) Are Collectives in Collectivism?"; Jai BP Sinha et al., "Collectivism Coexisting with Individualism: An Indian Scenario," *Asian Journal of Social Psychology* 4, no. 2 (2001): 133–45; M. Wetherell, "Cross-Cultural Studies of Minimal Groups: Implications for the Social Identity Theory of Intergroup Relations," in *Social Identity and Intergroup Relations*, ed. H. Tajfel (Cambridge, UK: Cambridge University Press, 1982), 207–40.

43. Brewer and Chen, "Where (Who) Are Collectives in Collectivism?"; Emiko S. F and Elizabeth A. Hardie, "The Development and Validation of the Relational, Individual, and Collective Self-Aspects (RIC) Scale," *Asian Journal of Social Psychology* 3, no. 1 (April 2000): 19–48.

44. Molefi Asante, *Afrocentric Idea Revised* (Philadelphia: Temple University Press, 2011).

45. Chen, "Toward an I Ching Model of Communication"; Wimal Dissanayake, "The Desire to Excavate Asian Theories of Communication: One Strand of the History," *Journal of Multicultural Discourses* 4, no. 1 (March 2009): 7–27; Wimal Dissanayake, "The Need for the Study of Asian Approaches to Communication,"

in *AMIC-Thammasat University Symposium on Mass Communication Theory: The Asian Perspective* (Bangkok: Singapore: Asian Mass Communication Research and Information Centre, 1985); Satoshi Ishii, "Conceptualising Asian Communication Ethics: A Buddhist Perspective," *Journal of Multicultural Discourses* 4, no. 1 (March 2009): 49–60; Ishii, "Complementing Contemporary Intercultural Communication Research with East Asian Sociocultural Perspectives and Practices"; Yoshitaka Miike, "Harmony without Uniformity": An Asiacentric Worldview and Its Communicative Implications," in *Intercultural Communication: A Reader*, ed. Larry A. Samovar, Richard E. Porter, and Edwin R. McDaniel, 2012, 65–80; Miike, "Theorizing Culture and Communication in the Asian Context: An Assumptive Foundation."

46. Kwasi Wiredu, *Cultural Universals and Particulars: An African Perspective* (Bloomington: Indiana University Press, 1996).

47. Georgette Wang, "Paradigm Shift and the Centrality of Communication Discipline," *International Journal of Communication* 5 (2011): 1461.

48. Wimal Dissanayake, "The Idea of Verbal Communication in Early Buddhism," *China Media Research* 4, no. 2 (2008): 8.

49. Brewer and Chen, "Where (Who) Are Collectives in Collectivism?"; Emiko S. Kashima and Elizabeth A. Hardie, "The Development and Validation of the Relational, Individual, and Collective Self-Aspects (RIC) Scale," *Asian Journal of Social Psychology* 3, no. 1 (2000): 19–48; George Ritzer and Pamela Gindoff, "Methodological Relationism: Lessons for and from Social Psychology," *Social Psychology Quarterly* 55, no. 2 (1992): 128–40, https://doi.org/10.2307/2786942; Ho et al., "Indigenization and Beyond"; David Y. F. Ho, "Interpersonal Relationships and Relationship Dominance: An Analysis Based on Methodological Relationism," *Asian Journal of Social Psychology* 1, no. 1 (1998): 1–16, https://doi.org/10.1111/1467-839X.00002; Hwang, "Chinese Relationalism."

50. Antjie Krog, "' . . . If It Means He Gets His Humanity Back . . .': The Worldview Underpinning the South African Truth and Reconciliation Commission," *Journal of Multicultural Discourses* 3, no. 3 (2008): 212.

51. Larry A. Samovar, Richard E. Porter, and Nemi C. Jain, *Understanding Intercultural Communication* (Belmont, CA: Wadsworth Publishing Company, 1981).

52. Andrew Kohut and Bruce Stokes, *America against the World: How We Are Different and Why We Are Disliked* (New York: Henry Holt and Co., 2007).

53. Betteke van Ruler and Dejan Verčič, "Overview of Public Relations and Communication Management in Europe," in *Public Relations and Communication Management in Europe*, ed. B. van Ruler and D. Verčič (Hague: Mouton de Gruyter, 2004), 1–11.

54. Felipe Korzenny and Betty Ann Korzenny, *Hispanic Marketing: A Cultural Perspective* (Burlington, MA: Elsevier/Butterworth-Heinemann, 2005).

55. Ibn Khaldun, *The Muqaddimah: An Introduction to History*, ed. N. J. Dawood, trans. Franz Rosenthal, Bollingen Series (Princeton, NJ: Princeton University Press, 1967).

56. Peter Ogom Nwosu, "Understanding Africans' Conceptualizations of Intercultural Competence," in *The Sage Handbook of Intercultural Competence*, ed. Darla Deardorff (Thousand Oaks, CA: Sage, 2009), 158–78.

57. Durganand Sinha, "Changing Perspectives in Social Psychology in India: A Journey towards Indigenization," *Asian Journal of Social Psychology* 1, no. 1 (1998): 19.

58. Miike, "Harmony without Uniformity": An Asiacentric Worldview and Its Communicative Implications."

59. This insight of the missing paired relations was highlighted by cross-cultural psychology research. See Brewer and Chen, "Where (Who) Are Collectives in Collectivism?"; Ho et al., "Indigenization and Beyond"; Kashima and Hardie, "The Development and Validation of the Relational, Individual, and Collective Self-Aspects (RIC) Scale," April 2000.

60. Xiao-Ping Chen and Chao C. Chen, "On the Intricacies of the Chinese Guanxi: A Process Model of Guanxi Development," *Asia Pacific Journal of Management* 21, no. 3 (September 8, 2004): 305–24.

61. Marshall McLuhan, *Understanding Media: The Extensions of Man* (Cambridge, MA: MIT Press, 1994).

62. S. A. Gunaratne, "De-Westernizing Communication/Social Science Research: Opportunities and Limitations," *Media, Culture & Society* 32, no. 3 (May 2010): 473–500.

63. Ronald D. Gordon, "Beyond the Failures of Western Communication Theory," *Journal of Multicultural Discourses* 2, no. 2 (November 15, 2007): 89–107, https://doi.org/10.2167/md090.0; Kim, *Non-Western Perspectives on Human Communication*.

64. Kejin Zhao, "China's Rise and Its Discursive Power Strategy," *Chinese Political Science Review*, April 19, 2016, https://doi.org/10.1007/s41111-016-0027-x.

65. Harry Charalambos Triandis, *Individualism and Collectivism*, 21; cited in Georgette Wang and Zhong-Bo Liu, "What Collective?"

66. Confucius, *The Analects*, trans. William E. Soothill, Dover Thrift Editions (New York: Dover Publications, 1910), chapter 9 https://www.amazon.com/Analects-Dover-Thrift-Editions-ebook/dp/B00A62Y3D2/ref=tmm_kin_swatch_0?_encoding=UTF8&qid=&sr=.

67. Marsh, "Converging on Harmony," 317–318,

68. Erin J. Rand, "'What One Voice Can Do': Civic Pedagogy and Choric Collectivity at Camp Courage," *Text and Performance Quarterly* 34, no. 1 (2014): 28–51.

69. Elleke Boehmer, *Nelson Mandela: A Very Short Introduction* (Oxford: Oxford University Press, 2008).

Chapter 2

1. Virginia Woolf, *Three Guineas*, Hogarth Critics (London: Hogarth, 1938).

2. Hall, *The Silent Language* (New York: Anchor Books, 1973); Hall, *Beyond Culture* (New York: Anchor Books, 1977); Hall, *The Dance of Life: The Other Dimension of Time* (Garden City, NY: Anchor Press/Doubleday, 1984); Hall, *Understanding Cultural Differences* (Yarmouth, ME: Intercultural Press, 1990); Hall, *An Anthropology of Everyday Life* (New York: Doubleday, 1992).

3. As Leeds-Hurwitz noted, "after WWII, Americans began to reevaluate their know-ledge and understanding of other countries, both in terms of their languages and in terms of their cultural assumptions. From 1951 to 1955, Hall was among the anthropologists and linguists brought to the newly established Foreign Service Institute to educate US diplomats about culture. Much to his surprise, Hall realized that the diplomats found his anthropological discussions of culture vague and "a waste of time." They wanted concrete information about how to interact with persons in the countries where they would be posted. In response, Hall began exploring "patterned distinctions." See Leeds-Hurwitz, Wendy. "Notes in the History of Intercultural Communication: The Foreign Service Institute and the Mandate for Intercultural Training," in *Readings in Cultural Contexts*, ed. Judith N. Martin, Thomas K. Nakayama, and Lisa A. Flores (Mountain View, CA: Mayfield Publishing, 1998), 15–28.

4. Hall, *Beyond Culture*, 105–116.

5. Donald Nathan Levine, *The Flight from Ambiguity: Essays in Social and Cultural Theory* (Chicago: University of Chicago Press, 1985); Stella Ting-Toomey, "Toward a Theory of Conflict and Culture," in *Communication, Culture, and Organization Processes*, ed. William B. Gudykunst, Lea Stewart, and Stella Ting-Toomey, International and Intercultural Communication Annual, Vol. 9 (Beverly Hills, CA: Sage Publications, 1985), 71–86.

6. Dorothy Lee, "A Lineal and Nonlineal Codification of Reality," in *The Production of Reality*, ed. P. Kollock and J. O'Brien (Thousand Oaks, CA: Pine-Forge Press, 1977), 101–11; Carley H. Dodd, *Dynamics of Intercultural Communication*, 4th ed. (Madison, WI: Brown and Benchmark, 1995).

7. Stephen Best, "Walter J. Ong, Orality and Literacy (1982)," *Public Culture* 32, no. 2 (2020): 431–39.

8. Hall, *Beyond Culture*, 91.

9. Hall, *Beyond Culture*, 98.

10. Harry Triandis, *Individualism and Collectivism* (Boulder, CO: Westview Press, 1995).

11. Geert Hofstede, *Culture's Consequences: National Differences in Thinking and Organizing*, (Beverly Hills, CA: Sage, 1980).

12. Florence Kluckhohn, "Dominant and Variant Value Orientations," in *Personality in Nature, Society and Culture*, ed. Clyde Kluckhohn and Henry A. Murray, 2nd ed. (New York: Alfred A. Knopf, 1953), 346.

13. Kluckhohn, 352.

14. Florence Rockwood Kluckhohn and Fred L. Strodtbeck, *Variations in Value Orientations* (Evanston, IL: Row, Peterson, 1961), 1–48..

15. Kluckhohn and Strodtbeck, 351.

16. Edward Stewart, *American Cultural Patterns: A Cross-Cultural Perspective* (Chicago: Intercultural Press, 1972), 36.

17. Roichi Okabe, "Cultural Assumptions of East and West: Japan and the U.S.," in *Theories in Intercultural Communication*, ed. Yun Kim and William B. Gudykunst (Newbury Park, CA: Sage Publications, 1988), 24.

18. Harold Adams Innis, *The Bias of Communication* (Toronto: University of Toronto Press, 1951).

19. James W. Carey, *Communication as Culture: Essays on Media and Society*, Media and Popular Culture 1 (Boston: Unwin Hyman, 1989), 15.

20. Carey, 18.

21. Carey, 18.

22. Marilynn B. Brewer and Ya-Ru Chen, "Where (Who) Are Collectives in Collectivism? Toward Conceptual Clarification of Individualism and Collectivism," *Psychological Review* 114, no. 1 (2007): 133–51; Emiko S. Kashima and Elizabeth A. Hardie, "The Development and Validation of the Relational, Individual, and Collective Self-Aspects (RIC) Scale," *Asian Journal of Social Psychology* 3, no. 1 (2000): 19–48.

23. Wetherell found that children with Polynesian background showed weaker ingroup bias than did those with European background, and they instead attempted to benefit both ingroup and outgroup members. M. Wetherell, "Cross-Cultural Studies of Minimal Groups: Implications for the Social Identity Theory of Intergroup Relations," in *Social Identity and Intergroup Relations*, ed. H. Tajfel (Cambridge, UK: Cambridge University Press, 1982), 147.

24. Harry C. Triandis et al., "Individualism and Collectivism: Cross-Cultural Perspectives on Self-Ingroup Relationships," *Journal of Personality and Social Psychology* 54, no. 2 (1988): 323–38; Vas Taras et al., "Opposite Ends of the Same Stick? Multi-Method Test of the Dimensionality of Individualism and Collectivism," *Journal of Cross-Cultural Psychology* 45, no. 2 (February 1, 2014): 213–45.

25. Jai B. P. Sinha et al., "Collectivism Coexisting with Individualism: An Indian Scenario," *Asian Journal of Social Psychology* 4 (2001): 133–45.

26. R. Kreuzbauer, S. Lin, and C-Y. Chiu, "Relational versus Group Collectivism and Optimal Distinctiveness in Consumption Context.," *Advances in Consumer Research* 36 (2009): 472.

27. Satoshi Ishii, "Complementing Contemporary Intercultural Communication Research with East Asian Sociocultural Perspectives and Practices," *China Media Research* 2, no. 1 (2006): 13–20; Min-Sun Kim, *Non-Western Perspectives on Human Communication: Implications for Theory and Practice* (Thousand Oaks: Sage Publications, 2002); Yoshitaka Miike, "Beyond Eurocentrism in the Intercultural Field," in *Ferment in the Intercultural Field*, ed. William J. Starosta and Gou-Ming Chen (Thousand Oaks, CA: Sage, 2003), 243–76; John C. Condon and Fathi S. Yousef, *An Introduction to Intercultural Communication* (Indianapolis: Bobbs-Merrill Educational Publishing, 1983); Edward C. Stewart and Milton J. Bennett, *American Cultural Patterns: A Cross-Cultural Perspective* (Yarmouth, ME: Intercultural Press, 1975).

28. Kim, 4.

29. Durganand Sinha, "Origins and Development of Psychology in India: Outgrowing the Alien Framework," *International Journal of Psychology* 29, no. 6 (1994): 695–705.

30. George Ritzer and Pamela Gindoff, "Methodological Relationism: Lessons for and from Social Psychology," *Social Psychology Quarterly* 55, no. 2 (1992): 128–40, https://doi.org/10.2307/2786942.

31. David Y. F. Ho et al., "Indigenization and beyond: Methodological Relationalism in the Study of Personality across Cultural Traditions," *Journal of Personality* 69, no. 6 (2001): 925–53.

32. Brewer and Chen, "Where (Who) Are Collectives in Collectivism? Toward Conceptual Clarification of Individualism and Collectivism"; Kashima and Hardie, "The Development and Validation of the Relational, Individual, and Collective Self-Aspects (RIC) Scale"; Ritzer and Gindoff, "Methodological Relationism."

33. Mustafa Emirbayer, "Manifesto for a Relational Sociology," *The American Journal of Sociology* 103, no. 2 (1997): 281–317.

34. Ho et al., "Indigenization and Beyond"; Yoshitaka Miike, "Non-Western Theory in Western Research? An Asiacentric Agenda for Asian Communication Studies," *Review of Communication* 6, no. 1–2 (2006): 4–31; Miike, "Beyond Eurocentrism in the Intercultural Field"; Kuang-Hui Yeh, "Relationalism: The Essence and Evolving Process of Chinese Interactive Relationships," *Chinese Journal of Communication* 3, no. 1 (2010): 76–94; Kwang-Kuo Hwang, "Chinese Relationalism: Theoretical Construction and Methodological Considerations," *Journal for the Theory of Social Behaviour* 30, no. 2 (December 25, 2001): 155–78; Georgette Wang and Zhong-Bo Liu, "What Collective? Collectivism and Relationalism from a Chinese Perspective," *Chinese Journal of Communication* 3, no. 1 (2010): 42–63.

35. Robert N. Bellah, Richard Madsen, William M. Sullivan, Ann Swidler, Steven M. Tipton, *Habits of the Heart: Individualism and Commitment in American Life: Updated Edition with a New Introduction* (Berkeley: University of California Press, 1996).

36. Larry A. Samovar, Richard E. Porter, and Nemi C. Jain, *Understanding Intercultural Communication* (Belmont, CA: Wadsworth Publishing Company, 1981), 65.

37. Alexis de Tocqueville, *Democracy in America Volume 2*, trans. Henry Reeve, revised Francis Bowen, editorial notes Phillips Bradley (New York: Vintage Books, 1945).

38. de Tocqueville, *Democracy in America*, Book 2, Chapter II, 104.

39. Clifford Geertz, *Local Knowledge: Further Essays in Interpretive Anthropology* (New York: Basic Books, 1983).

40. de Tocqueville, *Democracy in America*, Book 2, Chapter II, 104.

41. de Tocqueville, *Democracy in America*, Book 2, Chapter II, 105.

42. de Tocqueville, *Democracy in America*, Book 1, Chapter XXI, 94.

43. de Tocqueville, *Democracy in America*, Book 2, Chapter II, 105.

44. Andrew Kohut and Bruce Stokes, *America Against the World: How We Are Different and Why We Are Disliked* (New York: Holt, 2007).

45. Geertz, *Local Knowledge*, 59..

46. John C. Condon and Fathi S. Yousef, *An Introduction to Intercultural Communication*, (Indianapolis, IN: Bobbs-Merrill Series in Speech Communication, 1975), 65..

47. Harry C. Triandis, "Cross-Cultural Studies of Individualism and Collectivism," in *Nebraska Symposium on Motivation 1989: Cross-Cultural Perspectives*, ed. John J. Berman (Lincoln: University of Nebraska Press, 1990), 41–133.

48. de Tocqueville, *Democracy in America*, Book 1, Chapter 2, 11.

49. de Tocqueville, *Democracy in America*, Book 4, Chapter VII, 342.

50. Julia T. Wood, *Interpersonal Communication: Everyday Encounters*, 2nd ed. (Belmont, CA: Wadsworth Publishing, 1999).

51. de Tocqueville, *Democracy in America*, Book 2, Chapter V, 115.

52. de Tocqueville, *Democracy in America*, Book 2, Chapter V, 116.

53. de Tocqueville, *Democracy in America*, Book 2, Chapter VI, 119.

54. de Tocqueville, *Democracy in America*, Book 2, Chapter VI, 120.

55. Mark L. Knapp, *Interpersonal Communication and Human Relationships*, 3rd ed (Boston: Allyn and Bacon, 1996).

56. Geertz, *Local Knowledge*, 59.

57. Condon and Yousef, *An Introduction to Intercultural Communication*, 65.

58. New Zealand Ministry of Justice, *He Hinatore Ki Te Ao Māori; A Glimpse into the Māori World*, Māori Perspectives on Justice (Wellington, NZ: Ministry of Justice, 2001), https://www.justice.govt.nz/assets/Documents/Publications/he-hinatora-ki-te-ao-maori.pdf; James Graham, "Nā Rangi Tāua, Nā Tūānuku e Takoto Nei: Research Methodology Framed by Whakapapa," *MAI Review*, no. 1 (2009): 1–9; Di Pitama et al., *Guardianship, Custody and Access: Māori Perspectives and Experiences* (Wellington, NZ: Ministry of Justice, 2002), http://www.justice.govt.nz/pubs/reports/2002/guardianship-custody-access-maori/guardianship-custody-access-maori.pdf.

59. Felipe Korzenny and Betty Ann Korzenny, *Hispanic Marketing: A Cultural Perspective* (Burlington, MA: Elsevier/Butterworth-Heinemann, 2005).

60. *Constitution of Chile*, HeinOnline World Constitutions Illustrated. (Chicago: University of Chicago Press, 2010).

61. Rana Raddawi, "Teaching Critical Thinking Skills to Arab University Students," in *Teaching and Learning in the Arab World*, ed. Christina Gitsaki (Bern: P. Lang, 2011), 80.

62. Ubuntu is from the Zulu language; however, many scholars have described it as pan-African. See, for example, Betty Press, *I Am Because We Are: African Wisdom in Image and Proverb* (St. Paul, MN: Books for Africa, 2011); B. Nussbaum, "Ubuntu: Reflections of a South African on Our Common Humanity," *Reflections* 4, no. 4 (2003): 21; Pieter J. Fourie, "Communication, Cultural and Media Studies: Ubuntuism as a Framework for South African Media Practice and Performance: Can It Work?," *Communication* 34, no. 1 (2008): 53–79.

63. Antjie Krog, "'. . . If It Means He Gets His Humanity Back . . .': The Worldview Underpinning the South African Truth and Reconciliation Commission," *Journal of Multicultural Discourses* 3, no. 3 (2008), 207..

64. Peter Ogom Nwosu, "Understanding Africans' Conceptualizations of Intercultural Competence," in *The Sage Handbook of Intercultural Competence*, ed. Darla Deardorff (Thousand Oaks, CA: Sage Publications, 2009), 169.

65. Nwosu, "Understanding Africans' Conceptualizations of Intercultural Competence," 169.

66. Giorgia Nesti and Chiara Valentini, *Public Communication in the European Union: History, Perspectives and Challenges* (Newcastle upon Tyne: Cambridge Scholars, 2010).

67. Jurgen Habermas, *The Structural Transformation of the Public Sphere: An Inquiry into a Category of Bourgeois Society* (Cambridge, MA: MIT Press, 1991).

68. Dejan Verčič et al., "On the Definition of Public Relations: A European View," *Public Relations Review* 27, no. 4 (2001): 373–87.

69. Usha Vyasulu Reddi, "Communication Theory: An Indian Perspective," *Media Asia* 13, no. 1 (January 1986): 6.

70. Vyasulu Reddi, 6.

71. Xiaotong Fei, *From the Soil: The Foundations of Chinese Society; A Translation of Fei Xiaotong's* Xiangtu Zhongguo, *with an Introduction and Epilogue by Gary G. Hamilton and Wang Zheng* (Berkeley: University of California Press, 1992), 50.

72. Xiao-Ping Chen and Chao C. Chen, "On the Intricacies of the Chinese Guanxi: A Process Model of Guanxi Development," *Asia Pacific Journal of Management* 21, no. 3 (September 8, 2004): 305–24.

73. June Ock Yum, "Confucianism and Communication: Jen, Li, and Ubuntu," *China Media Research* 3, no. 4 (2007): 15–22.

74. Ibn Khaldun, *The Muqaddimah: An Introduction to History*, ed. N. J. Dawood, trans. Franz Rosenthal, Bollingen Series (Princeton, NJ: Princeton University Press, 1967).

75. Jonathan Mercer, "Feeling like a State: Social Emotion and Identity," *International Theory* 6, no. 3 (November 2014), 523.

76. Hui-Ching Chang and G. Richard Holt, "More than Relationship: Chinese Interaction and the Principle of Kuan-Hsi," *Communication Quarterly* 39, no. 3 (1991): 251–71.

77. Elza Venter, "The Notion of Ubuntu and Communalism in African Educational Discourse," *Studies in Philosophy and Education* 23, no. 2 (March 1, 2004): 149–60.

78. Nwosu, "Understanding Africans' Conceptualizations of Intercultural Competence," 169.

79. Edward Stewart, in one of the most comprehensive analyses of US cultural patterns, observed, "The American stress on the individual as a concrete point of reference begins at a very early age when the American child is encouraged to be autonomous . . . the American is not expected to bow to the wishes of authority, be it vested in family, tradition or some organizations." Stewart, *American Cultural Patterns: A Cross-Cultural Perspective*, 70.

80. Shi-Xu, "Reconstructing Eastern Paradigms of Discourse Studies," *Journal of Multicultural Discourses* 4, no. 1 (2009): 29–48; Ron Scollon and Suzie Wong Scollon, "Face Parameters in East-West Discourse," in *The Challenge of Facework: Cross-Cultural and Interpersonal Issues*, ed. Stella Ting-Toomey (Albany, NY: SUNY Press, 1994), 133–57; Satoshi Ishii, "Enryo-Sasshi Communication: A Key to Understanding Japanese Interpersonal Relations," *Cross Currents* 11, no. 1 (1984): 49–58.

81. Guo-Ming Chen, "Asian Communication Studies: What and Where to Now," *Review of Communication* 6, no. 4 (2006): 295–311.

82. D. Sinha's idea of "human in society" may well capture the idea of being imbedded in society, which is closer to the descriptions suggested by the intellectual heritage of Latin America and the Middle East. Durganand Sinha, "Changing Perspectives in Social Psychology in India: A Journey Towards Indigenization," *Asian Journal of Social Psychology* 1, no. 1 (1998): 17–31.

83. Samsup Jo and Yungwook Kim, "Media or Personal Relations? Exploring Media Relations Dimensions in South Korea," *Journalism and Mass Communication Quarterly* 81, no. 2 (June 1, 2004): 292–306, Ho et al., "Indigenization and Beyond," D. Sinha, "Changing Perspectives."

84. Samsup Jo and Yungwook Kim, "Media or Personal Relations? Exploring Media Relations Dimensions in South Korea," *Journalism and Mass Communication Quarterly* 81, no. 2 (June 1, 2004), 294.

85. Akira Miyahara, "Toward Theorizing Japanese Interpersonal Communication Competence from a Non-Western Perspective," *American Communication Journal* 3, no. 1 (2006), 9.

86. Uichol Kim, "Psychology, Science, and Culture: Cross-Cultural Analysis of National Psychologies," *International Journal of Psychology* 30, no. 6 (1995), 670.

87. Georgette Wang, "Paradigm Shift and the Centrality of Communication Discipline," *International Journal of Communication* 5 (2011), 1461.

88. Gayle L. Nelson, Mahmoud Al Batal, and Waguida El Bakary, "Directness vs. Indirectness: Egyptian Arabic and US English Communication Style," *International Journal of Intercultural Relations* 26, no. 1 (2002), 55..

89. Keith G. Provan, Amy Fish, and Joerg Sydow, "Interorganizational Networks at the Network Level: A Review of the Empirical Literature on Whole Networks," *Journal of Management* 33, no. 3 (2007): 479–516; Emilie M. Hafner-Burton, Miles Kahler, and Alexander H. Montgomery, "Network Analysis for International Relations," *International Organization* 63, no. 3 (July 2009): 559–92.

90. Krog, " '. . . If It Means He Gets His Humanity Back. . . .," 208.

91. Yaqing Qin, *A Relational Theory of World Politics* (Cambridge: Cambridge University Press, 2018).

92. Aimei Yang, Anna Klyueva, and Maureen Taylor, "Beyond a Dyadic Approach to Public Diplomacy: Understanding Relationships in Multipolar World," *Public Relations Review* 38, no. 5 (2012): 652–64.

93. James Der Derian, *On Diplomacy: A Genealogy of Western Estrangement* (Oxford: Blackwell, 1987), 27.

94. Ravi de Costa, "Indigenous Diplomacies before the Nation-State," in *Indigenous Diplomacies*, ed. J. Marshall Beier (New York: Palgrave Macmillan, 2009), 61–77.

95. Costas M. Constantinou and James Der Derian, *Sustainable Diplomacies* (London: Palgrave Macmillan, 2010), https://doi.org/10.1057/9780230297159.

Chapter 3

1. E. M. Cope, *An Introduction to Aristotle's Rhetoric with Analysis Notes and Appendices* (London: Macmillan and Co., 1867), 2.

2. Thucydides, Book II, cited in Cope, 9.

3. Robert T. Craig, "Communication," in *Encyclopedia of Rhetoric*, ed. Thomas O. Sloane (New York: Oxford University Press, 2001), 125–37.

4. "Aristotle," *Internet Encyclopedia of Philosophy*, accessed October 13, 2019, https://iep.utm.edu/aristotl/.

5. Cope, *An Introduction to Aristotle's Rhetoric*, 2.

6. Scott Porter Consigny, *Gorgias, Sophist and Artist* (Columbia: University of South Carolina Press, 2001).

7. George Alexander Kennedy, *Comparative Rhetoric: An Historical and Cross-Cultural Introduction* (New York: Oxford University Press, 1998).

8. Aristotle, *Rhetoric*, trans. W. Rhys Roberts, Provided by The Internet Classics Archive. Available online at http://classics.mit.edu/Aristotle/rhetoric.html Dover Thrift Editions (Mineola, NY: Dover Publications, 1946), Book I, part 1.

9. Aristotle, Book I, part 2.

10. Walter J. Ong, *Orality and Literacy: The Technologizing of the Word* (New York: Routledge, 1982), 111/master n6.

11. Christer Jönsson and Martin Hall, *Essence of Diplomacy* (Berlin: Springer, 2005), 87–88.

12. For historical overview, see, George R. Miller, "Taking Stock of a Discipline," *Journal of Communication* 33, no. 3 (1983): 31–41; Wilbur Schramm, Steven H. Chaffee, and Everett M. Rogers, *The Beginnings of Communication Study in America: A Personal Memoir* (Thousand Oaks: Sage, 1997); Pat Gehrke and William M. Keith, *A Century of Communication Studies: The Unfinished Conversation* (New York: Routledge, 2015).

13. Aristotle, *Rhetoric*, Book I, part 3.

14. T. Gulbrandsen and S. N. Just, "The Collaborative Paradigm: Towards an Invitational and Participatory Concept of Online Communication," *Media, Culture & Society* 33, no. 7 (2011): 1103.

15. Aristotle, *Rhetoric*, Book I, part 2.

16. Aristotle, Book II, part 2.

17. Laura K. Hahn, Lance Lippert, and Scott T. Paynton, *Survey of Communication Study* September 22, 2021 (https://en.wikibooks.org/wiki/Survey_of_Communication_St udy, 2017).

18. Charles U. Larson, *Persuasion: Reception and Responsibility*, 6th ed. (Belmont, CA: Wadsworth Publishing, 1992), 81.

19. Nathan Maccoby, "The New 'Scientific' Rhetoric," in *The Science of Human Communication: New Directions and New Findings in Communication Research*, ed. Wilbur Schramm (New York: Basic Books, 1963), 41–54.

20. Richard E. Nisbett et al., "Culture and Systems of Thought: Holistic versus Analytic Cognition," *Psychological Review* 108, no. 2 (2001): 292.

21. Clifford Geertz, *Local Knowledge: Further Essays in Interpretive Anthropology* (New York: Basic Books, 1983), 59.

22. Edward E. Sampson, "The Debate on Individualism: Indigenous Psychologies of the Individual and Their Role in Personal and Societal Functioning," *American Psychologist* 43, no. 1 (1988): 15–22, https://doi.org/10.1037/0003-066X.43.1.15.

23. Stephen W. Littlejohn and Karen A. Foss, *Theories of Human Communication*, 10th ed. (Long Grove, IL: Waveland Press, 2010), 79.

24. Geertz, *Local Knowledge*, 59.

25. James Carey, *Communication as Culture* (New York: Routledge, 1989), 15–18.

26. Geertz, *Local Knowledge*, 59.

27. Nisbett et al., "Culture and Systems of Thought."

28. Nisbett et al., 292; E. Hamilton, *The Greek Way* (New York: Avon, 1930), 25, cited by Nisbett et al. 2001, 292.

29. Aristotle, *Rhetoric*, Book I, part 1. Provided by The Internet Classics Archive. Available online at http://classics.mit.edu/Aristotle/rhetoric.html

30. David K. Berlo, *The Process of Communication* (New York: Holt, Rinehart and Winston, 1960), 10.

31. Berlo, 11.

32. Berlo, 11.

33. Berlo, 11–12.

34. Berlo, 12.

35. Keith Hamilton and Professor Richard Langhorne, *The Practice of Diplomacy: Its Evolution, Theory and Administration* (New York: Routledge, 2013), 33.

36. Hamilton and Langhorne, 232.

37. Jönsson and Hall, *Essence of Diplomacy*, 86.

38. Eban, *The New Diplomacy: International Affairs in the Modern Age* (1983), 393, cited in Jönsson and Hall, 86.

39. Joseph S. Nye, *Bound to Lead: The Changing Nature of American Power*, reprint ed. (New York: Basic Books, 1990).

40. Paul Watzlawick, Janet Beavin Bavelas, and Don D. Jackson, *Pragmatics of Human Communication: A Study of Interactional Patterns, Pathologies and Paradoxes* (New York: W. W. Norton & Company, 2011), 51.

41. Aristotle, *Rhetoric*, Book I, part 2, 1378a.

42. Aristotle, Book I, part 8. Provided by The Internet Classics Archive. Available online at http://classics.mit.edu/Aristotle/rhetoric.html.

43. Bruce E. Gronbeck, *The Articulate Person* (Glenview, IL: Scott, Foresman, 1983).

44. Nye focuses on soft power from the perspective of nation-states. Joseph S. Nye, *Soft Power: The Means to Success in World Politics* (New York: PublicAffairs, 2004).

45. Gary Rawnsley, "Approaches to Soft Power and Public Diplomacy in China and Taiwan," *Journal of International Communication* 18, no. 2 (August 1, 2012): 123, https://doi.org/10.1080/13216597.2012.695744.

46. Schramm, *The Science of Human Communication*, 7.

47. Ronald J. Deibert, *Parchment, Printing and Hypermedia: Communication and World Order Transformation* (New York: Columbia University Press, 1997), 21.

48. Aristotle, *Rhetoric*, 1356a.

49. 9/11 Commission, "The 9/11 Commission Report," 2004, 100, https://9-11commiss ion.gov/report/911Report.pdf.

50. 9/11 Commission, 376.

51. Alister Miskimmon, Ben O'Loughlin, and Laura Roselle, *Strategic Narratives: Communication Power and the New World Order* (New York: Routledge, 2013).

52. The word "sparse" derives from this stylistic trait.

53. Marshall McLuhan, *Understanding Media: The Extensions of Man* (New York: Signet Books 1964)..

54. Carlos Alberto Scolari, "Mapping Conversations about New Media: The Theoretical Field of Digital Communication," *New Media & Society* 11, no. 6 (2009): 943–64.

55. Donald A. Norman, "Affordance, Conventions and Design," *Interactions* 6, no. 3 (1999): 38–43.

56. Geoffrey Allen Pigman, *Contemporary Diplomacy: Representation and Communication in a Globalized World* (Cambridge, UK: Polity, 2010).

57. Fergus Hanson, "Baked in and Wired: EDiplomacy @ State," Foreign Policy Paper Series (Washington DC: The Brookings Institution, 2012), https://www.brookings.edu/research/baked-in-and-wired-ediplomacy-state/.

58. Shaun Riordan, "Digital Diplomacy 2.0: Beyond the Social Media Obsession," *CPD Blog* (blog), April 25, 2016, http://uscpublicdiplomacy.org/blog/digital-diplomacy-20-beyond-social-media-obsession.

59. John Louis Lucaites, Celeste Michelle Condit, and Sally Caudill, *Contemporary Rhetorical Theory: A Reader* (New York: Guilford Press, 1999).

60. Theresa Enos, *Encyclopedia of Rhetoric and Composition: Communication from Ancient Times to the Information Age* (New York: Taylor & Francis, 1996), 44–45.

61. Hahn, Lippert, and Paynton, *Survey of Communication Study*.

62. Kathy Fitzpatrick, *The Future of U.S. Public Diplomacy: An Uncertain Fate* (Leiden: Martinus Nijhoff, 2010), 200.

63. Ellen Huijgh, "Changing Tunes for Public Diplomacy: Exploring the Domestic Dimension," *Exchange: The Journal of Public Diplomacy* 2, no. 1 (2013): 1–12; Ellen Huijgh, "Indonesia's 'Intermestic' Public Diplomacy: Features and Future," *Politics & Policy* 45, no. 5 (2017): 762–92; Ellen Huijgh, *Public Diplomacy at Home: Domestic Dimensions* (The Netherlands: Brill Nijhoff University Press, 2019).

64. Tanina Zappone, "New Words for a New International Communication: The Case of Public Diplomacy" (London: Europe China Research and Advice Network, 2012), https://www.academia.edu/5235863/New_Words_for_A_New_International_Communication._The_Case_of_Public_Diplomacy; Zhao Qizheng, *One World: Bridging the Communication Gap* (Beijing: China Intercontinental Press, 2008); Y. Wang, "Relational Dimensions of a Chinese Model of Public Diplomacy," in *Relational, Networking and Collaborative Approaches to Public Diplomacy: The Connective Mindshift*, ed. R. Zaharna, A. Fisher, and A. Arsenault (New York: Routledge, 2013), 86–99; Yiwei Wang, "Public Diplomacy and the Rise of Chinese Soft Power," *The Annals of the American Academy of Political and Social Science* 616, no. 1 (March 1, 2008): 257–73, https://doi.org/10.1177/0002716207312757.

65. As Kennedy wrote: "If a speaker does not need to secure consensus, he need not try to conciliate the more extreme opponents, can largely ignore some of their concerns and concentrate of solidifying support with those already inclined to agree and winging over the doubtful. Vigorous, even personal, attack on opponents and their motives contributes to this end." George Alexander Kennedy, *Comparative Rhetoric: An Historical and Cross-Cultural Introduction* (New York: Oxford University Press, 1998), 201.

66. Nye, *Soft Power*, 4.

67. Craig Hayden, *The Rhetoric of Soft Power: Public Diplomacy in Global Contexts* (Lanham, MD: Lexington Books, 2012).

68. Patrick Jackson, "Twisting Tongues and Twisting Arms: The Power of Political Rhetoric," *Journal of International Relations* 13 (2006): 35.

69. Mathew G. Gerber, "On the Consideration of 'Public Diplomacy' as a Rhetorical Genre," *Contemporary Argumentation and Debate* 29 (2008): 123.

70. Harold D. Lasswell, "The Structure and Function of Communication in Society," *The Communication of Ideas* 37 (1948): 215–28.

71. Robert Banks, *A Resource Guide to Public Diplomacy Evaluation*, CPD Perspectives on Public Diplomacy (Los Angeles: Figueroa Press, 2011).

72. Nicholas Cull, "Introduction," in *Data Driven Public Diplomacy: Progress towards Measuring the Impact of Public Diplomacy and International Broadcasting Activities* (report), ed. Katherine Brown and Chris Hensman (Washington, DC: United States Advisory Commission on Public Diplomacy 2014), https://2009-2017.state.gov/documents/organization/231945.pdf.

73. Geertz, *Local Knowledge*, 59.

74. Intercultural scholars John Condon and Fathi Yousef raised the distinction between individualism and individuality. Their definition of individuality appears to fuse the two terms with its emphasis on agency: "Individuality refers to the person's *freedom to act* differently within the limits set by the social structure." John C. Condon and Fathi S. Yousef, *An Introduction to Intercultural Communication*, (Indianapolis, IN: Bobbs-Merrill Series in Speech Communication, 1975), 65.

75. Gary Althen, Amanda R. Doran, and Susan J. Szmania, *American Ways: A Guide for Foreigners in the United States* (London: Intercultural Press, 2003), 17.

76. "One who forms a judgement on any point but cannot explain himself clearly to the people might well have never thought at all upon the subject."

77. Kennedy, *Comparative Rhetoric*, 197.

78. Roumen Dimitrov, "Silence and Invisibility in Public Relations," *Public Relations Review* 41, no. 5 (December 2015): 636–51, https://doi.org/10.1016/j.pubrev.2014.02.019.

79. Min-Sun Kim, *Non-Western Perspectives on Human Communication: Implications for Theory and Practice* (Thousand Oaks, CA: Sage Publications, 2002), 131–39.

80. Kim, 137.

81. Nemi C. Jain and Anuradha Matukumalli, "The Functions of Silence in India: Implications for Intercultural Communication Research," in *The Global Intercultural Communication Reader 2nd Edition*, ed. Molefi Asante, Yoshitaka Miike, and J. Yin (New York: Routledge, 2014), 248–54.

82. Jain and Matukumalli, 253.

83. Charlotte Beers, Under Secretary for Public Diplomacy and Public Affairs, "Public Diplomacy after September 11" (Remarks to National Press Club, Washington, D.C., Department of State. The Office of Electronic Information, Bureau of Public Affairs, December 18, 2002), https://2001-2009.state.gov/r/us/16269.htm.

84. Patricia Harrison, "The 9/11 Commission Recommendations on Public Diplomacy: Defending Ideals and Defining the Message," § Subcommittee on National Security, Emerging Threats and International Relations, Committee on Government Reform, U.S. House of Representatives (2004), https://www.govinfo.gov/content/pkg/CHRG-108hhrg98211/html/CHRG-108hhrg98211.htm; Patricia Harrison, Acting under Secretary of State for Public Diplomacy and Public Affairs, Department of State.

85. Kenneth P. Todd, *A Capsule History of the Bell System* (American Telephone and Telegraph Company, 1975), https://www.beatriceco.com/bti/porticus/bell/capsule_bell_system.html#The%20Corporation%20Grows:

86. Uwe Vagelpohl, *Aristotle's Rhetoric in the East: The Syriac and Arabic Translation and Commentary Tradition* (Leiden, Netherlands: Brill, 2008), http://ebookcentral.proquest.com/lib/aul/detail.action?docID=682393; Lahcen E. Ezzaher et al., *Three Arabic Treatises on Aristotle's Rhetoric: The Commentaries of al-Fārābī, Avicenna, and Averroes*, Landmarks in Rhetoric and Public Address (Carbondale: Southern Illinois University Press, 2015).

87. Vagelpohl, *Aristotle's Rhetoric in the East*, vi.

88. Jonathan Lyons, *The House of Wisdom: How Arab Learning Transformed Western Civilization* (New York: Bloomsbury Press, 2009); Richard E. Rubenstein, *Aristotle's Children: How Christians, Muslims, and Jews Rediscovered Ancient Wisdom and Illuminated the Middle Ages* (San Diego, CA: Harcourt, 2004).

89. See, for example, Jönsson and Hall, *Essence of Diplomacy.*

Chapter 4

1. This incident is related by Podany. Amanda H. Podany, *Brotherhood of Kings: How International Relations Shaped the Ancient Near East* (New York: Oxford University Press, 2010), 173–76.

2. Hatti is located in modern Turkey; Babylonia in modern Iraq.

3. Raymond Cohen, "All in the Family: Ancient Near Eastern Diplomacy," *International Negotiation* 1, no. 1 (January 1, 1996): 11–28.

4. Christer Jönsson and Martin Hall, *Essence of Diplomacy* (Basingstokes: Palgrave-Macmillan, 2005).

5. Raymond Cohen and Raymond Westbrook, eds., *Amarna Diplomacy: The Beginnings of International Relations* (Baltimore, MD: Johns Hopkins University Press, 2002), 4.

6. Bertrand Lafont, "International Relations in the Ancient Near East: The Birth of a Complete Diplomatic System," *Diplomacy and Statecraft* 12, no. 1 (March 1, 2001): 39–60; Mario Liverani, "The Great Powers' Club," in *Amarna Diplomacy*, ed. Raymond Cohen and Raymond Westbrook (Baltimore, MD: Johns Hopkins University Press, 2000), 15–27.

7. Podany, *Brotherhood of Kings*, 10.

8. Christer Jönsson, "Diplomatic Signaling in the Amarna Letters," in *Amarna Diplomacy*, ed. Raymond Cohen and Raymond Westbrook (Baltimore, MD: Johns Hopkins University Press, 2000), 197.

9. William L. Moran, ed., *The Amarna Letters* (Baltimore, MD: Johns Hopkins University Press, 1992), xxiv.

10. Moran, EA 23, cited in Podany, *Royal Brotherhood of Kings*, 7.

11. For discussion, see Podany, *Brotherhood of Kings*, 219–224; Trevor Bryce, *Letters of the Great Kings of the Ancient Near East: The Royal Correspondence of the Late Bronze Age* (New York: Routledge, 2003).

12. Bryce, 91.

13. Moran, *Amarna Letters* EA 7: 61–62, cited by Bryce, *Letters of the Great Kings of the Ancient Near East*, 102.

14. Jönsson, "Diplomatic Signaling in the Amarna Letters," 200.

15. Moran, *Amarna Letters* EA 6: 13–17, cited by Bryce, *Letters of the Great Kings of the Ancient Near East*, 82.

16. Moran, *Amarna Letters* EA 3: 13–22, cited by Jönsson, "Diplomatic Signaling in the Amarna Letters," 197.

17. Jönsson, 197.

18. Podany, *Brotherhood of Kings*, 34.

19. Cohen, "All in the Family"; Lafont, "International Relations in the Ancient Near East."

20. Bryce, *Letters of the Great Kings of the Ancient Near East*, 76.

21. Yoshitaka Miike, "Harmony without Uniformity: An Asiacentric Worldview and Its Communicative Implications," in *Intercultural Communication: A Reader*, ed. Larry A. Samovar, Richard E. Porter, and Edwin R. McDaniel (Boston: Wadsworth, 2012), 73.

22. Virgilio G. Enriquez, "Developing a Filipino Psychology," in *Indigenous Psychologies: Research and Experience in Cultural Context*, ed. Uichol Kim and John Berry, Cross-Cultural Research and Methodology Series 17 (Thousand Oaks: Sage, 1993), 152–69; S. A. Gunaratne, "De-Westernizing Communication/Social Science Research: Opportunities and Limitations," *Media, Culture and Society* 32, no. 3 (May 2010): 473–500.

23. Muneo Jay Yoshikawa, "The Double-Swing Model of Intercultural Communication between the East and the West," in *Communication Theory: Eastern and Western Perspectives*, ed. D. Lawrence Kincaid (New York: Academic Press, 1987), 327.

24. We can see this blurring in the different understanding of the term "listener oriented" in communication. Contemporary communication scholarship breaks the parties into discrete units—sender/receiver or speaker/listener. Because the speaker is assumed to be responsible for the communicating, "listener centered" means the speaker adapts or tailors the message to the listener. The speaker, however, does not have to be in direct contact with the listener.

25. Martin Buber, *I And Thou*, trans. Walter Kaufmann (New York: Touchstone, 1971); M. M. Bakhtin, *The Dialogic Imagination: Four Essays*, ed. Michael Holquist, trans. Caryl Emerson, reprint ed. (Austin: University of Texas Press, 1983).

26. Cohen, "The Great Tradition," 25–26, draws upon the seminal work of Marcel Mauss' *The Gift: Forms and Functions of Exchange in Archaic Societies* (Glencoe, IL: The Free Press, 1954) to discuss "the moral and sacred obligation to give and receive" gifts and greets among the kings.

27. Jönsson, "Diplomatic Signaling in the Amarna Letters," 197–198.

28. Bryce, *Letters of the Great Kings of the Ancient Near East*, 83.

29. Cohen and Westbrook, *Amarna Diplomacy*, 227.

30. Cohen and Westbrook, 227.

31. Podany, *Brotherhood of Kings*, 173.

32. In English, the word "relationship" is used as a noun. In looking at the meaning or intent of "relationship" in other heritages, relationship suggests a dynamic similar to a verb. This is part of the difficulty in translating the relational terms from other languages, including guanxi (Chinese) or wasta (Arabic).

33. Betteke van Ruler and Dejan Vercic, *Public Relations and Communication Management in Europe: A Nation-by-Nation Introduction to Public Relations Theory and Practice* (Berlin: De Gruyter Mouton, 2008).

34. Ronél Rensburg, "Communications Management in the Africa Context: Implications for Theory, Research, and Practice," *International Journal of Strategic Communication* 1, no. 1 (2007): 46.

35. Personal conversation with Dr. K. Sundary, Emeritus Head, Department of Public Relations, Stella Maris College, Chennai, on June 22, 2010, International Communication Association conference, Singapore.

36. Kate Hutchings and David Weir, "Understanding Networking in China and the Arab World: Lessons for International Managers," *Journal of European Industrial Training* 30, no. 4 (2006): 272–90; Hutchings and Weir, "Guanxi and Wasta: A Comparison," *Thunderbird International Business Review* 48, no. 1 (2006): 141–56; Peter B. Smith et al., "How Distinctive Are Indigenous Ways of Achieving Influence? A Comparative Study of Guanxi, Wasta, Jeitinho, and 'Pulling Strings,'" *Journal of Cross-Cultural Psychology* 43, no. 1 (2012): 135–50; Robert B. Cunningham and Yasin K. Sarayrah, *Wasta: The Hidden Force in Middle Eastern Society* (Westport, CT: Praeger Publishers, 1993).

37. Hutchings and Weir, "Understanding Networking in China and the Arab World."

38. Rogier Van der Pluijm and Jan Melissen, *City Diplomacy: The Expanding Role of Cities in International Politics* (The Hague: Netherlands Institute of International Relations Clingendael, 2007).

39. Albert Mehrabian, *Silent Messages* (Belmont, CA: Wadsworth, 1971); Judee K. Burgoon and Jerold L. Hale, "The Fundamental Topoi of Relational Communication," *Communication Monographs* 51, no. 3 (1984): 193–214; Judith Burgoon, D. B. Buller, and W. G. Woodall, *Nonverbal Communication: The Unspoken Dialogue*, 2nd ed. (New York: McGraw-Hill, 1996).

40. Burgoon, Buller, and Woodall, *Nonverbal Communication*; Burgoon and Hale, "The Fundamental Topoi of Relational Communication"; Mark L. Knapp, *Nonverbal Communication in Human Interaction* (New York: Holt, Rinehart and Winston, 1972).

41. Mehrabian, *Silent Messages*, 2, 4; Michael Argyle and Mark Cook, *Gaze and Mutual Gaze* (Cambridge: Cambridge University Press, 1976); Ray L. Birdwhistell, *Kinesics and Context: Essays on Body Motion Communication* (Philadelphia: University of Pennsylvania Press, 1970).

42. Jönsson, "Diplomatic Signaling in the Amarna Letters."

43. Bryce, *Letters of the Great Kings of the Ancient Near East.*

44. Jarol B. Manheim, *Strategic Public Diplomacy and American Foreign Policy: The Evolution of Influence* (New York: Oxford University Press, 1994).

45. Kathy Fitzpatrick, *The Future of U.S. Public Diplomacy: An Uncertain Fate* (Leiden; Boston: Brill-Nijhoff, 2009).

46. John Urry, "Social Networks, Travel and Talk," *The British Journal of Sociology* 54, no. 2 (2003): 161.

47. Agneta H. Fischer et al., "Social Functions of Emotion," in *Handbook of Emotions*, 3rd. ed. (New York: Guilford, 2008), 456–70.

48. Moran, *The Amarna Letters*, 6–8.

49. *Letters of the Great Kings of the Ancient Near East*, 70.

50. Cohen, "All in the Family," 24.

51. Christian Reus-Smit, "Emotions and the Social," *International Theory* 6, no. 3 (November 2014): 568–74; Sarah Ellen Graham, "Emotion and Public Diplomacy: Dispositions in International Communications, Dialogue, and Persuasion," *International Studies Review* 16, no. 4 (December 1, 2014): 522–39.

52. Cynthia P. Schneider, "The Unrealized Potential of Cultural Diplomacy: 'Best Practices' and What Could Be, If Only. . .," *Journal of Arts Management, Law, and Society* 39, no. 4 (2009): 260–79.

53. Jian Wang, "Managing National Reputation and International Relations in the Global Era: Public Diplomacy Revisited," *Public Relations Review* 32, no. 2 (2006): 91–96.

54. Shali Wu and Boaz Keysar, "The Effect of Culture on Perspective Taking," *Psychological Science* 18, no. 7 (2007): 600–606.

55. Edward T. Hall, *Beyond Culture* (New York: Anchor Books, 1976), 98.

56. Satoshi Ishii, "Enryo-Sasshi Communication: A Key to Understanding Japanese Interpersonal Relations," *Cross Currents* 11, no. 1 (1984): 49–58.

57. Bryce, *Letters of the Great Kings of the Ancient Near East*, 70.

58. Georgette Wang and Zhong-Bo Liu, "What Collective? Collectivism and Relationalism from a Chinese Perspective," *Chinese Journal of Communication* 3, no. 1 (2010): 42–63.

59. Jonsson and Hall, *Essence of Diplomacy*, 29.

60. Jönsson, "Diplomatic Signaling in the Amarna Letters."

61. Bryce, *Letters of the Great Kings of the Ancient Near East*; Raymond Cohen, "The Great Tradition: The Spread of Diplomacy in the Ancient World," *Diplomacy and Statecraft* 12, no. 1 (March 1, 2001): 23–38; Podany, *Brotherhood of Kings*, 217–242.

62. Alvin W. Gouldner, "The Norm of Reciprocity: A Preliminary Statement," *American Sociological Review* 25, no. 2 (1960): 161.

63. Xiao-Ping Chen and Chao C. Chen, "On the Intricacies of the Chinese Guanxi: A Process Model of Guanxi Development," *Asia Pacific Journal of Management* 21, no. 3 (September 8, 2004): 305–24.

64. Leslie A. Baxter, "Symbols of Relationship Identity in Relationship Cultures," *Journal of Social and Personal Relationships* 4, no. 3 (August 1, 1987): 261–80.

65. Alisher Faizullaev, "Diplomacy and Symbolism," *The Hague Journal of Diplomacy* 8, no. 2 (January 1, 2013): 91–114.

66. Jönsson, "Diplomatic Signaling in the Amarna Letters," 195–196.

67. Lafont, "International Relations in the Ancient Near East," 43–44.

68. Podany, *Brotherhood of Kings*, 30.

69. The elaboration likelihood model (ELM), for example, distinguishes between the direct route that requires cognitive engagement and the peripheral route through emotions to make decisions and take action. Richard E. Petty, and John T. Cacioppo, *Attitudes and Persuasion: Classic and Contemporary Approaches* (Boulder, CO: Westview Press, 1996).

70. Ronald B. Adler, Lawrence B. Rosenfeld, and Russell F. Proctor, *Interplay: The Process of Interpersonal Communication*, 14th ed. (New York: Oxford University Press, 2017); Joseph A. DeVito, *The Interpersonal Communication Book*, 14th ed. (Boston: Pearson, 2015); Julia T. Wood, *Interpersonal Communication: Everyday Encounters*, 8th ed. (Boston, MA: Cengage Learning, 2015).

71. Wood, *Interpersonal Communication*.

72. Richard Ned Lebow, "Reason, Emotion and Cooperation," *International Politics* 42, no. 3 (September 2005): 283–313.

73. Neta C. Crawford, "The Passion of World Politics: Propositions on Emotion and Emotional Relationships," *International Security* 24, no. 4 (April 1, 2000), 119.

74. Reus-Smit, "Emotions and the Social."

75. N. Femenia, "Emotional Actor: Foreign Policy Decision-Making in the 1982 Falklands/Malvinas War," in *Social Conflicts and Collective Identities*, ed. P. Coy and L. Woehrle (Lanham, MD: Rowman & Littlefield, 2000), 41–66; Marcus Holmes, "Believing This and Alieving That: Theorizing Affect and Intuitions in International Politics," *International Studies Quarterly* 59, no. 4 (December 1, 2015): 706–20.

76. Seanon S. Wong, "Emotions and the Communication of Intentions in Face-to-Face Diplomacy," *European Journal of International Relations* 22, no. 1 (March 1, 2016): 144–67.

77. Jonathan Mercer, "Feeling like a State: Social Emotion and Identity," *International Theory* 6, no. 3 (November 2014): 517, 523.

78. Benedict Anderson, *Imagined Communities: Reflections on the Origin and Spread of Nationalism* (New York: Verso, 1983).

79. Mercer, "Feeling like a State."

80. See, for discussion, Antonio Damasio, Descartes' Error: Emotion, Reason, and the Human Brain, illustrated ed. (New York: Penguin Books, 2005); Joseph Ledoux, *The Emotional Brain: The Mysterious Underpinnings of Emotional Life*, (New York: Simon & Schuster, 1998); Loretta Graziano Breuning, *Habits of a Happy Brain: Retrain*

Your Brain to Boost Your Serotonin, Dopamine, Oxytocin, and Endorphin Levels (New York: Adams Media, 2015).

81. Trust and touch go together, beginning with the bonding through touch between the mother and infant, Loretta Graziano Breuning, *Habits of a Happy Brain*, 71–73. The simple gesture of shaking hands, even in a pre-Covid world, was an acknowledgment of trust.

82. Damasio, *Descartes' Error*, 127–165.

83. Ledoux, *The Emotional Brain*, 90–98.

84. If we look closely at works on emotional intelligence, they are in essence ways to express or put into words what we are feeling—as opposed to emoting. See, for example, Daniel Goleman, Emotional Intelligence: Why It Can Matter More than IQ. (New York: Bantam, 2005).

85. Durganand Sinha, "Origins and Development of Psychology in India: Outgrowing the Alien Framework," *International Journal of Psychology* 29, no. 6 (1994): 695.

86. Sinha, 695.

87. Michael Gershon, *The Second Brain: A Groundbreaking New Understanding of Nervous Disorders of the Stomach and Intestine*, (New York: Harper Perennial, 1998), 12–20.

88. Marco Iacoboni, *Mirroring People: The Science of Empathy and How We Connect with Others* (New York: Picador, 2009).

89. J. M. Kilner and R. N. Lemon, "What We Know Currently about Mirror Neurons," *Current Biology* 23, no. 23 (December 2, 2013): R1057–62, https://doi.org/10.1016/j.cub.2013.10.051; Martin Schulte-Rüther et al., "Mirror Neuron and Theory of Mind Mechanisms Involved in Face-to-Face Interactions: A Functional Magnetic Resonance Imaging Approach to Empathy," *Journal of Cognitive Neuroscience* 19, no. 8 (August 1, 2007): 1354–72.

90. Holmes, "Believing This and Alieving That"; Marcus Holmes, *Face-to-Face Diplomacy: Social Neuroscience and International Relations* (New York: Cambridge University Press, 2018).

91. Marcus Holmes, "The Force of Face-to-Face Diplomacy: Mirror Neurons and the Problem of Intentions," *International Organization* 67, no. 4 (October 2013), 833.

Chapter 5

1. G. S. Kirk, J. E. Raven, and M. Schofield, *The Presocratic Philosophers: A Critical History with a Selection of Texts* (Cambridge: Cambridge University Press, 1983); William Smith, *Dictionary of Greek and Roman Biography and Mythology* (London: Perseus Digital Library, 1873).

2. Robert Thomas Rundle Clark, *Myth and Symbol in Ancient Egypt*, new impression ed. (London: Thames & Hudson, 1991); Vincent A. Tobin, *Theological Principles of Egyptian Religion* (New York: Peter Lang, 1989); Tobin, "Mytho-Theology in Ancient Egypt," *Journal of the American Research Center in Egypt* 25 (1988): 169–83; Denise Martin, "Maat and Order in African Cosmology: A Conceptual Tool

for Understanding Indigenous Knowledge," *Journal of Black Studies* 38, no. 6 (2008): 951–67.

3. James Evans, *The History and Practice of Ancient Astronomy* (New York: Oxford University Press, 1998); Andrew Gregory, *Ancient Greek Cosmogony* (London: Bloomsbury Academic, 2013); Geoffrey Ernest Richard Lloyd, *Magic, Reason and Experience: Studies in the Origins and Development of Greek Science* (London: Duckworth, 1999).

4. E. J. Michael Witzel, *The Origins of the World's Mythologies*, illustrated ed. (Oxford: Oxford University Press, 2013); David A. Leeming and Margaret Adams Leeming, *Encyclopedia of Creation Myths* (Santa Barbara, CA: ABC-CLIO, 1994).

5. Wyatt MacGaffey, *Religion and Society in Central Africa* (Chicago: University of Chicago Press, 1986); MacGaffey, "Constructing a Kongo Identity: Scholarship and Mythopoesis," *Comparative Studies in Society and History* 58, no. 1 (2016): 159–80; Robert Farris Thompson and J. Cornet, *The Four Moments of the Sun: Kongo Art in Two Worlds* (Washington, DC: National Gallery of Art, 1981); John S. Mbiti, *African Religions and Philosophy* (London: Longman, 1970); Mbiti, *Introduction to African Religion* (Oxford: Heinemann, 1991).

6. Miguel León-Portilla, *Aztec Thought and Culture: A Study of the Ancient Nahuatl Mind*, trans. Jack Emory Davis, rev. ed. (Norman: University of Oklahoma Press, 1990); James Maffie, *Aztec Philosophy: Understanding a World in Motion* (Boulder: University Press of Colorado, 2015); Maffie, "Pre-Columbian Philosophies," in *A Companion to Latin American Philosophy*, ed. Susana Nuccetelli, Ofelia Schutte, and Otávio Bueno, 9–22 (New York: Wiley & Sons, 2013); Emma Kirk, "Peace in the Chaos: Implications of the Conscious Elimination of Conflict in Divinely Designed and Spontaneous Creation from the Hebrew and Chinese Traditions," PhD thesis, Macquarie University, 2015; Anne M. Birrell, *Chinese Mythology: An Introduction*, rev. ed. (Baltimore: Johns Hopkins University Press, 1999); Mark Edward Lewis, *The Flood Myths of Early China* (Albany: State University of New York Press, 2006); John S. Major et al., eds. and trans., *The Huainanzi* (New York: Columbia University Press, 2010).

7. Nikos Papastergiadis, "Hiding in the Cosmos," in *Camouflage Cultures: Beyond the Art of Disappearance*, ed. Ann Elias, Ross Harley, and Nicholas Tsoutas (Sydney: Sydney University Press, 2015), 193–200.

8. Fu-Kiau Bunseki, *African Cosmology of the Bantu-Kongo: Tying the Spiritual Knot, Principles of Life and Living*, 2nd ed. (Brooklyn, NY: Athelia Henrietta Press, 2001).

9. Ross Hassig, *Time, History, and Belief in Aztec and Colonial Mexico*, illustrated ed. (Austin: University of Texas Press, 2001); León-Portilla, *Aztec Thought and Culture*; Maffie, "Pre-Columbian Philosophies."

10. Jose Barreiro and Carol Cornelius (eds.), *Knowledge of the Elders: The Iroquois Condolence Cane Tradition* (Ithaca, NY: *Northeast Indian Quarterly*, Cornell University, 1991), 1–31; Francis Jennings, *The History and Culture of Iroquois Diplomacy: An Interdisciplinary Guide to the Treaties of the Six Nations and Their League* (Syracuse: Syracuse University Press, 1995); Timothy J. Shannon and

Colin Calloway, *Iroquois Diplomacy on the Early American Frontier*, reprint ed. (New York: Penguin Books, 2009).

11. D. M. Dusty Gruver, "The Earth as Family: A Traditional Hawaiian View with Current Applications," in *Philosophy, Humanity and Ecology: Philosophy of Nature and Environmental Ethics*, ed. H. Odera Oruka (Darby, PA: Diane Publishing, 1996), 301–305; Miguel León-Portilla, *The Broken Spears: The Aztec Account of the Conquest of Mexico* (Boston: Beacon Press, 1992).

12. Marco A. Almazán, "The Aztec States-Society: Roots of Civil Society and Social Capital," *The Annals of the American Academy of Political and Social Science* 565, no. 1 (1999): 162–75; León-Portilla, *Aztec Thought and Culture*.

13. León-Portilla, *The Broken Spears*.

14. F. Shroff, "We Are All One: Holistic Thought-Forms within Indigenous Societies, Indigeneity and Holism," in *Indigenous Philosophies and Critical Education*, ed. George Sefa Dei (New York: Peter Lang, 2011).

15. Maffie, "Pre-Columbian Philosophies," 11.

16. "Harmony of the Spheres," *Ancient Wisdom* (blog), accessed April 22, 2021 www.ancient-wisdom.com/harmonics.htm.

17. Kenneth Sylvan Guthrie, *The Pythagorean Sourcebook and Library: An Anthology of Ancient Writings Which Relate to Pythagoras and Pythagorean Philosophy*, ed. David Fideler, rev. ed. (Grand Rapids: Phanes Press, 1987).

18. Because of the importance of harmony, harmony transcends the individual experience, implying awareness of a larger relational universe. We see the idea of "cosmic duty" in the Hindu concept of dharma, the Maori idea of "stewardship," African ubuntu, and Confucian "li" propriety.

19. Maffie, *Aztec Philosophy*, 11.

20. Leeming, *Creation Myths of the World* (2 vols.).

21. Papastergiadis, "Hiding in the Cosmos," 197.

22. The unique and personal quality of the paired relations that serve as the building blocks for the Holistic relational structure help differentiate it from abstract and impersonal notions that plague understandings of "the collective."

23. Yoshitaka Miike, "Harmony without Uniformity: An Asiacentric Worldview and Its Communicative Implications," in *Intercultural Communication: A Reader*, ed. Larry A. Samovar, Richard E. Porter, and Edwin R. McDaniel (Boston: Wadsworth, 2012), 71.

24. Relational connectivity expands across time and space to encompass all relations— near and far, direct and indirect, seen and unseen. Even the most distant entities are connected. Relational connectivity is unbounded by time. Past relations may be immediate, such as a felt ancestral spirit, while unseen future relations such as a hostile enemy may transform into a vital ally. While the nature of the relational connections may change, the idea of being in a perpetual state of relational connectivity with all others remains constant.

25. David Bowles, *Flower, Song, Dance: Aztec and Mayan Poetry* (Lamar, TX: Lamar University Press, 2013).

26. Marieke de Mooij, *Human and Mediated Communication around the World: A Comprehensive Review and Analysis* (New York: Springer, 2014), 98.
27. Richard Fletcher and Tony Fang, "Assessing the Impact of Culture on Relationship Creation and Network Formation in Emerging Asian Markets," *European Journal of Marketing* 40, no. 3/4 (2006): 435.
28. Guo-Ming Chen, "Toward an I Ching Model of Communication," *China Media Research* 5, no. 3 (2009): 72–81.
29. Any single snapshot of inter-connections in a network is fundamentally flawed because it fails to articulate the dynamic and constantly changing interactivity of connected but diverse entities. The idea of a circuit more accurately depicts the Holistic logic of a relational universe.
30. Charles Marsh, "Converging on Harmony: Idealism, Evolution, and the Theory of Mutual Aid," *Public Relations Inquiry* 1, no. 3 (September 1, 2012): 313–35.
31. Gou-Ming Chen, "An Introduction to Key Concepts in Understanding the Chinese: Harmony as the Foundation of Chinese Communication," *China Media Research* 7, no. 4 (2011): 3.
32. Richard E. Nisbett, "Living Together versus Going It Alone," in *Intercultural Communication: A Reader*, eds. Larry Samovar, Richard Porter, McDaniel, 134–54 (Boston: Wadsworth, 2009), 135.
33. Again, the universe is not a collection of random or separate individuals but an integrated, indivisible whole, and relational bonds are what make it so. Thus, we would expect to see or assume familiar relationship-defining and -building dynamics, such as identifying contact points, co-presence, emotion, perspective-taking, reciprocity, and symbolism.
34. Yaqing Qin, *A Relational Theory of World Politics* (Cambridge: Cambridge University Press, 2018).
35. Qin, *A Relational Theory of World Politics*, 258–88.
36. Xiaotong Fei, *From the Soil, the Foundations of Chinese Society: A Translation of Fei Xiaotong's Xiangtu Zhongguo, with an Introduction and Epilogue* (Berkeley: University of California Press, 1992).
37. Shi-Xu, "Reconstructing Eastern Paradigms of Discourse Studies," *Journal of Multicultural Discourses* 4, no. 1 (2009): 34. .
38. Rosita Dellios, "Mandala: From Sacred Origins to Sovereign Affairs in Traditional Southeast Asia," Centre for East-West Cultural and Economic Studies, Research Paper No. 10 (2003), http://www.international-relations.com/rp/WBrp10.html.
39. Iver B. Neumann and Einar Wigen, *The Steppe Tradition in International Relations: Russians, Turks and European State Building 4000 BCE–2017 CE* (Cambridge: Cambridge University Press, 2018); Neumann and Wigen, "The Importance of the Eurasian Steppe to the Study of International Relations," *Journal of International Relations and Development* 16, no. 3 (July 1, 2013): 311–30.
40. Wimal Dissanayake, "The Need for the Study of Asian Approaches to Communication," in *AMIC-Thammasat University Symposium on Mass Communication Theory: The Asian Perspective*, Bangkok, Oct 15–17, 1985 (Singapore: Asian Mass Communication Research and Information Centre, 1985), 15.

41. Akira Miyahara, "Toward Theorizing Japanese Interpersonal Communication Competence from a Non-Western Perspective," *American Communication Journal* 3, no. 1 (2006): 9.

42. Jai B. P. Sinha and Rajesh Kumar, "Methodology for Understanding Indian Culture," *Copenhagen Journal of Asian Studies* 19 (2004): 89–104; Xu Wu, "Doing PR in China: A 2001 Version—Concepts, Practices and Some Misperceptions," *Public Relations Quarterly* 47, no. 2 (Summer 2002): 10–20.

43. Guo-Ming Chen, "An Introduction to Key Concepts in Understanding the Chinese: Harmony as the Foundation of Chinese Communication," *China Media Research* 7, no. 4 (2011), 5..

44. William W. Maddux and Masaki Yuki, "The Ripple Effect: Cultural Differences in Perceptions of the Consequences of Events," *Personality and Social Psychology Bulletin* 32, no. 5 (May 2006): 669–83.

45. The mandala is adapted from the work of Shamsiddin Kamoliddin, "On the Religion of the Samanid Ancestors," *Transoxiana, Journal Libre de Estudios Orientales* 11 (July 2006), http://www.transoxiana.org/11/kamoliddin-samanids.html.

46. Yoshitaka Miike, "Beyond Eurocentrism in the Intercultural Field," in *Ferment in the Intercultural Field*, ed. William J. Starosta and Guo-Ming Chen (Thousand Oaks, CA: Sage, 2003), 243–76.

47. Gou-Ming Chen. "Toward Transcultural Understanding: A Harmony Theory of Chinese Communication," in *Transcultural Realities: Interdisciplinary Perspectives on Cross-Cultural Relations*, ed. Virginia Milhouse, Molefi Asante, and Peter Nwosu (Thousand Oaks, CA: Sage, 2001), 57.

48. Young Yun Kim, "Achieving Synchrony: A Foundational Dimension of Intercultural Communication Competence," *International Journal of Intercultural Relations* 48 (September 1, 2015): 27–37.

49. The Individual logic assumes arriving at commonality through dialogue, speech, words, and shared understanding.

50. The holistic imperative for mutual alignment and adaptation is reflected in the many references to "self-cultivation" and "other orientation" in traditional texts and scholarship (Guo-Ming Chen, "Asian Communication Studies: What and Where to Now," *Review of Communication* 6, no. 4 (2006): 295–311; Chen, "Toward an I Ching Model of Communication"; Miike, "Harmony without Uniformity." Confucian learning calls for people to engage in ceaseless self-cultivation and creative self-transformation. The logic of connectivity and mutual alignment suggests that one can change or influence others by first changing oneself. Once one individual changes, connectivity compels the other to change or realign as well.

51. Geoffrey Cowan and Amelia Arsenault, "Moving from Monologue to Dialogue to Collaboration: The Three Layers of Public Diplomacy," *The Annals of the American Academy of Political and Social Science* 616, no. 1 (2008): 10–30.

52. Cowan and Arsenault, 10.

53. Xu Wu, "Doing PR in China: A 2001 Version, Concepts, Practices and Some Misperceptions," *Public Relations Quarterly* 47, no. 2 (2002): 11..

54. The yin-yang symbol is illustrative. Yaqing Qin called the yin-yang relationship "the relationship of relationships," or a "meta-relationship"; for discussion, see pp. 169–94; Qin, *A Relational Theory of World Politics*; for "continuity through change," see also Qin, "International Society as a Process: Institutions, Identities, and China's Peaceful Rise," *The Chinese Journal of International Politics* 3, no. 2 (June 1, 2010): 140–41 .

55. Usha Vyasulu Reddi, "Communication Theory: An Indian Perspective," *Media Asia* 13, no. 1 (January 1986), 25–28.

56. Nan Lin, "Building a Network Theory of Social Capital," *Connections* 22, no. 1 (1999): 28–51.

57. Di Wu, "Assessing Resource Transactions in Partnership Networks: US 100,000 Strong Network of Public Diplomacy," *Public Relations Review* 42, no. 1 (March 2016): 120–34; Maureen Taylor and Michael L. Kent, "Building and Measuring Sustainable Networks of Organizations and Social Capital: Postwar Public Diplomacy in Croatia," in *Relational, Networked, and Collaborative Approaches to Public Diplomacy*, ed. R. S. Zaharna, Amelia Arsenault, and Ali Fisher (New York: Routledge, 2013), 103–16.

58. "Qin, "A Relational Theory of World Politics," *International Studies Review* 18 (2016): 37–39, spoke of the "logic of relationality"; Shi-Xu wrote: "The ontology and axiology of social and natural interconnections and harmony . . . would compel one to strive for humanness in relations with others" ("Reconstructing Eastern Paradigm," 38).

59. Mbiti, *African Religions and Philosophy*, 109.

60. Confucius, *The Analects*, trans. William E. Soothill, Dover Thrift ed. (New York: Dover Publications, 1910).

61. See, for example, Shi-Xu, "Reconstructing Eastern Paradigms,"; Qin, "A Relational Theory of World Politics"; Chen, "A Harmony Theory of Communication."

62. Katherine A. Cronin et al., "Hierarchy Is Detrimental for Human Cooperation," *Scientific Reports* 5, no. 1 (December 22, 2015): 18634.

63. Melvyn L. Fein, *Human Hierarchies: A General Theory* (New Brunswick: Transaction Publishers, 2012); Christopher Boehm, *Hierarchy in the Forest: The Evolution of Egalitarian Behavior*, rev. ed. (Cambridge, MA: Harvard University Press, 2001); Steven Peterson and Albert Somit, *Darwinism, Dominance, and Democracy: The Biological Bases of Authoritarianism* (Westport, CT: Praeger, 1997); Harold J. Leavitt, "Why Hierarchies Thrive," *Harvard Business Review* 81, no. 3 (2003): 96–102, 141.

64. Shuang Liu, "Hierarchy (Dengji)—A Pyramid of Interconnected Relationships," *China Media Research* 7, no. 4 (2011): 77–84.

65. Leavitt, "Why Hierarchies Thrive."

66. Leavitt, 102.

67. Chen, "An Introduction to Key Concepts in Understanding the Chinese."

68. The physical presence includes the spiritual realm. In the ancient world, the gods were perceived as real. The ancients often created symbolic physical representation. As we saw in Amarna diplomacy, the gods took the form of statutes and accompanied the envoys on their missions. For the role of the gods, see Lafont, "International Relations in the Ancient Near East," 41–44.

69. Edward T. Hall, *Beyond Culture* (New York: Anchor Books, 1976); Hall, *The Dance of Life: The Other Dimension of Time* (New York: Anchor Books, 1984); Jürgen Streeck, "Embodiment in Human Communication," *Annual Review of Anthropology* 44, no. 1 (2015): 419–38; Ipke Wachsmuth, Manuela Lenzen, and Gunther Knoblich, "Introduction to Embodied Communication: Why Communication Needs the Body," in *Embodied Communication in Humans and Machines*, ed. Ipke Wachsmuth, Manuela Lenzen, and Guenther Knoblich (New York: Oxford University Press, 2008), 1–28.

70. Marcus Holmes, "The Force of Face-to-Face Diplomacy: Mirror Neurons and the Problem of Intentions," *International Organization* 67, no. 4 (October 2013), 838–41.

71. Harold H. Saunders, "The Relational Paradigm and Sustained Dialogue," in *Relational, Networked and Collaborative Approaches to Public Diplomacy*, ed. R. S. Zaharna, Amelia Arsenault, and Ali Fisher (New York: Routledge, 2013), 132–44; Marcus Holmes, *Face-to-Face Diplomacy: Social Neuroscience and International Relations* (Cambridge: Cambridge University Press, 2018).

72. Fred Cummins, "Voice, (Inter-)subjectivity, and Real Time Recurrent Interaction," *Frontiers in Psychology* 5 (2014): 760. doi: 10.3389/fpsyg.2014.00760.

73. Jorina von Zimmermann and Daniel C. Richardson, "Verbal Synchrony and Action Dynamics in Large Groups," *Frontiers in Psychology* 7, no. 2034 (December 26, 2016): 1–10, doi: 10.3389/fpsyg.2016.02034.

74. William S. Condon and Louis W. Sander, "Synchrony Demonstrated between Movements of the Neonate and Adult Speech," *Child Development* 45, no. 2 (1974): 456–62.

75. Condon and Sander, "Synchrony Demonstrated."

76. Hall, *The Dance of Life*, 177.

77. N. Katherine Hayles, *How We Became Posthuman: Virtual Bodies in Cybernetics, Literature, and Informatics* (Chicago: University of Chicago Press, 1999); Ray Kurzweil, *The Singularity Is Near: When Humans Transcend Biology* (New York: Viking Press, 2005).

78. Marc Fabri, David J. Moore, and Dave J. Hobbs, "The Emotional Avatar: Non-Verbal Communication between Inhabitants of Collaborative Virtual Environments," in *Gesture-Based Communication in Human-Computer Interaction*, ed. Annelies Braffort et al (Berlin: Springer, 1999), 269–73.

79. Gregor Schoner, "Embodied Communication: Looking for Systems That Mean What They Say," Robohub. March 14, 2014, https://robohub.org/embodied-communicat ion-looking-for-systems-that-mean-what-they-say/ .

80. John Durham Peters, *Speaking into the Air: A History of the Idea of Communication* (Chicago: University of Chicago Press, 2001), 33–45..

81. Barreiro and Cornelius, "Knowledge of the Elders"; Jennings, *The History and Culture of Iroquois Diplomacy*; Shannon and Calloway, *Iroquois Diplomacy on the Early American Frontier.*

82. Dissanayake, "The Need for the Study of Asian Approaches to Communication"; Dissanayake, "Nagarjuna and Modern Communication Theory," *China Media Research* 3, no. 4 (2007): 34–41; Dissanayake, "The Desire to Excavate Asian Theories

of Communication: One Strand of the History," *Journal of Multicultural Discourses* 4, no. 1 (March 2009): 7–27.

83. Satoshi Ishii, "Conceptualising Asian Communication Ethics: A Buddhist Perspective," *Journal of Multicultural Discourses* 4, no. 1 (March 2009): 49–60; Ishii, "Enryo-Sasshi Communication: A Key to Understanding Japanese Interpersonal Relations," *Cross Currents* 11, no. 1 (1984): 49–58; Ishii, "Complementing Contemporary Intercultural Communication Research with East Asian Sociocultural Perspectives and Practices," *China Media Research* 2, no. 1 (2006): 13–20.

84. Yoshitaka Miike, "Asian Contributions to Communication Theory: An Introduction," *China Media Research* 3, no. 4 (2007); Miike, "Non-Western Theory in Western Research? An Asiacentric Agenda for Asian Communication Studies," *Review of Communication* 6, nos. 1 and 2 (2006): 4–31; Miike, "New Frontiers in Asian Communication Theory: An Introduction," *Journal of Multicultural Discourses* 4, no. 1 (2009): 1–5; Miike, "Theorizing Culture and Communication in the Asian Context: An Assumptive Foundation," *Intercultural Communication Studies* 11, no. 1 (2002): 1–22; Miike, "Harmony without Uniformity."

85. Guo-Ming Chen, "A Model of Global Communication Competence," *China Media Research* 1, no. 1 (2005): 3–11; Chen, "Toward an I Ching Model of Communication"; Chen, "An Introduction to Key Concepts in Understanding the Chinese."

Chapter 6

1. The story is from Rumi's *Masnavi I Ma'navi*, Book 1, Story XIV. Rumi favored the Greeks, though. See, Maulana Jalalu-'d-din Muhammad Rumi, *Masnavi I Ma'navi: Teachings of Rumi*, trans. Edward Henry. Whinfield (Originally published by Kegan Paul, Trench, Trübner & Co, London, 1898), available online at wikisource, https://en.wikisource.org/wiki/Masnavi_I_Ma%27navi.

2. Geert Hofstede, *Culture's Consequences: National Differences in Thinking and Organizing*, (Beverly Hills, CA: Sage, 1980).

3. Charlotte Alter, Suyin Haynes, and Justin Worland, "TIME 2019 Person of the Year: Greta Thunberg," December 23, 2019, https://time.com/person-of-the-year-2019-greta-thunberg/.

4. Charles Marsh, "Converging on Harmony: Idealism, Evolution, and the Theory of Mutual Aid," *Public Relations Inquiry* 1, no. 3 (September 1, 2012): 327.

5. Christer Jönsson and Martin Hall, *Essence of Diplomacy* (Basingstoke: Palgrave-Macmillan, 2005).

6. Roger Boesche, "Kautilya's Arthasastra on War and Diplomacy in Ancient India," *Journal of Military History* 67, no. 1 (2003): 9–37; Aabid Majeed Sheikh and Saima Rashid, "Kautilya, the Indian Machiavelli; On War and Diplomacy in Ancient India," *Journal of Humanities and Education Development* 2, no. 1 (2020): 29; Pradeep Kumar Gautam, Saurabh Mishra, and Arvind Gupta, *Indigenous Historical*

Knowledge: Kautilya and His Vocabulary, vol. 1 (New Delhi: Pentagon Press, 2015), https://idsa.in/system/files/book/book_IndigenousHistoricalKnowledge_Vol-I.pdf.

7. Tran Van Dinh, *Communication and Diplomacy in a Changing World* (Norwood, NJ: Ablex, 1987), 16–17.

8. Mark Pagel, "Q&A: What Is Human Language, When Did It Evolve and Why Should We Care?," *BMC Biology* 15, no. 1 (July 24, 2017): 64; Asif A. Ghazanfar and Daniel Y. Takahashi, "The Evolution of Speech: Vision, Rhythm, Cooperation," *Trends in Cognitive Sciences* 18, no. 10 (October 2014): 543–53.

9. Daniel Smith et al., "Cooperation and the Evolution of Hunter-Gatherer Storytelling," *Nature Communications* 8, no. 1 (December 5, 2017): 201.

10. Walter R. Fisher, *Human Communication as Narration: Toward a Philosophy of Reason, Value, and Action* (Columbia: University of South Carolina Press, 1987).

11. Jonathan Gottschall, *The Storytelling Animal: How Stories Make Us Human* (New York: Mariner Books, 2013).

12. Frank Rose, "The Art of Immersion: Why Do We Tell Stories?," *Wired*, March 8, 2011.

13. Kathryn Coe, Nancy E. Aiken, and Craig T. Palmer, "Once Upon a Time: Ancestors and the Evolutionary Significance of Stories," *Anthropological Forum* 16, no. 1 (March 1, 2006): 21–40, https://doi.org/10.1080/00664670600572421.

14. Coe, Aiken, and Palmer, 36.

15. Smith et al., "Cooperation and the Evolution of Hunter-Gatherer Storytelling."

16. Smith et al., 2.

17. Ilan Manor, *The Digitalization of Public Diplomacy* (New York: Palgrave Macmillan, 2019); Nicholas J. Cull, "The Long Road to Public Diplomacy 2.0: The Internet in US Public Diplomacy," *International Studies Review* 15, no. 1 (March 2013): 123–39; Fergus Hanson, "Baked in and Wired: eDiplomacy @ State," The Brookings Institution, Foreign Policy Paper Series, October 25, 2012, https://www.brookings.edu/research/baked-in-and-wired-ediplomacy-state/.

18. Anne-Marie Slaughter, *The Chessboard and the Web: Strategies of Connection in a Networked World* (New Haven, CT: Yale University Press, 2017).

19. Serge Schmemann, "A New Rule Book for the Great Game," *New York Times*, April 12, 2017, sec. Books, https://www.nytimes.com/2017/04/12/books/review/chessboard-and-the-web-anne-marie-slaughter.html; Ali Wyne, "Anne-Marie Slaughter Tries to Make Sense of the New Global Order," *The New Republic*, September 22, 2017, https://newrepublic.com/article/144930/anne-marie-slaughter-tries-make-sense-new-global-order; Samprity Biswas, "Book Review: Anne-Marie Slaughter, The Chessboard and the Web: Strategies of Connection in a Networked World," *International Studies* 55, no. 2 (April 1, 2018): 211–12, https://doi.org/10.1177/0020881718792111.

20. Fisher speaks of the trade-off between how collaboration or connections with others can restrict and why he calls it "increasing the odds." Ali Fisher, *Collaborative Public Diplomacy: How Transnational Networks Influenced American Studies in Europe* (New York: Palgrave Macmillan, 2013).

21. Emilie M. Hafner-Burton, Miles Kahler, and Alexander H. Montgomery, "Network Analysis for International Relations," *International Organization* 63, no. 3 (July 2009): 559–92; Keith G. Provan, Amy Fish, and Joerg Sydow, "Interorganizational

Networks at the Network Level: A Review of the Empirical Literature on Whole Networks," *Journal of Management* 33, no. 3 (2007): 479–516.

22. Howard Rheingold, *The Virtual Community: Homesteading on the Electronic Frontier* (MIT Press eBooks, 2000), http://www.rheingold.com/vc/book/; P. Seargeant and C. Tagg, *The Language of Social Media: Identity and Community on the Internet* (Berlin: Springer, 2014); Anatoliy Gruzd, Barry Wellman, and Yuri Takhteyev, "Imagining Twitter as an Imagined Community," *American Behavioral Scientist* 55, no. 10 (October 1, 2011): 1294–1318.

23. R. S. Zaharna, "Network Purpose, Network Design: Dimensions of Network and Collaborative Public Diplomacy," in *Relational, Networked and Collaborative Approaches to Public Diplomacy: The Connective Mindshift*, ed. R. S. Zaharna, Amelia Arsenault, and Ali Fisher (New York: Routledge, 2013), 173–91.

24. Alister Miskimmon, Ben O'Loughlin, and Laura Roselle, *Strategic Narratives: Communication Power and the New World Order* (New York: Routledge, 2013).

25. Miskimmon, O'Loughlin, and Roselle, 4.

26. John Arquilla and David Ronfeldt, *Networks and Netwars: The Future of Terror, Crime, and Militancy* (Santa Monica, CA: RAND Corporation, 2001); John Arquilla and David Ronfeldt, *The Emergence of Noopolitik: Toward an American Information Strategy* (Santa Monica, CA: RAND Corporation, 1999).

27. R. S. Zaharna, "The Soft Power Differential: Network Communication and Mass Communication in Public Diplomacy," *The Hague Journal of Diplomacy* 2, no. 3 (October 1, 2007): 213–28, .

28. Philip N. Howard and Malcolm R. Parks, "Social Media and Political Change: Capacity, Constraint, and Consequence," *Journal of Communication* 62, no. 2 (2012): 359–62.

29. Zizi Papacharissi and Maria de Fatima Oliveira, "Affective News and Networked Publics: The Rhythms of News Storytelling on #Egypt," *Journal of Communication* 62, no. 2 (April 1, 2012): 266–82.

30. Papacharissi and de Fatima Oliveira, 267.

31. Zizi Papacharissi, *Affective Publics: Sentiment, Technology, and Politics* (New York: Oxford University Press, 2015).

32. Wael Ghonim, *Revolution 2.0: The Power of the People Is Greater Than the People in Power: A Memoir* (Boston: Houghton Mifflin Harcourt, 2012).

33. The relationship between language and emotion has become a very active area of research, with conventional ideas of separate brain regions of speech and emotion (see Ledoux, 1998) being challenged by new research that suggests greater interaction (see Barrett, 2017 and Lindquist, 2021).Joseph Ledoux, *The Emotional Brain: The Mysterious Underpinnings of Emotional Life* (New York: Simon & Schuster, 1998). Lisa Feldman Barrett, *How Emotions are Made: The Secret Life of the Brain*, (New York: Houghton Mifflin Harcourt, 2017); and Kristen A. Lindquist, "Language and Emotion: Introduction to the Special Issue," *Affective Science*, 2 (2021): 91–98.

34. There is a rich body of literature on nonverbal behaviors and impression formation and management. For an overview, see, for example: Albert Mehrabian, *Silent Messages* (Belmont, CA: Wadsworth, 1971); Judee K. Burgoon, Laura K. Guerrero,

and Kory Floyd, "Social Cognition and Impression Formation," in *Nonverbal Communication* (New York: Routledge, 2010), 229–260; Dale Leathers and Michael H. Eaves, "Impression Management," in *Successful Nonverbal Communication: Principles and Applications*, 4th ed. (New York: Pearson, 2007), 187–208.

35. Erin Hawley, "The Story behind a Viral Photo of an Arkansas Doctor and His Son" (Little Rock, AR, March 27, 2020), https://katv.com/news/local/the-story-behind-a-viral-photo-of-an-arkansas-doctor-and-his-son.

36. Angela Dobele et al., "Why Pass on Viral Messages? Because They Connect Emotionally," *Business Horizons* 50, no. 4 (July 2007): 50.

37. Daantje Derks, Agneta H. Fischer, and Arjan E. R. Bos, "The Role of Emotion in Computer-Mediated Communication: A Review," *Computers in Human Behavior* 24, no. 3 (2008): 766–85; T. Benski and E. Fisher, *Internet and Emotions* (New York: Routledge, 2014); Javier Serrano-Puche, "Emotions and Digital Technologies: Mapping the Field of Research in Media Studies.," MEDIA@LSE Working Papers #33, 2015, https://www.lse.ac.uk/media-and-communications/assets/documents/research/working-paper-series/EWP33.pdf; R. S. Zaharna, "Emotion, Identity & Social Media: Developing a New Awareness, Lens & Vocabulary for Diplomacy 21," Working Paper, "Diplomacy in the 21st Century" (Berlin: German Institute for International and Security Affairs, January 2017),https://www.swp-berlin.org/fileadmin/contents/products/arbeitspapiere/WP_Diplomacy21_No2_RS_Zaharna.pdf.

38. Ancient texts spoke of basic pan-human emotional expression and recognition. From the Chinese classic Li-Chi: "What are the feelings of men? They are joy, anger, sadness, fear, love, disliking, and liking. These seven feelings belong to men without their learning them." Ch'u Chai and Winberg Chai, eds., *Li Chi Book of Rites. An Encyclopedia of Ancient Ceremonial Usages, Religious Creeds, and Social Institutions*, trans. James Legge (New Hyde Park: University Books, 1967), 379 ; The Natyashastra, the oldest surviving ancient Indian work on performance arts (1st millennium BCE), detailed a taxonomy of emotions. Kathleen Marie Higgins, "An Alchemy of Emotion: Rasa and Aesthetic Breakthroughs," *The Journal of Aesthetics and Art Criticism* 65, no. 1 (2007): 43–54.

39. Charles Darwin, with Paul Ekman Introduction, *The Expression of the Emotions in Man and Animals*, 3rd ed. (New York: Oxford University Press, 1872/1998).

40. Paul Ekman, "Darwin's Contributions to Our Understanding of Emotional Expressions," *Philosophical Transactions of the Royal Society B: Biological Sciences* 364, no. 1535 (December 12, 2009): 3449–51; Paul Ekman, "Darwin's Compassionate View of Human Nature," *JAMA* 303, no. 6 (February 10, 2010): 557.

41. Antonio Damasio, *Descartes' Error: Emotion, Reason, and the Human Brain*, reprint ed. (London: Penguin Books, 2005); Dylan Evans and Pierre Cruse, *Emotion, Evolution and Rationality* (Oxford: Oxford University Press, 2004).

42. Paul Ekman and Wallace V. Friesen, "The Repertoire of Nonverbal Behavior: Categories, Origins, Usage, and Coding," *Semiotica* 1, no. 1 (1969): 49–98; Paul Ekman and Wallace Friesen, "Constants across Cultures in the Face and Emotion.," *Journal of Personality and Social Psychology* 17, no. 2 (1971): 124–129;

Paul Ekman, E. Richard Sorenson, and Wallace V. Friesen, "Pan-Cultural Elements in Facial Displays of Emotion," *Science* 164, no. 3875 (April 4, 1969): 86–88; Paul Ekman, Wallace V. Friesen, and Phoebe Ellsworth, *Emotion in the Human Face* (New York: Pergamon, 1972).

43. Paul Ekman, "What Scientists Who Study Emotion Agree About," *Perspectives on Psychological Science* 11, no. 1 (January 1, 2016): 31–34; David Matsumoto and Hyi Sung Hwang, "Reading Facial Expressions of Emotion," *Psychological Science Agenda*, May 2011; Michael Price, "Facial Expressions—Including Fear—May Not Be as Universal as We Thought," *Science | AAAS*, 2016, https://www.sciencemag.org/news/2016/10/facial-expressions-including-fear-may-not-be-universal-we-thought; James A. Russell, "Is There Universal Recognition of Emotion from Facial Expression? A Review of the Cross-Cultural Studies," *Psychological Bulletin* 115, no. 1 (1994): 102–41, https://doi.org/10.1037/0033-2909.115.1.102; Carlos Crivelli et al., "The Fear Gasping Face as a Threat Display in a Melanesian Society," *Proceedings of the National Academy of Sciences* 113, no. 44 (November 1, 2016): 12403–7, https://doi.org/10.1073/pnas.1611622113.

44. Charles Darwin, *The Expression of Emotion in Man and Animals (with an Introduction by Paul Ekman* (New York: Oxford University Press, 1998), 130.

45. Alan Kam-leung Chan, *Mencius: Contexts and Interpretations* (Honolulu: University of Hawaii Press, 2002), 6.

46. Wm. Theodore de Bary and Irene Bloom, eds., *Sources of Chinese Tradition: From Earliest Times to 1600,* 2nd ed. (New York: Columbia University Press, 1999), 129.

47. H. Saunders, *Politics Is about Relationship: A Blueprint for the Citizens' Century* (New York: Palgrave Macmillan, 2006); Harold H. Saunders, "The Relational Paradigm and Sustained Dialogue," in *Relational, Networked and Collaborative Approaches to Public Diplomacy.*, ed. R. S. Zaharna, Amelia Arsenault, and Ali Fisher (New York: Routledge, 2013), 132–44.

48. Matsumoto and Hwang, "Reading Facial Expressions of Emotion."

49. Daniel Goleman, *Emotional Intelligence: Why It Can Matter More Than IQ*, 10th anniversary ed. (New York: Bantam, 2005).

50. The biological effects of oxytocin and mirror neuron in the human brain are particularly important for understanding how people are able to gain a sense of trust, affinity, and even pleasure in working with others despite vast differences in languages or traditions. See Chapter 4.

51. Andreas Fulda, "The Emergence of Citizen Diplomacy in European Union–China Relations: Principles, Pillars, Pioneers, Paradoxes," *Diplomacy & Statecraft* 30, no. 1 (2019): 188–216.

52. Nicholas J. Cull, *Public Diplomacy: Foundations for Global Engagement in the Digital Age* (Cambridge, UK: Polity, 2019); Cull, "Public Diplomacy: Taxonomies and Histories," *The Annals of the American Academy of Political and Social Science* 616 (2008): 31–54.

53. Matthew W. Seeger, "Best Practices in Crisis Communication: An Expert Panel Process," *Journal of Applied Communication Research* 34, no. 3 (August 1, 2006): 232–44.

54. Cheryl Snapp Conner, "In a Crisis, Use These 3 Forms of Empathy to Serve Your Customers Well," *Mission.Org* (blog), June 29, 2017, https://medium.com/the-mission/in-a-crisis-use-these-3-forms-of-empathy-to-serve-your-customers-well-35722ec88590.

55. Jonny Dymond, "Queen's Coronavirus Speech: 'Ambitious' Words 'to Reassure and Inspire,'" BBC News, April 5, 2020, sec. UK, https://www.bbc.com/news/uk-52176209.

56. Nina Goswami, "Have Female CEOs Coped Better with Covid than Men?," BBC News, November 19, 2020, sec. Business, https://www.bbc.com/news/business-54974132; Michal Katz, "Commentary: The COVID Crisis Shows Why We Need More Female Leadership," *Fortune*, March 17, 2020, https://fortune.com/2021/03/17/covid-female-women-leadership-jacinda-ardern/; Kathy Caprino, "How Women Leaders Are Rising to the Unique Challenges They're Facing from the Pandemic," *Forbes*, May 18, 2020, https://www.forbes.com/sites/kathycaprino/2020/05/18/how-women-leaders-are-rising-to-the-unique-challenges-theyre-facing-from-the-pandemic/.

57. Supriya Garikipati and Uma Kambhampati, "Leading the Fight against the Pandemic: Does Gender 'Really' Matter?," SSRN Scholarly Paper (Rochester, NY: Social Science Research Network, June 3, 2020); Joana Probert, "Leading with Empathy in the Pandemic," *Saïd Business School, University of Oxford*, July 1, 2020, https://www.sbs.ox.ac.uk/oxford-answers/leading-empathy-pandemic; Kayla Sergent and Alexander D. Stajkovic, "Women's Leadership Is Associated with Fewer Deaths during the COVID-19 Crisis: Quantitative and Qualitative Analyses of United States Governors," *Journal of Applied Psychology* 105, no. 8 (August 2020): 771–83.

58. Carolyn Childers, "Why Coronavirus Demands Women's Leadership," April 22, 2020, https://milkeninstitute.org/power-of-ideas/why-coronavirus-demands-womens-leadership.

59. Edward T. Hall, *Beyond Culture* (New York: Anchor Books, 1976), 71.

60. Edward T. Hall, *The Dance of Life: The Other Dimension of Time* (New York: Anchor Books, 1984), 177.

61. Researchers link this unique human ability to the whites of the eye, which other primates lack. For discussion, see Fred Cummins, "Voice, (Inter-)Subjectivity, and Real Time Recurrent Interaction," *Frontiers in Psychology*, July 18, 2014; Michael Tomasello et al., "Two Key Steps in the Evolution of Human Cooperation: The Interdependence Hypothesis," *Current Anthropology* 53, no. 6 (December 1, 2012): 673–92.

62. Alexandra Paxton and Rick Dale, "Interpersonal Movement Synchrony Responds to High- and Low-Level Conversational Constraints," *Frontiers in Psychology* 8, no. 1135 (July 28, 2017); Cummins, "Voice, (Inter-)Subjectivity, and Real Time Recurrent Interaction."

63. Jorina von Zimmermann and Daniel C. Richardson, "Verbal Synchrony and Action Dynamics in Large Groups," *Frontiers in Psychology* 7, no. 2034 (December 26, 2016).

64. William H. McNeill, *Together in Time: Dance and Drill in Human History* (Cambridge, MA: Harvard University Press, 1995).

65. McNeill, 2.

66. William Booth, Karla Adam, and Pamela Rolfe, "In Fight against Coronavirus, the World Gives Medical Heroes a Standing Ovation," *Washington Post*, March 26, 2020, https://www.washingtonpost.com/world/europe/clap-for-carers/2020/03/26/3d05e b9c-6f66-11ea-a156-0048b62cdb51_story.html.

67. Kari Paul, "Please Don't Stop the Music: How Choirs Are Singing through the Pandemic," *The Guardian*, April 22, 2021, sec. Music, http://www.theguardian.com/ music/2021/apr/22/choirs-coronavirus-covid-19-us-virtual-singing; Jasmine Garsd, "Musicians Are Doing Virtual Concerts during COVID-19," *Marketplace* (blog), April 27, 2020, https://www.marketplace.org/2020/04/27/musicians-virtual-conce rts-covid19-pandemic/.

68. Amanda Holpuch, "'A Lifesaver': US Seniors Turn to Zoom to Connect with Friends and Family," *The Guardian*, September 18, 2020, sec. US news, http://www.theguard ian.com/us-news/2020/sep/18/us-seniors-video-calls-zoom-coronavirus;   Clare Ansberry, "Zoom Reconnects Family and Friends in the Coronavirus Pandemic—but Will It Last?," *Wall Street Journal*, July 22, 2020, sec. Life, https://www.wsj.com/artic les/zoom-reconnects-family-and-friends-in-the-coronavirus-pandemicbut-will-it-last-11595379600.

69. Fong, cited in "Games Industry Unites to Promote World Health Organization Messages against COVID-19; Launch #PlayApartTogether Campaign," Bloomberg. com, April 10, 2020, https://www.bloomberg.com/press-releases/2020-04-10/games-industry-unites-to-promote-world-health-organization-messages-against-covid-19-launch-playaparttogether-campaign.

70. Andy Phelps, "Gaming Fosters Social Connection at a Time of Physical Distance," *The Conversation* (blog), April 13, 2020, https://theconversation.com/gaming-fosters-soc ial-connection-at-a-time-of-physical-distance-135809.

71. Hall, *Beyond Culture*, 170.

72. Young Yun Kim, "Achieving Synchrony: A Foundational Dimension of Intercultural Communication Competence," *International Journal of Intercultural Relations*, Intercultural Competence 48 (September 1, 2015): 27.

73. Léopold Sédar Senghor (1964), "Je pense donc je suis, crivait Descartes. . . . Le Negro-africain pourrait dire: 'Je sens l'Autre, je danse l'Autre, donc je suis,'" *Libertd* 1:259, cited in Peter Aberger, "Leopold Senghor and the Issue of Reverse Racism," *Phylon* 41, no. 3 (1980): 277.

74. John Carlin, *Playing the Enemy: Nelson Mandela and the Game That Made a Nation* (New York: Penguin, 2008); Claire E. Oppenheim, "Nelson Mandela and the Power of Ubuntu," *Religions* 3 (2012): 369–88.

75. Marshall Ganz, "Leading Change: Leadership, Organization, and Social Movements," ed. Nitin Nohria and Rakesh Khurana (Cambridge, MA: Harvard Business School Press, 2010), 509–50.

76. Erin J. Rand, "'What One Voice Can Do': Civic Pedagogy and Choric Collectivity at Camp Courage," *Text and Performance Quarterly* 34, no. 1 (2014): 28–51.

77. Bernard De Koven, *The Well-Played Game: A Player's Philosophy*, illustrated ed. (Cambridge, MA: MIT Press, 2013).

78. Bernard De Koven, "Confluence," *DeepFUN* (blog), 2018, https://www.deepfun.com/confluence/.

79. Benjamin Stokes, *Locally Played: Real-World Games for Stronger Places and Communities* (Cambridge, MA: MIT Press, 2020).

Conclusion

1. Iver B. Neumann, "A Prehistorical Evolutionary View of Diplomacy," *Place Branding and Public Diplomacy* 14 (2018), 4.

2. Yoshitaka Miike, "Harmony without Uniformity": An Asiacentric Worldview and Its Communicative Implications," in *Intercultural Communication: A Reader*, ed. Larry A. Samovar, Richard E. Porter, and Edwin R. McDaniel (Boston: Wadsworth, 2012), 65–80.

3. Nancy E. Aiken and Kathryn Coe, "Promoting Cooperation among Humans: The Arts as the Ties That Bind," *Bulletin of Psychology and the Arts* 5, no. 1 (2004): 5–20; Viva Ona Bartkus and James H. Davis, *Social Capital: Reaching Out, Reaching In* (Camberley, Surrey: Edward Elgar Publishing, 2010); Dirk Messner and Silke Weinlich, *Global Cooperation and the Human Factor in International Relations* (New York: Routledge, 2015); Richard Sennett, *Together: The Rituals, Pleasures and Politics of Cooperation* (New Haven, CT: Yale University Press, 2013); Michael Tomasello et al., "Two Key Steps in the Evolution of Human Cooperation: The Interdependence Hypothesis," *Current Anthropology* 53, no. 6 (2012): 673–92.

4. Bartkus and Davis, *Social Capital*, 4–5.

5. Tomasello et al., "Two Key Steps in the Evolution of Human Cooperation"; Babak Fotouhi et al., "Conjoining Uncooperative Societies Facilitates Evolution of Cooperation," *Nature Human Behaviour* 2, no. 7 (July 2018): 492–99, https://doi.org/10.1038/s41562-018-0368-6; Samuel Bowles and Herbert Gintis, *A Cooperative Species: Human Reciprocity and Its Evolution*, reprint ed. (Princeton, NJ: Princeton University Press, 2013); J. M. Burkart et al., "The Evolutionary Origin of Human Hyper-Cooperation," *Nature Communications* 5, no. 1 (December 2014): 4747; Charles Darwin, *The Descent of Man and Selection in Relation to Sex*, new rev, ed. (New York: D. Appleton, 1896).

6. Neumann, "A Prehistorical Evolutionary View of Diplomacy."

7. Charles R. DiSalvo, *Gandhi: The Man before the Mahatma* (Berkeley: University of California Press, 2013), https://www.wvpublic.org/post/gandhis-life-lawyer-revealed.

8. Peter Kropotkin, *Mutual Aid: A Factor of Evolution* (New York: Black Rose Books, 1902).

9. Jeremy Roschelle and Stephanie D. Teasley, "The Construction of Shared Knowledge in Collaborative Problem Solving," in *Computer Supported Collaborative Learning*, ed. Claire O'Malley, NATO ASI Series (Berlin, Heidelberg: Springer, 1995), 69–97, https://doi.org/10.1007/978-3-642-85098-1_5.

10. Roschelle and Teasley, 70.

11. See Spencer's writing at john@spencerauthor.com. and http://www.spencerauthor. com/about-me/. The drawing is taken from http://www.spencerauthor.com/designt hinking/https://www.youtube.com/watch?v=Gr5mAboH1Kk&vl=en.

12. Lucian J. Hudson, *The Enabling State: Collaborating for Success* (London: Foreign Commonwealth Office, 2009), https://webarchive.nationalarchives.gov.uk/2010051 3203926/http://www.fco.gov.uk/resources/en/pdf/pdf9/enabling-state-v3.

13. Ali Fisher, *Collaborative Public Diplomacy: How Transnational Networks Influenced American Studies in Europe* (New York: Palgrave Macmillan, 2013).

14. Thomas S. Kuhn, *The Structure of Scientific Revolutions*, 3rd ed. (Chicago: University of Chicago Press, 1996).

15. Donald E. Brown, "Human Universals, Human Nature and Human Culture," *Daedalus* 133, no. 4 (2004), 48.

16. Costa M. Constantinou, "Everyday Diplomacy: Mission, Spectacle and the Remaking of Diplomatic Culture," in *Diplomatic Cultures and International Politics: Translations, Spaces and Alternatives* (New York: Routledge, 2016); Magnus Marsden, Diana Ibañez-Tirado, and David Henig, "Everyday Diplomacy," *Cambridge Journal of Anthropology* 34, no. 2 (September 1, 2016): 2–22.

17. Christer Jönsson, "Relationships between Negotiators: A Neglected Topic in the Study of Negotiation," *International Negotiation* 20 (2015), 14.

18. Tran Van Dinh, *Communication and Diplomacy in a Changing World* (Norwood, NJ: Ablex, 1987), 4.

19. Richard Ned Lebow, "Reason, Emotion and Cooperation," *International Politics* 42, no. 3 (September 2005): 283–313; Richard Ned Lebow, "Fear, Interest and Honour: Outlines of a Theory of International Relations," *International Affairs* 82, no. 3 (May 2006): 431–48, https://doi.org/10.1111/j.1468-2346.2006.00543.x.

20. Jonathan Mercer, "Rationality and Psychology in International Politics," *International Organization* 59, no. 1 (January 2005): 77–106; Mercer, "Feeling like a State: Social Emotion and Identity," *International Theory* 6, no. 03 (November 2014): 515–35; Yohan Ariffin, Jean-Marc Coicaud, and Vesselin Popovski, *Emotions in International Politics: Beyond Mainstream International Relations* (Cambridge: Cambridge University Press, 2016); Emma Hutchison and Roland Bleiker, "Theorizing Emotions in World Politics," *International Theory* 6, no. 3 (November 2014): 491–514, https:// doi.org/10.1017/S1752971914000232; Roland Bleiker and Emma Hutchison, "Fear No More: Emotions and World Politics," *Review of International Studies* 34, no. S1 (January 2008): 115–35, https://doi.org/10.1017/S0260210508007821; Neta C. Crawford, "Institutionalizing Passion in World Politics: Fear and Empathy," *International Theory* 6, no. 3 (November 2014): 535–57, https://doi.org/10.1017/ S1752971914000256; Crawford, "The Passion of World Politics: Propositions on Emotion and Emotional Relationships," *International Security* 24, no. 4 (April 1, 2000): 116–56; Christian Reus-Smit, "Emotions and the Social," *International Theory* 6, no. 03 (November 2014): 568–74.

21. Hyunjin Seo and Stuart Thorson, "Empathy in Public Diplomacy: Strategic Academic Engagement with North Korea," in *Intersections between Public Diplomacy*

and International Development: Case Studies in Converging Fields, ed. James Pamment (Los Angeles: Figueroa Press, 2016), 19–34; Seanon S. Wong, "Emotions and the Communication of Intentions in Face-to-Face Diplomacy," *European Journal of International Relations* 22, no. 1 (March 1, 2016): 144–67; David Kang, "Korea's Emotional Diplomacy," *Center on Public Diplomacy, Public Diplomacy Magazine*, 2009.

22. Sarah Ellen Graham, "Emotion and Public Diplomacy: Dispositions in International Communications, Dialogue, and Persuasion," *International Studies Review* 16, no. 4 (December 1, 2014): 522–39; Constance Duncombe, "Digital Diplomacy: Emotion and Identity in the Public Realm," *The Hague Journal of Diplomacy* 14, nos. 1 and 2 (April 22, 2019): 102–16, https://doi.org/10.1163/1871191X-14101016.

23. Douglas Johnston, *Faith-Based Diplomacy Trumping Realpolitik, Faith-Based Diplomacy Trumping Realpolitik* (New York: Oxford University Press, 2003), https://oxford.universitypressscholarship.com/view/10.1093/acprof:oso/9780195367 935.001.0001/acprof-9780195367935; Costas M. Constantinou, "Human Diplomacy and Spirituality," Discussion Papers in Diplomacy (Netherlands Institute of International Relations Clingendael, 2006).

References

Aberger, Peter. "Leopold Senghor and the Issue of Reverse Racism." *Phylon* 41, no. 3 (1980): 276–83.

Abu-Lugod, Lila. "Writing against Culture." In *Recapturing Anthropology: Working in the Present*, ed., Richard G. Fox, 137–62. Santa Fe, NM: School of American Research, 1991.

Adam, Barbara, and Stuart Allan. *Theorizing Culture: An Interdisciplinary Critique after Postmodernism*. New York: NYU Press, 1995.

Adler, Ronald B., Lawrence B. Rosenfeld, and Russell F. Proctor. *Interplay: The Process of Interpersonal Communication*. 14th ed. New York: Oxford University Press, 2017.

Aiken, Nancy E., and Kathryn Coe. "Promoting Cooperation among Humans: The Arts as the Ties That Bind." *Bulletin of Psychology and the Arts* 5, no. 1 (2004): 5–20.

Al Kabalan, Marwan. "Al Hurra's Chances of Success Are Remote." *Gulf News*, February 20, 2004. https://gulfnews.com/uae/dr-marwan-al-kabalan-al-hurras-chances-of-success-are-remote-1.314218.

Almazán, Marco A. "The Aztec States-Society: Roots of Civil Society and Social Capital." *The Annals of the American Academy of Political and Social Science* 565, no. 1 (1999): 162–75.

Alter, Charlotte, Suyin Haynes, and Justin Worland. "TIME 2019 Person of the Year: Greta Thunberg," *TIME*, December 23, 2019. https://time.com/person-of-the-year-2019-greta-thunberg/.

Althen, Gary, Amanda R. Doran, and Susan J. Szmania. *American Ways: A Guide for Foreigners in the United States*. Yarmouth, ME: Intercultural Press, 2003.

Anderson, Benedict. *Imagined Communities: Reflections on the Origin and Spread of Nationalism*. New York: Verso, 1983.

Anholt, Simon. *The Good Country Equation: How We Can Repair the World in One Generation*. New York: Berrett-Koehler, 2020.

Ansberry, Clare. "Zoom Reconnects Family and Friends in the Coronavirus Pandemic—but Will It Last?" *Wall Street Journal*, July 22, 2020, sec. Life. https://www.wsj.com/articles/zoom-reconnects-family-and-friends-in-the-coronavirus-pandemicbut-will-it-last-11595379600.

Appadurai, Arjun. *Modernity at Large: Cultural Dimensions of Globalization*. Public Worlds 1. Minneapolis: University of Minnesota Press, 1996.

Appiah, Kwame Anthony. *The Ethics of Identity*. Princeton, NJ: Princeton University Press, 2010. https://doi.org/10.1515/9781400826193.

Argyle, Michael, and Mark Cook. *Gaze and Mutual Gaze*. New York: Cambridge University Press, 1976.

Ariffin, Yohan, Jean-Marc Coicaud, and Vesselin Popovski. *Emotions in International Politics: Beyond Mainstream International Relations*. New York: Cambridge University Press, 2016.

Aristotle. *Rhetoric*, translated by W. Rhys Roberts. Dover Thrift ed. New York: Dover Publications, 1946.

"Aristotle." Internet Encyclopedia of Philosophy, n.d. Accessed October 13, 2019. https://www.iep.utm.edu/aristotl/.

Armstrong, John A. *Nations before Nationalism*. Chapel Hill: UNC Press Books, 2017.

Arquilla, John and David Ronfeldt. *The Emergence of Noopolitik: Toward an American Information Strategy*. Santa Monica, CA: RAND Corporation, 1999.

Arquilla, John, and David Ronfeldt. *Networks and Netwars: The Future of Terror, Crime, and Militancy*. Santa Monica, CA: RAND Corporation, 2001.

Asante, Molefi. *Afrocentric Idea Revised*. Philadelphia, PA: Temple University Press, 2011.

Badie, Bertrand. "The European Challenge to Bismarckian Diplomacy." *International Politics* 46, no. 5 (2009): 517–26.

Bakhtin, M. M. *The Dialogic Imagination: Four Essays*, ed., Michael Holquist, translated by Caryl Emerson. Reprint ed. Austin: University of Texas Press, 1983.

Banks, Robert. *A Resource Guide to Public Diplomacy Evaluation*. CPD Perspectives on Public Diplomacy. Los Angeles: Figueroa Press, 2011.

Barreiro, Jose, and Carol Cornelius. "Knowledge of the Elders: The Iroquois Condolence Cane Tradition." *Northeast Indian Quarterly*, 1991, 1–31.

Barrett, Lisa Feldman. *How Emotions are Made: The Secret Life of the Brain*. New York: Houghton Mifflin Harcourt, 2017.

Bartkus, Viva Ona, and James H. Davis. *Social Capital: Reaching out, Reaching in*. Camberley, Surrey: Edward Elgar Publishing, 2010.

Baxter, Leslie A. "Symbols of Relationship Identity in Relationship Cultures." *Journal of Social and Personal Relationships* 4, no. 3 (August 1, 1987): 261–80.

Beers, Charlotte, Under Secretary for Public Diplomacy and Public Affairs. "American Public Diplomacy and Islam." Department of State, Office of Electronic Information, Bureau of Public Affairs, February 27, 2003. https://2001-2009.state.gov/r/us/18098.htm.

Beers, Charlotte. "Public Diplomacy after September 11." Presented at the Remarks to National Press Club, Washington, DC, December 18, 2002. https://2001-2009.state.gov/r/us/16269.htm.

Beers, Charlotte. "Public Service and Public Diplomacy." Department of State, Office of Electronic Information, Bureau of Public Affairs, October 17, 2002. https://2001-2009.state.gov/r/us/15912.htm.

Beers, Charlotte. "U.S. Public Diplomacy in the Arab and Muslim Worlds." Department of State, Office of Electronic Information, Bureau of Public Affairs, May 7, 2002. https://2001-2009.state.gov/r/us/10424.htm.

Bellah, Robert N., Richard Madsen, William M. Sullivan, Ann Swidler, and Steven M. Tipton. *Habits of the Heart: Individualim and Commitment in American Life: Updated Edition with a New Introduction*. Berkeley: University of California Press, 1996.

Benski, Tova, and Eran Fisher. *Internet and Emotions*. New York: Routledge, 2014.

Berlo, David K. *The Process of Communication*. New York: Holt, Rinehart and Winston, 1960.

Berridge, G. R. *Diplomacy: Theory and Practice*. New York: NY: Palgrave MacMillan, 2015.

Best, Stephen. "Walter J. Ong, Orality and Literacy (1982)." *Public Culture* 32, no. 2 (2020): 431–39.

Bhabha, Homi K. *The Location of Culture*. 2nd ed. New York: Routledge, 2004.

Billig, Michael. *Banal Nationalism*. Thousand Oaks, CA: Sage Publications Ltd., 1995.

Birdwhistell, Ray L. *Kinesics and Context: Essays on Body Motion Communication*. Philadelphia: University of Pennsylvania Press, 1970.

Birrell, Anne M. *Chinese Mythology: An Introduction*. Revised ed. Baltimore: Johns Hopkins University Press, 1999.

Bishara, Marwan. "Washington's New Channel: Propaganda TV Won't Help the U.S." *New York Times*, February 23, 2004, sec. Opinion. https://www.nytimes.com/2004/02/23/opinion/washingtons-new-channel-propaganda-tv-wont-help-the-us.html.

Biswas, Samprity. "Book Review: Anne-Marie Slaughter, The Chessboard and the Web: Strategies of Connection in a Networked World." *International Studies* 55, no. 2 (April 1, 2018): 211–12. https://doi.org/10.1177/0020881718792111.

Bleiker, Roland, and Emma Hutchison. "Fear No More: Emotions and World Politics." *Review of International Studies* 34, no. SI (January 2008): 115–35. https://doi.org/10.1017/S0260210508007821.

Boehm, Christopher. *Hierarchy in the Forest: The Evolution of Egalitarian Behavior*. Revised ed. Cambridge, MA: Harvard University Press, 2001.

Boehmer, Elleke. *Nelson Mandela: A Very Short Introduction*. Oxford: Oxford University Press, 2008.

Boesche, Roger. "Kautilya's Arthasastra on War and Diplomacy in Ancient India." *The Journal of Military History* 67, no. 1 (2003): 9–37.

Booth, William, Karla Adam, and Pamela Rolfe. "In Fight against Coronavirus, the World Gives Medical Heroes a Standing Ovation." *Washington Post*, March 26, 2020. https://www.washingtonpost.com/world/europe/clap-for-carers/2020/03/26/3d05eb9c-6f66-11ea-a156-0048b62cdb51_story.html.

Bowles, David. *Flower, Song, Dance: Aztec and Mayan Poetry*. Lamar, TX: Lamar University Press, 2013.

Bowles, Samuel, and Herbert Gintis. *A Cooperative Species: Human Reciprocity and Its Evolution*. Reprint ed. Princeton, NJ: Princeton University Press, 2013.

Breuning, Loretta Graziano. *Habits of a Happy Brain: Retrain Your Brain to Boost Your Serotonin, Dopamine, Oxytocin, and Endorphin Levels*. New York: Adams Media, 2015.

Brewer, Marilynn B., and Ya-Ru Chen. "Where (Who) Are Collectives in Collectivism? Toward Conceptual Clarification of Individualism and Collectivism." *Psychological Review* 114, no. 1 (2007): 133–51.

Brown, Donald E. "Human Universals, Human Nature and Human Culture." *Daedalus* 133, no. 4 (2004): 47–54.

Bryce, Trevor. *Letters of the Great Kings of the Ancient Near East: The Royal Correspondence of the Late Bronze Age*. New York: Routledge, 2003.

Buber, Martin. *I and Thou*, translated by Walter Kaufmann. 1st Touchstone ed. New York: Touchstone, 1971.

Buhmann, Alexander, and Diana Ingenhoff. "The 4D Model of the Country Image: An Integrative Approach from the Perspective of Communication Management." *International Communication Gazette* 77, no. 1 (February 1, 2015): 102–24.

Bunseki, Fu-Kiau. *African Cosmology of the Bantu-Kongo: Tying the Spiritual Knot, Principles of Life and Living*. 2nd ed. Brooklyn, NY: Athelia Henrietta Press, 2001.

Burdett, Carolyn. "Post Darwin: Social Darwinism, Degeneration, Eugenics." *British Library, Discovering Literature: Romantics and Victorians* (blog), May 15, 2014. https://www.bl.uk/romantics-and-victorians/articles/post-darwin-social-darwinism-degeneration-eugenics#.

Burgoon, Judee K., Laura K. Guerrero, and Kory Floyd. "Social Cognition and Impression Formation." In *Nonverbal Communication,* 229–60. New York: Routledge: Taylor and Francis, 2010.

Burgoon, Judee K., and Jerold L. Hale. "The Fundamental Topoi of Relational Communication." *Communication Monographs* 51, no. 3 (1984): 193–214.

Burgoon, Judith, D. B. Buller, and W. G. Woodall. *Nonverbal Communication: The Unspoken Dialogue.* 2nd ed. New York: McGraw-Hill, 1996.

Burkart, J. M., O. Allon, F. Amici, C. Fichtel, C. Finkenwirth, A. Heschl, J. Huber, et al. "The Evolutionary Origin of Human Hyper-Cooperation." *Nature Communications* 5, no. 1 (August 27, 2014): 4747.

Bush, George W. "Press Conference," October 11, 2001. http://www.washingtonpost.com/wp-srv/nation/specials/attacked/transcripts/bush_text101101.html.

Buzan, Barry, and George Lawson. *The Global Transformation.* Cambridge: Cambridge University Press, 2015. https://doi.org/10.1017/CBO9781139565073.

Caprino, Kathy. "How Women Leaders Are Rising to the Unique Challenges They're Facing from the Pandemic." *Forbes,* May 18, 2020. https://www.forbes.com/sites/kathycaprino/2020/05/18/how-women-leaders-are-rising-to-the-unique-challenges-theyre-facing-from-the-pandemic/.

Carey, James W. *Communication as Culture: Essays on Media and Society.* Boston: Unwin Hyman, 1989.

Carlin, John. *Playing the Enemy: Nelson Mandela and the Game That Made a Nation.* New York: Penguin, 2008.

Carlson, Peter. "America's Glossy Envoy." *Washington Post,* August 9, 2003. https://www.washingtonpost.com/archive/politics/2003/08/09/americas-glossy-envoy/94567794-380c-4aad-b007-e324fe596145/.

Castells, Manuel. "The New Public Sphere: Global Civil Society, Communication Networks, and Global Governance." *The Annals of the American Academy of Political and Social Science* 616, no. 1 (March 1, 2008): 78–93.

Cavanaugh, Tim. "Hi Times: Citizen Powell's State Department Publishing Adventure." *Reason,* September 30, 2003. https://reason.com/2003/09/30/hi-times/.

CBS News. "Babies Help Unlock the Origins of Morality." *60 Minutes,* 2012. https://www.cbsnews.com/news/babies-help-unlock-the-origins-of-morality/.

Chai, Ch'u, and Winberg Chai, eds. *Li Chi Book of Rites: An Encyclopedia of Ancient Ceremonial Usages, Religious Creeds, and Social Institutions,* translated by James Legge 2 vols. New Hyde Park, NY: University Books, 1967. https://www.abebooks.com/Book-Rites-Encyclopedia-Ancient-Ceremonial-Usages/11814458402/bd.

Chan, Alan Kam-leung. *Mencius: Contexts and Interpretations.* Honolulu: University of Hawaii Press, 2002.

Chang, Hui-Ching, and G. Richard Holt. "More than Relationship: Chinese Interaction and the Principle of Kuan-Hsi." *Communication Quarterly* 39, no. 3 (1991): 251–71.

Chen, Guo-Ming. "Asian Communication Studies: What and Where to Now." *The Review of Communication* 6, no. 4 (2006): 295–311.

Chen, Guo-Ming. "An Introduction to Key Concepts in Understanding the Chinese: Harmony as the Foundation of Chinese Communication." *China Media Research* 7 (2011): 1–12.

Chen, Guo-Ming. "A Model of Global Communication Competence." *China Media Research* 1, no. 1 (2005): 3–11.

Chen, Guo-Ming. "Toward an I Ching Model of Communication." *China Media Research* 5, no. 3 (2009): 72–81.

Chen, Gou-Ming. "Toward Transcultural Understanding: A Harmony Theory of Chinese Communication." In *Transcultural Realities: Interdisciplinary Perspectives on Cross-Cultural Relations*, ed. Virginia Milhouse, Molefi Asante, and Peter Nwosu, 55–70. Thousand Oaks, CA: Sage, 2001.

Chen, Guo-Ming, and William J. Starosta. *Foundations of Intercultural Communication*. Boston: Allyn and Bacon, 1998.

Chen, Xiao-Ping, and Chao C. Chen. "On the Intricacies of the Chinese Guanxi: A Process Model of Guanxi Development." *Asia Pacific Journal of Management* 21, no. 3 (September 8, 2004): 305–24.

Childers, Carolyn. "Why Coronavirus Demands Women's Leadership," April 22, 2020. https://milkeninstitute.org/power-of-ideas/why-coronavirus-demands-womens-leadership.

Constitution of Chile. In *HeinOnline World Constitutions Illustrated*, s.v. "Chile". Chicago: University of Chicago Press, 2010.

Christakis, Nicholas A. *Blueprint: The Evolutionary Origins of a Good Society*. New York: Little, Brown Spark, 2019.

Clark, R. T. Rundle. *Myth and Symbol in Ancient Egypt*. New Impression ed. London: Thames & Hudson, 1991.

Coe, Kathryn, Nancy E. Aiken, and Craig T. Palmer. "Once upon a Time: Ancestors and the Evolutionary Significance of Stories." *Anthropological Forum* 16, no. 1 (March 1, 2006): 21–40. https://doi.org/10.1080/00664670600572421.

Cohen, Raymond. "All in the Family: Ancient Near Eastern Diplomacy." *International Negotiation* 1, no. 1 (January 1, 1996): 11–28.

Cohen, Raymond. "The Great Tradition: The Spread of Diplomacy in the Ancient World." *Diplomacy and Statecraft* 12, no. 1 (March 1, 2001): 23–38.

Cohen, Raymond, and Raymond Westbrook, eds. *Amarna Diplomacy: The Beginnings of International Relations*. Baltimore, MD: Johns Hopkins University Press, 2002.

9/11 Commission. "The 9/11 Commission Report," 2004. https://9-11commission.gov/report/911Report.pdf.

Comor, Edward, and Hamilton Bean. "America's 'Engagement' Delusion: Critiquing a Public Diplomacy Consensus." *International Communication Gazette* 74, no. 3 (April 1, 2012): 203–20. https://doi.org/10.1177/1748048511432603.

Condon, John C., and Fathi S. Yousef. *An Introduction to Intercultural Communication*. Indianapolis, IN: Bobbs-Merrill Series in Speech Communication, 1975.

Condon, William S., and Louis W. Sander. "Synchrony Demonstrated between Movements of the Neonate and Adult Speech." *Child Development* 45, no. 2 (1974): 456–62.

Confucius. *The Analects*, translated by William E. Soothill. Dover Thrift ed. New York: Dover Publications, 1910.

Conner, Cheryl Snapp. "In a Crisis, Use These 3 Forms of Empathy to Serve Your Customers Well." *Mission.Org* (blog), June 29, 2017. https://medium.com/the-mission/in-a-crisis-use-these-3-forms-of-empathy-to-serve-your-customers-well-35722ec88590.

Connor, Walker. "When Is a Nation?" In *Nationalism*, ed. John Hutchinson and Anthony D. Smith, 154–59. Oxford: Oxford University Press, 1994.

Conrad, Sebastian, Jürgen Osterhammel, and Akira Iriye. *An Emerging Modern World: 1750–1870*. A History of the World 4. Cambridge, MA: Harvard University Press, 2018.

Consigny, Scott Porter. *Gorgias, Sophist and Artist*. Columbia: University of South Carolina Press, 2001.

Constantinou, Costas M. "Everyday Diplomacy: Mission, Spectacle and the Remaking of Diplomatic Culture." In *Diplomatic Cultures and International Politics: Translations, Spaces and Alternatives*, ed. Jason Dittmer and Fiona McConnel, 23–40. New York: Routledge, 2016.

Constantinou, Costas M. "Between Statecraft and Humanism: Diplomacy and Its Forms of Knowledge." *International Studies Review* 15, no. 2 (June 1, 2013): 141–62.

Constantinou, Costas M. "Human Diplomacy and Spirituality." Discussion Papers in Diplomacy. Netherlands Institute of International Relations 'Clingendael,' 2006. https://www.google.com/books/edition/Human_Diplomacy_and_Spirituality/g-P3GgAACAAJ?hl=en

Constantinou, Costas M., and James Der Derian. "Introduction: Sustaining Global Hope: Sovereignty, Power and the Transformation of Diplomacy." In *Sustainable Diplomacies*, ed. Costas M. Constantinou and James Der Derian, 1–22. London: Palgrave Macmillan, 2010.

Constantinou, Costas M., and James Der Derian. *Sustainable Diplomacies*. London: Palgrave Macmillan, 2010. https://doi.org/10.1057/9780230297159.

Cooper, Andrew F., Brian Hocking, and William Maley, eds. *Global Governance and Diplomacy: Worlds Apart?* Houndmills: Palgrave Macmillan, 2008.

Cope, E. M. *An Introduction to Aristotle's Rhetoric: With Analysis, Notes and Appendices*. London: Macmillan and Co., 1867.

Copeland, Daryl. *Guerrilla Diplomacy: Rethinking International Relations*. New York: Lynne Rienner, 2009.

Cornago, Noé. *Plural Diplomacies: Normative Predicaments and Functional Imperatives*. Diplomatic Studies 8. Leiden: Martinus Nijhoff Publishers, 2013.

Council on Foreign Relations. "Public Diplomacy: A Strategy for Reform." Council on Foreign Relations, July 30, 2002. http://www.cfr.org/diplomacy-and-statecraft/public-diplomacy-strategy-reform/p4697.

Cowan, Geoffrey, and Amelia Arsenault. "Moving from Monologue to Dialogue to Collaboration: The Three Layers of Public Diplomacy." *The Annals of the American Academy of Political and Social Science* 616, no. 1 (2008): 10–30.

Craig, Robert T. "Communication." In *Encyclopedia of Rhetoric*, ed., Thomas O. Sloane, 125–37. New York: Oxford University Press, 2001.

Crawford, Neta C. "Institutionalizing Passion in World Politics: Fear and Empathy." *International Theory* 6, no. 3 (November 2014): 535–57. https://doi.org/10.1017/S1752971914000256.

Crawford, Neta C. "The Passion of World Politics: Propositions on Emotion and Emotional Relationships." *International Security* 24, no. 4 (April 1, 2000): 116–56.

Crivelli, Carlos, James A. Russell, Sergio Jarillo, and José-Miguel Fernández-Dols. "The Fear Gasping Face as a Threat Display in a Melanesian Society." *Proceedings of the National Academy of Sciences* 113, no. 44 (November 1, 2016): 12403–7. https://doi.org/10.1073/pnas.1611622113.

Cronin, Katherine A., Daniel J. Acheson, Penélope Hernández, and Angel Sánchez. "Hierarchy Is Detrimental for Human Cooperation." *Scientific Reports* 5, no. 1 (December 22, 2015): 18634.

Cull, Nicholas. "Introduction. Data Driven Public Diplomacy: Progress towards Measuring the Impact of Public Diplomacy and International Broadcasting Activities,"

2014. Accessed April 15, 2021. http://www.state.gov/documents/organization/231
945.pdf.

Cull, Nicholas J. *Public Diplomacy: Foundations for Global Engagement in the Digital Age.*
Cambridge: Polity, 2019.

Cull, Nicholas J. "Public Diplomacy: Taxonomies and Histories." *The Annals of the
American Academy of Political and Social Science* 616, no. 1 (2008): 31–54.

Cull, Nicholas J. "The Long Road to Public Diplomacy 2.0: The Internet in US Public
Diplomacy." *International Studies Review* 15, no. 1 (March 2013): 123–39.

Cull, Nicholas J., and Michael K. Hawes, eds. *Canada's Public Diplomacy.* Palgrave
Macmillan Series in Global Public Diplomacy. Switzerland: Palgrave Macmillan, 2021.

Cummins, Fred. "Voice, (Inter-)Subjectivity, and Real Time Recurrent Interaction."
Frontiers in Psychology 5 (2014): 1–10.

Cunningham, Robert B., and Yasin K. Sarayrah. *Wasta: The Hidden Force in Middle
Eastern Society.* Westport, CT: Praeger Publishers, 1993.

Damasio, Antonio. *Descartes' Error: Emotion, Reason, and the Human Brain.* Reprint ed.
London: Penguin Books, 2005.

Dance, Frank E. X. "The 'Concept' of Communication." *Journal of Communication* 20
(1970): 201–10.

Darwin, Charles. *The Descent of Man, and Selection in Relation to Sex.* United Kingdom: J.
Murray, 1871.

Darwin, Charles. *The Descent of Man and Selection in Relation to Sex.* New revised ed.
New York: D. Appleton, 1896.

Darwin, Charles. *The Expression of Emotion in Man and Animals (with an Introduction by
Paul Ekman).* New York: Oxford University Press, 1998. First published in 1872 by John
Murray, London.

Daya Kishan Thussu. *Communicating India's Soft Power: Buddha to Bollywood.* Palgrave
Macmillan Series in Global Public Diplomacy. New York: Palgrave Macmillan, 2013.
https://doi.org/10.1057/9781137027894.

de Bary, Wm Theodore, and Irene Bloom, eds. *Sources of Chinese Tradition: From Earliest
Times to 1600.* 2nd ed. New York: Columbia University Press, 1999.

de Costa, Ravi. "Indigenous Diplomacies before the Nation-State." In *Indigenous
Diplomacies,* ed., J. Marshall Beier, 61–77. New York: Palgrave Macmillan, 2009.

De Koven, Bernard. "Confluence." *DeepFUN* (blog), 2018. https://www.deepfun.com/con
fluence/. Accessed April 22, 2021.

De Koven, Bernard. *The Well-Played Game: A Player's Philosophy.* Illustrated ed.
Cambridge, MA: MIT Press, 2013.

de Mooij, Marieke. *Human and Mediated Communication around the World: A
Comprehensive Review and Analysis.* New York: Springer, 2014.

de Tocqueville, Alexis. *Democracy in America, Volume 2,* translated by Henry Reeve, revised Francis Bowen, editorial notes Phillips Bradley. New York: Vintage Books, 1945.

Deibert, Ronald J. *Parchment, Printing and Hypermedia: Communication and World
Order Transformation.* New York: Columbia University Press, 1997.

Dellios, Rosita. "Mandala: From Sacred Origins to Sovereign Affairs in Traditional
Southeast Asia." The Centre for East-West Cultural and Economic Studies, Research
Paper No. 10, 2003. http://www.international-relations.com/rp/WBrp10.html.

Der Derian, James. *On Diplomacy: A Genealogy of Western Estrangement.*
Oxford: Blackwell, 1987.

Derks, Daantje, Agneta H. Fischer, and Arjan E. R. Bos. "The Role of Emotion in Computer-Mediated Communication: A Review." *Computers in Human Behavior* 24, no. 3 (2008): 766–85.

DeVito, Joseph A. *The Interpersonal Communication Book*. 14th ed. Boston: Pearson, 2015.

Dimitrov, Roumen. "Silence and Invisibility in Public Relations." *Public Relations Review* 41, no. 5 (December 2015): 636–51. https://doi.org/10.1016/j.pubrev.2014.02.019.

Dinnie, Keith. *Nation Branding: Concepts, Issues, Practice*. London: Routledge, 2015.

DiSalvo, Charles R. *Gandhi: The Man before the Mahatma*. Berkeley: University of California Press, 2013.

Dissanayake, Wimal. "The Need for the Study of Asian Approaches to Communication." In *AMIC-Thammasat University Symposium on Mass Communication Theory*, 1–17. Bangkok: Singapore: Asian Mass Communication Research and Information Centre, 1985.

Dissanayake, Wimal. "Nagarjuna and Modern Communication Theory." *China Media Research* 3, no. 4 (2007): 34–41.

Dissanayake, Wimal. "The Desire to Excavate Asian Theories of Communication: One Strand of the History." *Journal of Multicultural Discourses* 4, no. 1 (2009): 7–27.

Dissanayake, Wimal. "The Idea of Verbal Communication in Early Buddhism." *China Media Research* 4, no. 2 (2008): 69–76.

Djerejian, Edward P. "Changing Minds, Winning Peace: A New Strategic Direction for US Public Diplomacy in the Arab and Muslim World." Washington, DC: Advisory Group on Public Diplomacy, U.S. Department of State, October 2003.

Dobele, Angela, Adam Lindgreen, Michael Beverland, Joëlle Vanhamme, and Robert van Wijk. "Why Pass on Viral Messages? Because They Connect Emotionally." *Business Horizons* 50, no. 4 (July 2007): 291–304.

Dodd, Carley. *Dynamics of Intercultural Communication*. Dubuque, IA: William C. Brown, 1982.

Duncombe, Constance. "Digital Diplomacy: Emotion and Identity in the Public Realm." *The Hague Journal of Diplomacy* 14, no. 1–2 (April 22, 2019): 102–16. https://doi.org/10.1163/1871191X-14101016.

Dutta-Bergman, Mohan J. "U.S. Public Diplomacy in the Middle East." *Journal of Communication Inquiry* 30, no. 2 (April 2006): 102–24. https://doi.org/10.1177/0196859905285286.

Dymond, Jonny. "Queen's Coronavirus Speech: 'Ambitious' Words 'to Reassure and Inspire.'" *BBC News*, April 5, 2020, sec. UK. https://www.bbc.com/news/uk-52176209.

Earley, P. Christopher, and Cristina B. Gibson. "Taking Stock in Our Progress on Individualism-Collectivism: 100 Years of Solidarity and Community." *Journal of Management* 24, no. 3 (1998): 265–304.

Ekman, Paul. "Darwin's Compassionate View of Human Nature." *JAMA* 303, no. 6 (February 10, 2010): 557.

Ekman, Paul. "Darwin's Contributions to Our Understanding of Emotional Expressions." *Philosophical Transactions of the Royal Society B: Biological Sciences* 364, no. 1535 (December 12, 2009): 3449–51.

Ekman, Paul. "What Scientists Who Study Emotion Agree about." *Perspectives on Psychological Science* 11, no. 1 (January 1, 2016): 31–34.

Ekman, Paul, and Wallace V. Friesen. "The Repertoire of Nonverbal Behavior: Categories, Origins, Usage and Coding." *Semiotica* 1 (1969): 49–98.

Ekman, Paul, and Wallace V. Friesen. "Constants across Cultures in the Face and Emotion." *Journal of Personality and Social Psychology* 17, no. 2 (1971): 124–9.

Ekman, Paul, Wallace V. Friesen, and Phoebe Ellsworth. *Emotion in the Human Face*. New York: Pergamon, 1972.

Ekman, Paul, E. Richard Sorenson, and Wallace V. Friesen. "Pan-Cultural Elements in Facial Displays of Emotion." *Science* 164, no. 3875 (April 4, 1969): 86–88.

Emirbayer, Mustafa. "Manifesto for a Relational Sociology." *American Journal of Sociology* 103, no. 2 (1997): 281–317.

Enos, Theresa. *Encyclopedia of Rhetoric and Composition: Communication from Ancient Times to the Information Age*. New York: Taylor & Francis, 1996.

Enriquez, Virgilio G. "Developing a Filipino Psychology." In *Indigenous Psychologies: Research and Experience in Cultural Context*, ed. Uichol Kim and John Berry, 152–69. Cross-Cultural Research and Methodology Series 17. Thousand Oaks: Sage, 1993.

Evans, Dylan, and Pierre Cruse. *Emotion, Evolution and Rationality*. Oxford: Oxford University Press, 2004.

Evans, James. *The History and Practice of Ancient Astronomy*. New York: Oxford University Press, 1998.

Ezzaher, Lahcen E., Fārābī, Avicenna, and Averroës. *Three Arabic Treatises on Aristotle's Rhetoric: The Commentaries of al-Fārābī, Avicenna, and Averroes*. Landmarks in Rhetoric and Public Address. Carbondale: Southern Illinois University Press, 2015.

Fabri, Marc, David J. Moore, and Dave J. Hobbs. "The Emotional Avatar: Non-Verbal Communication between Inhabitants of Collaborative Virtual Environments." In *Gesture-Based Communication in Human-Computer Interaction*, ed. Annelies Braffort, Rachid Gherbi, Sylvie Gibet, Daniel Teil, and James Richardson, 269–73. Lecture Notes in Computer Science. Berlin: Springer, 1999.

Faizullaev, Alisher. "Diplomacy and Symbolism." *The Hague Journal of Diplomacy* 8, no. 2 (January 1, 2013): 91–114.

Fakhreddine, Jihad. "US Public Diplomacy in Broken Arabic: Evaluating the Shared Values Advertising Campaign Targeting Arab and Muslim Worlds." *Global Media Journal* 2, no. 4 (Spring 2004): 1–5. https://www.globalmediajournal.com/open-acc ess/us-public-diplomacy-in-broken-arabic.pdf.

Fei, Xiaotong. *From the Soil, the Foundations of Chinese Society: A Translation of Fei Xiaotong's Xiangtu Zhongguo, with an Introduction and Epilogue*. Berkeley: University of California Press, 1992.

Fein, Melvyn L. *Human Hierarchies: A General Theory*. New Brunswick, NJ: Transaction Publishers, 2012.

Femenia, N. "Emotional Actor: Foreign Policy Decision-Making in the 1982 Falklands/ Malvinas War." In *Social Conflicts and Collective Identities*, ed. P. Coy and L. Woehrle, 41–66. Lanham, MD: Rowman & Littlefield, 2000.

Finn, Ed. "Unhip, Unhip Al Hurra, The Middle East Hates Its New TV Station." *Slate*, February 20, 2004. https://slate.com/news-and-politics/2004/02/the-middle-east-hates-its-new-tv-station.html.

Fischer, Agneta H., Antony S. R. Manstead, Michael Lewis, Jannette Haviland-Jones, and Lisa Feldman Barrett. "Social Functions of Emotion." In *Handbook of Emotions*, 3rd ed., ed. Michael Lewis, Jannette Haviland-Jones, and Lisa Feldman Barrett, 456–70. New York: Guilford, 2008.

Fisher, Ali. *Collaborative Public Diplomacy: How Transnational Networks Influenced American Studies in Europe.* New York: Palgrave Macmillan, 2013.

Fisher, Walter R. *Human Communication as Narration: Toward a Philosophy of Reason, Value, and Action.* Columbia: University of South Carolina Press, 1987.

Fitzpatrick, Kathy. *The Future of U.S. Public Diplomacy: An Uncertain Fate.* Leiden; Boston: Brill–Nijhoff, 2010.

Fitzpatrick, Kathy R. "Public Diplomacy in the Public Interest." *Journal of Public Interest Communication* 1, no. 1 (2017): 78–93.

Fletcher, Richard, and Tony Fang. "Assessing the Impact of Culture on Relationship Creation and Network Formation in Emerging Asian Markets." *European Journal of Marketing* 40, no. 3/4 (2006): 430–46.

Fotouhi, Babak, Naghmeh Momeni, Benjamin Allen, Martin A. Nowak, Naghmeh Momeni, Benjamin Allen, and Martin A. Nowak. "Conjoining Uncooperative Societies Facilitates Evolution of Cooperation." *Nature Human Behaviour* 2, no. 7 (July 2018): 492–99. https://doi.org/10.1038/s41562-018-0368-6.

Fourie, Pieter J. "Communication, Cultural and Media Studies: Ubuntuism as a Framework for South African Media Practice and Performance: Can It Work?" *Communication* 34, no. 1 (2008): 53–79.

"Games Industry Unites to Promote World Health Organization Messages against COVID-19; Launch #PlayApartTogether Campaign." *Bloomberg.Com*, April 10, 2020. https://www.bloomberg.com/press-releases/2020-04-10/games-industry-unites-to-promote-world-health-organization-messages-against-covid-19-launch-playapart together-campaign.

Ganz, Marshall. "Leading Change: Leadership, Organization, and Social Movements," in *Handbook of Leadership Theory and Practice: A Harvard Business School Centennial Colloquium* ed. Nitin Nohria and Rakesh Khurana, 509–50. Cambridge, MA: Harvard Business School Press, 2010.

Garikipati, Supriya, and Uma Kambhampati. "Leading the Fight against the Pandemic: Does Gender 'Really' Matter?" SSRN Scholarly Paper. Rochester, NY: Social Science Research Network, June 3, 2020.

Garsd, Jasmine. "Musicians Are Doing Virtual Concerts during COVID-19." *Marketplace* (blog), April 27, 2020. https://www.marketplace.org/2020/04/27/musicians-virtual-concerts-covid19-pandemic/.

Gautam, Pradeep Kumar, Saurabh Mishra, and Arvind Gupta. *Indigenous Historical Knowledge: Kautilya and His Vocabulary.* Vol. 1. New Delhi: Pentagon Press, 2015. https://idsa.in/system/files/book/book_IndigenousHistoricalKnowledge_Vol-I.pdf.

Geertz, Clifford. *Local Knowledge: Further Essays in Interpretive Anthropology.* New York: Basic Books, 1983.

Gehrke, Pat, and William M. Keith. *A Century of Communication Studies: The Unfinished Conversation.* New York: Routledge, 2015.

Gerber, Matthew G. "On the Consideration of 'Public Diplomacy' as a Rhetorical Genre." *Contemporary Argumentation and Debate* 29 (2008): 118–33.

Gerring, John. "What Makes a Concept Good? A Criterial Framework for Understanding Concept Formation in the Social Sciences." *Polity* 31, no. 3 (1999): 357–93.

Gershon, Michael. *The Second Brain: A Groundbreaking New Understanding of Nervous Disorders of the Stomach and Intestine.* New York: Harper Perennial, 1998.

Ghazanfar, Asif A., and Daniel Y. Takahashi. "The Evolution of Speech: Vision, Rhythm, Cooperation." *Trends in Cognitive Sciences* 18, no. 10 (October 2014): 543–53.

Ghonim, Wael. *Revolution 2.0: The Power of the People Is Greater Than the People in Power: A Memoir*. Boston: Houghton Mifflin Harcourt, 2012.

Goleman, Daniel. *Emotional Intelligence: Why It Can Matter More Than IQ*. 10th Anniversary ed. New York: Bantam, 2005.

Good Country Index. Good Country, (website) 2021. https://www.goodcountry.org/.

Gordon, Ronald D. "Beyond the Failures of Western Communication Theory." *Journal of Multicultural Discourses* 2, no. 2 (2007): 89–107. https://doi.org/10.2167/md090.0.

Goswami, Nina. "Have Female CEOs Coped Better with Covid Than Men?" *BBC News*, November 19, 2020, sec. Business. https://www.bbc.com/news/business-54974132.

Gottschall, Jonathan. *The Storytelling Animal: How Stories Make Us Human*. New York: Mariner Books, 2013.

Gouldner, Alvin W. "The Norm of Reciprocity: A Preliminary Statement." *American Sociological Review* 25, no. 2 (1960): 161–78.

Graham, James. "Nā Rangi Tāua, Nā Tūānuku e Takoto Nei: Research Methodology Framed by Whakapapa." *MAI Review*, no. 1 (2009): 1–9.

Graham, Sarah Ellen. "Emotion and Public Diplomacy: Dispositions in International Communications, Dialogue, and Persuasion." *International Studies Review* 16, no. 4 (2014): 522–39.

Grandados, Samuel, Zoeann Murphy, Kevin Schaul, and Anthony Faiola. "Raising Barriers: A New Age of Walls." *Washington Post*, October 12, 2016. https://www.was hingtonpost.com/graphics/world/border-barriers/global-illegal-immigration-pre vention/.

Gregory, Andrew. *Ancient Greek Cosmogony*. London: Bloomsbury Academic, 2013.

Gregory, Bruce. "American Public Diplomacy: Enduring Characteristics, Elusive Transformation." *The Hague Journal of Diplomacy* 6, no. 3 (2011): 351–72. https://doi. org/10.1163/187119111X583941.

Gronbeck, Bruce E. *The Articulate Person*. Glenview, IL: Scott, Foresman, 1983.

Gruver, D. M. Dusty. "The Earth as Family: A Traditional Hawaiian View with Current Applications." In *Philosophy, Humanity and Ecology: Philosophy of Nature and Environmental Ethics*, ed., H. Odera Oruka, 301–5. Darby, PA: DIANE Publishing, 1996.

Gruzd, Anatoliy, Barry Wellman, and Yuri Takhteyev. "Imagining Twitter as an Imagined Community." *American Behavioral Scientist* 55, no. 10 (2011): 1294–318.

Gulbrandsen, Ib Tunby, and Sine Nørholm Just. "The Collaborative Paradigm: Towards an Invitational and Participatory Concept of Online Communication." *Media, Culture & Society* 33, no. 7 (2011): 1095–1108.

Gulmez, Seçkin Barış. "Cosmopolitan Diplomacy." In *Routledge International Handbook of Cosmopolitanism Studies*, ed., Gerard Delanty, 430–439. New York: Routledge, 2018.

Gunaratne, Shelton A. "De-Westernizing Communication/Social Science Research: Opportunities and Limitations." *Media, Culture & Society* 32, no. 3 (2010): 473–500.

Guthrie, Kenneth Sylvan (compiled and trans.). *The Pythagorean Sourcebook and Library: An Anthology of Ancient Writings Which Relate to Pythagoras and Pythagorean Philosophy*, ed., David Fideler. Revised ed. Grand Rapids: Phanes Press, 1987.

Habermas, Jurgen. *The Structural Transformation of the Public Sphere: An Inquiry into a Category of Bourgeois Society*. Cambridge, MA: MIT Press, 1991.

Hafner-Burton, Emilie M., Miles Kahler, and Alexander H. Montgomery. "Network Analysis for International Relations." *International Organization* 63, no. 3 (2009): 559–92.

Hahn, Laura K., Lance Lippert, and Scott T. Paynton. *Survey of Communication Study*. Wikibooks, 2014. https://en.wikibooks.org/wiki/Survey_of_Communication_Study, 2017. http://www.csus.edu/indiv/s/stonerm/coms5surveyofcommunicationtextb ook.pdf.

Hall, Edward T. *An Anthropology of Everyday Life*. New York: Doubleday, 1992.

Hall, Edward T. *Beyond Culture*. (Anchor Books Edition). New York: Anchor Books, 1977.

Hall, Edward T. *The Dance of Life: The Other Dimension of Time*. New York: Anchor Books, 1984.

Hall, Edward T. *The Silent Language*. (originally published Doubleday, 1959) New York: Anchor Books, 1973.

Hall, Edward T. *Understanding Cultural Differences*. Yarmouth, ME: Intercultural Press, 1990.

Hamilton, Edith. *The Greek Way*. New York: Avon, 1930.

Hamilton, Keith, and Richard Langhorne. *The Practice of Diplomacy: Its Evolution, Theory and Administration*. New York: Routledge, 2013.

Hanson, Fergus. "Baked in and Wired: eDiplomacy @State." Foreign Policy Paper Series. Washington DC: The Brookings Institution, 2012. https://www.brookings.edu/resea rch/baked-in-and-wired-ediplomacy-state/.

Harari, Yuval Noah. *Sapiens: A Brief History of Humankind*. Reprint ed. New York: Harper Perennial, 2018.

"Harmony of the Spheres." Ancient Wisdom. www.ancient-wisdom.com/harmonics.htm, Accessed April 22, 2021.

Harrison, Patricia. The 9/11 Commission Recommendations on Public Diplomacy: Defending Ideals and Defining the Message, § Subcommittee on National Security, Emerging Threats and International Relations, Committee on Government Reform, U.S. House of Representatives (2004). https://www.govinfo.gov/content/pkg/ CHRG-108hhrg98211/html/CHRG-108hhrg98211.htm.

Hassig, Ross. *Time, History, and Belief in Aztec and Colonial Mexico*. Illustrated ed. Austin: University of Texas Press, 2001.

Hayden, Craig. *The Rhetoric of Soft Power: Public Diplomacy in Global Contexts*. Lanham, MD: Lexington Books, 2012.

Hayles, N. Katherine. *How We Became Posthuman: Virtual Bodies in Cybernetics, Literature, and Informatics*. Chicago, IL: University of Chicago Press, 1999.

Higgins, Kathleen Marie. "An Alchemy of Emotion: Rasa and Aesthetic Breakthroughs." *The Journal of Aesthetics and Art Criticism* 65, no. 1 (2007): 43–54.

Ho, David Y. F. "Interpersonal Relationships and Relationship Dominance: An Analysis Based on Methodological Relationism." *Asian Journal of Social Psychology* 1, no. 1 (1998): 1–16. https://doi.org/10.1111/1467-839X.00002.

Ho, David Y. F., Si-qing Peng, Alice Cheng Lai, and Shui-fun F. Chan. "Indigenization and beyond: Methodological Relationalism in the Study of Personality across Cultural Traditions." *Journal of Personality* 69, no. 6 (2001): 925–53. https://doi.org/10.1111/ 1467-6494.696170.

Hocking, Brian L. "Introduction: Gatekeepers and Boundary-Spanners: Thinking about Foreign Ministries in the European Union." In *Foreign Ministries in the European Union: Integrating Diplomats*, ed. Brian Hocking and David Spence, 1–16. Basingstoke: Palgrave, 2005.

Hofstede, Geert. *Culture's Consequences: National Differences in Thinking and Organizing*. Beverly Hills, CA: Sage, 1980.

Holmes, Marcus. "Believing This and Alieving That: Theorizing Affect and Intuitions in International Politics." *International Studies Quarterly* 59, no. 4 (2015): 706–20.

Holmes, Marcus. *Face-to-Face Diplomacy: Social Neuroscience and International Relations.* Cambridge, UK: Cambridge University Press, 2018.

Holmes, Marcus. "The Force of Face-to-Face Diplomacy: Mirror Neurons and the Problem of Intentions." *International Organization* 67, no. 4 (2013): 829–61.

Holpuch, Amanda. "'A Lifesaver': US Seniors Turn to Zoom to Connect with Friends and Family." *The Guardian*, September 18, 2020, sec. US news. http://www.theguardian.com/us-news/2020/sep/18/us-seniors-video-calls-zoom-coronavirus.

Horst W. J. Rittel and Melvin M. Webber. "Dilemmas in a General Theory of Planning." *Policy Sciences* 4, no. 2 (1973): 155–69.

Howard, Philip N., and Malcolm R. Parks. "Social Media and Political Change: Capacity, Constraint, and Consequence." *Journal of Communication* 62, no. 2 (2012): 359–62.

Hudson, Lucian J. "The Enabling State: Collaborating for Success." London: Foreign Commonwealth Office, 2009. https://webarchive.nationalarchives.gov.uk/2010051 3203926/http://www.fco.gov.uk/resources/en/pdf/pdf9/enabling-state-v3.

Huijgh, Ellen. "Changing Tunes for Public Diplomacy: Exploring the Domestic Dimension." *Exchange: The Journal of Public Diplomacy* 2, no. 1 (2013): 1–12.

Huijgh, Ellen. "Indonesia's 'Intermestic' Public Diplomacy: Features and Future." *Policy & Politics* 45, no. 5 (2017): 762–92.

Huijgh, Ellen. *Public Diplomacy at Home: Domestic Dimensions.* Leiden; Boston: Brill–Nijhoff, 2019.

Hung, F. C. "Toward the Theory of Relationship Management in Public Relations: How to Cultivate Quality in Relationships?" In *The Future of Excellence in Public Relations and Communication Management*, ed., E. L. Toth, 443–476. Mahwah, NJ: Lawrence Erlbaum, 2007.

Hurteau, Robert. "Navigating the Limitations of Western Approaches to the Intercultural Encounter: The Works of Walter Ong and Harry Triandis." *Missiology* 34, no. 2 (2006): 201–17.

Hutchings, Kate, and David Weir. "Guanxi and Wasta: A Comparison." *Thunderbird International Business Review* 48, no. 1 (2006): 141–56.

Hutchings, Kate, and David Weir. "Understanding Networking in China and the Arab World: Lessons for International Managers." *Journal of European Industrial Training* 30, no. 4 (2006): 272–90.

Hutchinson, John, and Anthony D. Smith. "The Rise of Nations" In *Nationalism*, ed. John Hutchinson and Anthony D. Smith, 113–132. Oxford: Oxford University Press, 1994.

Hutchison, Emma, and Roland Bleiker. "Theorizing Emotions in World Politics." *International Theory* 6, no. 3 (2014): 491–514. https://doi.org/10.1017/S175297191 4000232.

Hwang, Kwang-Kuo. "Chinese Relationalism: Theoretical Construction and Methodological Considerations." *Journal for the Theory of Social Behaviour* 30, no. 2 (2000): 155–78.

Iacoboni, Marco. *Mirroring People: The Science of Empathy and How We Connect with Others.* New York: Picador, 2009.

Ibn Khaldun. *The Muqaddimah: An Introduction to History*, ed., N. J. Dawood, translated by Franz Rosenthal. Bollingen Series. Princeton, NJ: Princeton University Press, 1967.

Innis, Harold Adams. *The Bias of Communication.* Toronto: University of Toronto Press, 1951.

International Social Science Council, and UNESCO's Director-General, 2009–2017. *World Social Science Report, 2010: Knowledge Divides*. Paris: UNESCO, 2010. https://unesdoc.unesco.org/ark:/48223/pf0000188333.

Iriye, Akira. *Global Community: The Role of International Organizations in the Making of the Contemporary World*. Berkeley: University of California Press, 2002.

Iriye, Akira, Jürgen Osterhammel, Wilfried Loth, Thomas W. Zeiler, and J. R. Mcneill. *Global Interdependence: The World after 1945*. Cambridge, MA: Harvard University Press, 2014.

Ishii, Satoshi. "Complementing Contemporary Intercultural Communication Research with East Asian Sociocultural Perspectives and Practices." *China Media Research* 2, no. 1 (2006): 13–20.

Ishii, Satoshi. "Conceptualising Asian Communication Ethics: A Buddhist Perspective." *Journal of Multicultural Discourses* 4, no. 1 (March 2009): 49–60. https://doi.org/10.1080/17447140802651645.

Ishii, Satoshi. "Enryo-Sasshi Communication: A Key to Understanding Japanese Interpersonal Relations." *Cross Currents* 11, no. 1 (1984): 49–58.

Ito, Y. "Mass Communication Theories from a Japanese Perspective." *Media, Culture & Society* 12 (1990): 423–64.

Jackson, Patrick. "Twisting Tongues and Twisting Arms: The Power of Political Rhetoric." *Journal of International Relations* 13 (2006): 35–66.

Jain, Nemi C., and Anuradha Matukumalli. "The Functions of Silence in India: Implications for Intercultural Communication Research." In *The Global Intercultural Communication Reader*, ed. Molefi Asante, Yoshitaka Miike, and J. Yin, 248–54. New York: Routledge, (2008).

Jennings, Francis. *The History and Culture of Iroquois Diplomacy: An Interdisciplinary Guide to the Treaties of the Six Nations and Their League*. Syracuse, NY: Syracuse University Press, 1995.

Jo, Samsup, and Yungwook Kim. "Media or Personal Relations? Exploring Media Relations Dimensions in South Korea." *Journalism & Mass Communication Quarterly* 81, no. 2 (2004): 292–306.

Johnston, Douglas. *Faith-Based Diplomacy: Trumping Realpolitik*. New York: Oxford University Press, 2003. https://oxford.universitypressscholarship.com/view/10.1093/acprof:oso/9780195367935.001.0001/acprof-9780195367935.

Jones, Reece. "Borders and Walls: Do Barriers Deter Unauthorized Migration?" migrationpolicy.org, 2016. https://www.migrationpolicy.org/article/borders-and-walls-do-barriers-deter-unauthorized-migration.

Jönsson, Christer. "Diplomatic Signaling in the Amarna Letters." In *Amarna Diplomacy*, ed. Raymond Cohen and Raymond Westbrook, 191–204. Baltimore, MD: Johns Hopkins University Press, 2000.

Jönsson, Christer. Relationships between Negotiators: A Neglected Topic in the Study of Negotiation. *International Negotiation* 20 (2015): 7–24.

Jönsson, Christer, and Martin Hall. *Essence of Diplomacy*. Basingstoke: Palgrave MacMillan, 2005.

Kamoliddin, Shamsiddin. "On the Religion of the Samanid Ancestors." *Transoxiana, Journal Libre de Estudios Orientales* 11 (July 2006). http://www.transoxiana.org/11/kamoliddin-samanids.html.

Kampf, Ronit, Ilan Manor, and Elad Segev. "Digital Diplomacy 2.0? A Cross-National Comparison of Public Engagement in Facebook and Twitter." *The Hague Journal of Diplomacy* 10, no. 4 (2015): 331–62.

Kang, David. "Korea's Emotional Diplomacy." *Public Diplomacy Magazine*, no. 2 (2009): 64–67.

Kashima, Emiko S., and Elizabeth A. Hardie. "The Development and Validation of the Relational, Individual, and Collective Self-Aspects (RIC) Scale." *Asian Journal of Social Psychology* 3, no. 1 (2000): 19–48.

Katz, Michal. "Commentary: The COVID Crisis Shows Why We Need More Female Leadership." *Fortune*, March 17, 2020. https://fortune.com/2021/03/17/covid-female-women-leadership-jacinda-ardern/.

Kelley, John Robert. *Agency Change: Diplomatic Action beyond the State*. Lanham, MD: Rowman & Littlefield, 2014.

Kennedy, George Alexander. *Comparative Rhetoric: An Historical and Cross-Cultural Introduction*. New York: Oxford University Press, 1998.

Khouri, Rami. "The US Public Diplomacy Hoax: Why Do They Keep Insulting Us?" *The Daily Star*. February 11, 2004. http://www.dailystar.com.lb//Opinion/Comment ary/2004/Feb-11/92631-the-us-public-diplomacy-hoax-why-do-they-keep-insult ing-us.ashx.

Khoury-Machool, Makram. "Losing Iraqi Hearts and Minds." Iraqi Crisis Report. Global Vision News Network, June 11, 2003. https://iwpr.net/global-voices/losing-iraqi-hearts-and-minds

Kilner, J. M., and R. N. Lemon. "What We Know Currently about Mirror Neurons." *Current Biology* 23, no. 23 (2013): R1057–62. https://doi.org/10.1016/j.cub.2013.10.051.

Kim, Min-Sun. *Non-Western Perspectives on Human Communication: Implications for Theory and Practice*. Thousand Oaks, CA: Sage Publications, 2002.

Kim, Uichol. "Psychology, Science, and Culture: Cross-Cultural Analysis of National Psychologies." *International Journal of Psychology* 30, no. 6 (1995): 663–79.

Kim, Young Yun. "Achieving Synchrony: A Foundational Dimension of Intercultural Communication Competence." *International Journal of Intercultural Relations*, 48 (2015): 27–37.

Kincaid, D. Lawrence. *Communication Theory: Eastern and Western Perspectives*. San Diego: Academic Press, 2013.

Kirk, Emma. "Peace in the Chaos: Implications of the Conscious Elimination of Conflict in Divinely Designed and Spontaneous Creation from the Hebrew and Chinese Traditions." Sydney: Macquarie University, 2015.

Kirk, G. S., J. E. Raven, and M. Schofield. *The Presocratic Philosophers: A Critical History with a Selection of Texts*. United Kingdom: Cambridge University Press, 1983.

Kluckhohn, Florence. "Dominant and Variant Value Orientations." In *Personality in Nature, Society and Culture*, ed. Clyde Kluckhohn and Henry A. Murray, 2nd ed., 342–355. New York: Alfred A. Knopf, 1953.

Kluckhohn, Florence Rockwood, and Fred L. Strodtbeck. *Variations in Value Orientations*. Evanston, IL: Row, Peterson, 1961.

Knapp, Mark L. *Interpersonal Communication and Human Relationships*. 3rd ed. Boston: Allyn and Bacon, 1996.

Knapp, Mark L. *Nonverbal Communication in Human Interaction*. New York: Holt, Rinehart and Winston. Inc., 1972.

Brian Knowlton, "Lugar Says U.S. is All Thumbs in Dealing with Muslims," *The New York Times*, October 29, 2003, https://www.nytimes.com/2003/10/29/international/middleeast/lugar-says-us-is-all-thumbs-in-dealing-with-muslims.html.

Kohut, Andrew, and Bruce Stokes. *America against the World: How We Are Different and Why We Are Disliked*. New York: Henry Holt and Co., 2007.

Korzenny, Felipe, and Betty Ann Korzenny. *Hispanic Marketing: A Cultural Perspective*. Burlington, MA: Elsevier/Butterworth-Heinemann, 2005.

Kraidy, Marwan M. *Hybridity: The Cultural Logic of Globalization*. Philadelphia: Temple University Press, 2005.

Kreuzbauer, R., S. Lin, and C-Y. Chiu. "Relational versus Group Collectivism and Optimal Distinctiveness in Consumption Context." *Advances in Consumer Research* 36 (2009): 472.

Krog, Antjie. "'. . . If It Means He Gets His Humanity Back . . .': The Worldview Underpinning the South African Truth and Reconciliation Commission." *Journal of Multicultural Discourses* 3, no. 3 (2008): 204–20.

Kuhn, Thomas S. *The Structure of Scientific Revolutions*. 3rd ed. Chicago, IL: University of Chicago Press, 1996.

Kunczik, Michael. *Images of Nations and International Public Relations*. Mahwah, NJ: Routledge, 1996.

Kurzweil, Ray. *The Singularity Is Near: When Humans Transcend Biology*. New York: The Viking Press, 2005.

Lafont, Bertrand. "International Relations in the Ancient Near East: The Birth of a Complete Diplomatic System." *Diplomacy and Statecraft* 12, no. 1 (2001): 39–60.

Larson, Charles U. *Persuasion: Reception and Responsibility*. 6th ed. Belmont, CA: Wadsworth Publishing, 1992.

Lasswell, Harold D. "The Structure and Function of Communication in Society." *The Communication of Ideas* 37 (1948): 215–28.

Leathers, Dale, and Michael H. Eaves. "Impression Management." In *Successful Nonverbal Communication: Principles and Applications* ed. Dale Leathers and Michael H. Eaves, 4th ed., 187–208. New York: Pearsons, 2007.

Leavitt, Harold J. "Why Hierarchies Thrive." *Harvard Business Review* 81, no. 3 (2003): 96–102, 141.

Lebow, Richard Ned. "Reason, Emotion and Cooperation." *International Politics* 42, no. 3 (2005): 283–313.

Ledoux, Joseph. *The Emotional Brain: The Mysterious Underpinnings of Emotional Life*. New York: Simon & Schuster, 1998.

Lee, Dorothy. "A Lineal and Nonlineal Codification of Reality." In *The Production of Reality*, ed. P. Kollock and J. O'Brien, 101–11. Thousand Oaks, CA: Pine-Forge Press, 1977.

Leeds-Hurwitz, Wendy. "Notes in the History of Intercultural Communication: The Foreign Service Institute and the Mandate for Intercultural Training." In *Readings in Cultural Contexts*, ed. Judith N. Martin, Thomas K. Nakayama, and Lisa A. Flores, 15–28. Mountain View, CA: Mayfield Publishing, 1998.

Leeming, David A., and Margaret Adams Leeming. *Encyclopedia of Creation Myths*. Santa Barbara, CA: ABC-CLIO, 1994.

León-Portilla, Miguel. *Aztec Thought and Culture: A Study of the Ancient Nahuatl Mind*. Translated by Jack Emory Davis. Revised ed. Norman: University of Oklahoma Press, 1990.

León-Portilla, Miguel. *The Broken Spears: The Aztec Account of the Conquest of Mexico.* Boston: Beacon Press, 2006.

Levine, Donald Nathan. *The Flight from Ambiguity: Essays in Social and Cultural Theory.* Chicago: University of Chicago Press, 1985.

Lewis, Mark Edward. *The Flood Myths of Early China.* Albany: State University of New York Press, 2006.

Lin, Nan. "Building a Network Theory of Social Capital." *Connections* 22, no. 1 (1999): 28–51.

Lindquist, Kristen A. "Language and Emotion: Introduction to the Special Issue," *Affective Science* 2 (2021): 91–98.

Lindquist, Kristen A. and Maria Gendron, and Ajay B. Satpute, "Language and Emotion: Putting Words into Feelings and Feelings into Words," in *Handbook of Emotions*, 4th ed., ed. Lisa Feldman Barrett, Michael Lewis, and Jeannette Haviland-Jones, 579–594. New York: Guilford Press, 2016.

Littlejohn, Stephen W., and Karen A. Foss. *Theories of Human Communication.* 10th ed. Long Grove, IL: Waveland Press, 2010.

Liu, Shuang. "Hierarchy (Dengji): A Pyramid of Interconnected Relationships." *China Media Research* 7, no. 4 (2011): 77–84.

Liverani, Mario. "The Great Powers' Club." In *Amarna Diplomacy*, ed. Raymond Cohen and Raymond Westbrook, 15–27. Baltimore, MD: Johns Hopkins University Press, 2000.

Lloyd, G. E. R. *Magic, Reason and Experience: Studies in the Origins and Development of Greek Science.* London, Duckworth: 1999.

Lucaites, John Louis, Celeste Michelle Condit, and Sally Caudill. *Contemporary Rhetorical Theory: A Reader.* New York: Guilford Press, 1999.

Lugar, Richard. U.S. Senate Foreign Relations Committee, "Opening Statement for Nomination Hearings for Margaret D. Tutwiler for Undersecretary of State for Public Diplomacy," October 29, 2003, https://www.foreign.senate.gov/hearings/2003/10/29/nomination

Lyons, Jonathan. *The House of Wisdom: How Arab Learning Transformed Western Civilization.* New York: Bloomsbury Press, 2009.

Maccoby, Nathan. "The New 'Scientific' Rhetoric." In *The Science of Human Communication: New Directions and New Findings in Communication Research*, ed., Wilbur Schramm, 41–54. New York: Basic Books, 1963.

MacGaffey, Wyatt. "Constructing a Kongo Identity: Scholarship and Mythopoesis." *Comparative Studies in Society and History* 58, no. 1 (2016): 159–80.

MacGaffey, Wyatt. *Religion and Society in Central Africa.* Chicago: University of Chicago Press, 1986.

Maddux, William W., and Masaki Yuki. "The Ripple Effect: Cultural Differences in Perceptions of the Consequences of Events." *Personality and Social Psychology Bulletin* 32, no. 5 (2006): 669–83.

Maffie, James. *Aztec Philosophy: Understanding a World in Motion.* Boulder: University Press of Colorado, 2015.

Maffie, James. "Pre-Columbian Philosophies." In *A Companion to Latin American Philosophy*, ed. Susana Nuccetelli, Ofelia Schutte, and Otávio Bueno, 9–22. New York,:Wiley & Sons, 2013.

Major, John S. *The Huainanzi*, translated and eds., Sarah A. Queen, Andrew Seth Meyer, and Harold D. Roth, with additional contributions by Michael Puett and Judson Murray. New York: Columbia University Press, 2010.

Manheim, Jarol B. *Strategic Public Diplomacy and American Foreign Policy: The Evolution of Influence*. New York: Oxford University Press, 1994.

Manor, Ilan. *The Digitalization of Public Diplomacy*. New York: Palgrave Macmillan, 2019.

Marsden, Magnus, Diana Ibañez-Tirado, and David Henig. "Everyday Diplomacy." *The Cambridge Journal of Anthropology* 34, no. 2 (2016): 2–22.

Marsh, Charles. "Converging on Harmony: Idealism, Evolution, and the Theory of Mutual Aid." *Public Relations Inquiry* 1, no. 3 (2012): 313–35.

Martin, Denise. "Maat and Order in African Cosmology: A Conceptual Tool for Understanding Indigenous Knowledge." *Journal of Black Studies* 38, no. 6 (2008): 951–67.

Matsumoto, David, and Hyi Sung Hwang. "Reading Facial Expressions of Emotion." *Psychological Science Agenda*, May 2011, https://www.apa.org/science/about/psa/2011/05/facial-expressions#.

Mauss, Marcel. *The Gift : Forms and Functions of Exchange in Archaic Societies*. Glencoe, IL: The Free Press, 1954.

Mayer, Emeran. *The Mind-Gut Connection: How the Hidden Conversation within Our Bodies Impacts Our Mood, Our Choices, and Our Overall Health*. Reprint ed. New York: Harper Wave, 2018.

Mazumdar, B. Theo. "Digital Diplomacy: Internet-Based Public Diplomacy Activities or Novel Forms of Public Engagement?" *Place Branding and Public Diplomacy* (2021), 1–20. https://doi.org/10.1057/s41254-021-00208-4.

Mbiti, John S. *African Religions and Philosophy*. London: Longman, 1970.

Mbiti, John S. *Introduction to African Religion*. Oxford: Heinemann, 1991.

McDaniel, Edwin, and Larry A. Samovar. "Understanding and Applying Intercultural Communication in the Global Community: The Fundamentals." In *Intercultural Communication: A Reader*, ed. Larry A. Samovar, Richard E. Porter, Edwin R. McDaniel, and Carolyn Sexton Roy, 5–15. Boston: Cengage Learning, 2014.

McLuhan, Marshall. *Understanding Media: The Extensions of Man*. New York: Signet Books, 1964.

McNeill, William H. *Together in Time: Dance and Drill in Human History*. Cambridge, MA: Harvard University Press, 1995.

Mehrabian, Albert. *Silent Messages*. Belmont, CA: Wadsworth, 1971.

Melissen, Jan. "The New Public Diplomacy: Between Theory and Practice." In *The New Public Diplomacy: Soft Power in International Relations*, ed., Jan Melissen, 3–27. New York: Palgrave Macmillan, 2005.

Mercer, Jonathan. "Feeling Like a State: Social Emotion and Identity." *International Theory* 6, no. 03 (2014): 515–35.

Mercer, Jonathan. "Rationality and Psychology in International Politics." *International Organization* 59, no. 1 (2005): 77–106.

Messner, Dirk, and Silke Weinlich. *Global Cooperation and the Human Factor in International Relations*. New York: Routledge, 2015.

Miike, Yoshitaka. "Asian Contributions to Communication Theory: An Introduction." *China Media Research* 3, no. 4 (2007): 1–6.

Miike, Yoshitaka. "Beyond Eurocentrism in the Intercultural Field." In *Ferment in the Intercultural Field*, ed. William J. Starosta and Guo-Ming Chen, 243–76. Thousand Oaks, CA: Sage, 2003.

Miike, Yoshitaka. "Harmony without Uniformity": An Asiacentric Worldview and Its Communicative Implications." In *Intercultural Communication: A Reader*, ed. Larry A. Samovar, Richard E. Porter, and Edwin R. McDaniel, 65–80. Boston: Wadsworth, 2012.

Miike, Yoshitaka. "New Frontiers in Asian Communication Theory: An Introduction." *Journal of Multicultural Discourses* 4, no. 1 (2009): 1–5.

Miike, Yoshitaka. "Non-Western Theory in Western Research? An Asiacentric Agenda for Asian Communication Studies." *The Review of Communication* 6, no. 1–2 (2006): 4–31.

Miike, Yoshitaka. "Theorizing Culture and Communication in the Asian Context: An Assumptive Foundation." *Intercultural Communication Studies* 11, no. 1 (2002): 1–22.

Miller, George R. "Taking Stock of a Discipline." *Journal of Communication* 33, no. 3 (1983): 31–41.

Miskimmon, Alister, Ben O'Loughlin, and Laura Roselle. *Strategic Narratives: Communication Power and the New World Order*. London: Routledge, 2013.

Miyahara, Akira. "Toward Theorizing Japanese Interpersonal Communication Competence from a Non-Western Perspective." *American Communication Journal* 3, no. 1 (2006), 1–17.

Moffett, Mark W. *The Human Swarm: How Our Societies Arise, Thrive, and Fall*. New York: Basic Books, 2019.

Moran, William L., ed. *The Amarna Letters*. Baltimore, MD: Johns Hopkins University Press, 1992.

Mowlana, Hamid, and William B. Gudykunst. "Mass Media and Culture: Toward an Integrated Theory." In *Intercultural Communication Theory: Current Perspectives*, ed., William B. Gudykunst,149–70. Beverly Hills, CA: Sage, 1983.

Naupa, Anna. "Indo-Pacific Diplomacy: A View from the Pacific Islands." *Politics & Policy* 45, no. 5 (2017): 902–17.

Nelson, Gayle L., Mahmoud Al Batal, and Waguida El Bakary. "Directness vs. Indirectness: Egyptian Arabic and US English Communication Style." *International Journal of Intercultural Relations* 26, no. 1 (2002): 39–57.

Nesti, Giorgia, and Chiara Valentini. *Public Communication in the European Union: History, Perspectives and Challenges*. Newcastle upon Tyne: Cambridge Scholars, 2010.

Neumann, Iver B., and Einar Wigen. "The Importance of the Eurasian Steppe to the Study of International Relations." *Journal of International Relations and Development* 16, no. 3 (2013): 311–30.

Neumann, Iver B., and Einar Wigen. *The Steppe Tradition in International Relations: Russians, Turks and European State Building 4000 BCE–2017 CE*. Cambridge: Cambridge University Press, 2018.

Neumann, Iver B. "A Prehistorical Evolutionary View of Diplomacy." *Place Branding and Public Diplomacy* 14 (2018): 4–10.

New Zealand Ministry of Justice. *He Hinatore Ki Te Ao Maori; A Glimpse into the Mäori World: Mäori Perspectives on Justice*. Wellington, NZ: Ministry of Justice, 2001. https://www.justice.govt.nz/assets/Documents/Publications/he-hinatora-ki-te-ao-maori.pdf.

Nisbett, Richard E. "Living Together versus Going It Alone," in *Intercultural Communication: A Reader*, 12th ed., ed. Larry Samovar, Richard Porter, and Edwin R. McDaniel, 134–154. Boston: Wadsworth, 2009.

Nisbett, Richard E., Kaiping Peng, Incheol Choi, and Ara Norenzayan. "Culture and Systems of Thought: Holistic versus Analytic Cognition." *Psychological Review* 108, no. 2 (2001): 291–310.

Norman, Donald A. "Affordance, Conventions and Design." *Interactions* 6, no. 3 (1999): 38–43.

Maffie, James. "Pre-Columbian Philosophies." In *A Companion to Latin American Philosophy*, ed. Susana Nuccetelli, Ofelia Schutte, and Otávio Bueno, 9–22. New York: Wiley & Sons, 2013.

Nussbaum, B. "Ubuntu: Reflections of a South African on Our Common Humanity." *Reflections* 4, no. 4 (2003): 21–26.

Nwosu, Peter Ogom. "Understanding Africans' Conceptualizations of Intercultural Competence." In *The Sage Handbook of Intercultural Competence*, ed., Darla K. Deardorff, 158–78. SAGE Publications, Inc. Thousand Oaks, CA: 2009..

Nye, Joseph S. *Bound to Lead: The Changing Nature of American Power*. Reprint ed. New York: Basic Books, 1990.

Nye, Joseph S. *Soft Power: The Means to Success in World Politics*. New York: PublicAffairs, 2004.

Oglesby, Donna Marie. "Spectacle in Copenhagen: Public Diplomacy on Parade." *CPD Perspectives on Public Diplomacy*, Paper 4, December 2010, https://uscpublicdiplomacy.org/sites/uscpublicdiplomacy.org/files/useruploads/u35361/2010%20Paper%204.pdf.

Okabe, Roichi. "Cultural Assumptions of East and West: Japan and the U.S." In *Intercultural Communication Theory: Current Perspectives*, ed., William B. Gudykunst, 21–44. Newbury Park, CA: Sage Publications, 1983.

Ong, W. "Literacy and Orality in Our Times." *Journal of Communication* 30 (1980): 197–204.

Ong, Walter J. *Orality and Literacy: The Technologizing of the Word*. New York: Routledge, 1982.

Oppenheim, Claire E. "Nelson Mandela and the Power of Ubuntu." *Religions* 3 (2012): 369–88.

Otoide, Leo E. "Re-Thinking the Subject of Africa's International Relations." *Voice of History (Nepal)* 16, no. 2 (2001): 43–56, https://doi.org/10.3126/voh.v16i2.77.

Oyserman, Daphna, Heather M. Coon, and Markus Kemmelmeier. "Rethinking Individualism and Collectivism: Evaluation of Theoretical Assumptions and Meta-Analyses." *Psychological Bulletin* 128, no. 1 (2002): 3–72.

Page, Scott E. *The Difference: How the Power of Diversity Creates Better Groups, Firms, Schools, and Societies*. New ed. Princeton, NJ: Princeton University Press, 2008.

Pagel, Mark. "Q&A: What Is Human Language, When Did It Evolve and Why Should We Care?" *BMC Biology* 15, no. 64 (2017): 1–6, DOI 10.1186/s12915-017-0405-3.

Papacharissi, Zizi. *Affective Publics: Sentiment, Technology, and Politics*. New York: Oxford University Press, 2015.

Papacharissi, Zizi, and Maria de Fatima Oliveira. "Affective News and Networked Publics: The Rhythms of News Storytelling on #Egypt." *Journal of Communication* 62, no. 2 (2012): 266–82.

Papastergiadis, Nikos. "Hiding in the Cosmos." In *Camouflage Cultures: Beyond the Art of Disappearance*, ed. Ann Elias, Ross Harley, and Nicholas Tsoutas, 193–200. New South Wales, AU: Sydney University Press, 2015.

Paul, Kari. "Please Don't Stop the Music: How Choirs Are Singing through the Pandemic." *The Guardian*, April 22, 2021, sec. Music. http://www.theguardian.com/music/2021/apr/22/choirs-coronavirus-covid-19-us-virtual-singing.

Paxton, Alexandra, and Rick Dale. "Interpersonal Movement Synchrony Responds to High- and Low-Level Conversational Constraints." *Frontiers in Psychology* 8 (July 28, 2017): 1–16, https://doi.org/10.3389/fpsyg.2017.01135.

Peters, John Durham. *Speaking into the Air: A History of the Idea of Communication.* Chicago, IL: University of Chicago Press, 2001.

Peterson, Peter G. "Public Diplomacy and the War on Terrorism." *Foreign Affairs* 81, no. 5 (2002): 74–94. https://doi.org/10.2307/20033270.

Peterson, Steven, and Albert Somit. *Darwinism, Dominance, and Democracy: The Biological Bases of Authoritarianism.* Westport, CT: Praeger, 1997.

Petty, Richard E., and John T. Cacioppo. *Attitudes and Persuasion: Classic and Contemporary Approaches.* Boulder, CO: Westview Press, 1996.

Pew Research Center. "A Year after Iraq War: Mistrust of America in Europe Ever Higher, Muslim Anger Persists." The Pew Global Attitudes Project, March 16, 2004. https://www.pewresearch.org/global/2004/03/16/a-year-after-iraq-war/.

Pew Research Center. "America's Image Further Erodes, Europeans Want Weaker Ties But Post-War Iraq Will Be Better Off, Most Say," March 18, 2003. https://www.pewresearch.org/politics/2003/03/18/americas-image-further-erodes-europeans-want-weaker-ties/.

Pew Research Center. "Views of a Changing World 2003 War With Iraq Further Divides Global Publics," June 3, 2003. https://www.pewresearch.org/politics/2003/06/03/views-of-a-changing-world-2003/.

Pew Research Center. "What the World Thinks in 2002." The Pew Global Attitudes Project, December 4, 2002. https://www.pewresearch.org/global/2002/12/04/what-the-world-thinks-in-2002/.

Phelps, Andy. "Gaming Fosters Social Connection at Ate of Physical Distance." *The Conversation* (blog), April 13, 2020. https://theconversation.com/gaming-fosters-social-connection-at-a-time-of-physical-distance-135809.

Pigman, Geoffrey Allen. *Contemporary Diplomacy: Representation and Communication in a Globalized World.* Cambridge, UK: Polity, 2010.

Piller, Ingrid. *Intercultural Communication: A Critical Introduction.* 2nd ed. Edinburgh: Edinburgh University Press, 2017.

Pitama, Di, George Ririnui, Annabel Mikaere. *Guardianship, Custody and Access: Māori Perspectives and Experiences.* Wellington, NZ: Ministry of Justice, 2002. http://www.justice.govt.nz/pubs/reports/2002/guardianship-custody-access-maori/guardianship-custody-access-maori.pdf.

Podany, Amanda H. *Brotherhood of Kings: How International Relations Shaped the Ancient Near East.* New York: Oxford University Press, 2010.

Press, Betty. *I Am Because We Are: African Wisdom in Image and Proverb.* St. Paul, MN: Books for Africa, 2011.

Price, Michael. "Facial Expressions—Including Fear—May Not Be as Universal as We Thought." *Science | AAAS*, October 17, 2016, 1–2, doi: 10.1126/science.aal0271 .

Probert, Joana. "Leading with Empathy in the Pandemic." *Saïd Business School, University of Oxford*, July 1, 2020. https://www.sbs.ox.ac.uk/oxford-answers/leading-empathy-pandemic.

Provan, Keith G., Amy Fish, and Joerg Sydow. "Interorganizational Networks at the Network Level: A Review of the Empirical Literature on Whole Networks." *Journal of Management* 33, no. 3 (2007): 479–516.

Qin, Yaqing. "International Society as a Process: Institutions, Identities, and China's Peaceful Rise." *The Chinese Journal of International Politics* 3, no. 2 (2010): 129–53.

Qin, Yaqing. *A Relational Theory of World Politics*. Cambridge: Cambridge University Press, 2018.

Qizheng, Zhao. *One World: Bridging the Communication Gap*. Beijing: China Intercontinental Press, 2008.

Raddawi, Rana. "Teaching Critical Thinking Skills to Arab University Students." In *Teaching and Learning in the Arab World*, ed., Christina Gitsaki, 71–91. Bern: P. Lang, 2011.

Rand, Erin J. "'What One Voice Can Do': Civic Pedagogy and Choric Collectivity at Camp Courage." *Text and Performance Quarterly* 34, no. 1 (2014): 28–51.

Rawnsley, Gary. "Approaches to Soft Power and Public Diplomacy in China and Taiwan." *The Journal of International Communication* 18, no. 2 (2012): 121–35. https://doi.org/ 10.1080/13216597.2012.695744.

Refugees International. "COVID-19 and the Displaced: Addressing the Threat of the Novel Coronavirus in Humanitarian Emergencies." Washington DC: Refugees International, March 30, 2020. https://www.refugeesinternational.org/reports/2020/3/ 29/covid-19-and-the-displaced-addressing-the-threat-of-the-novel-coronavirus-in- humanitarian-emergencies.

Rensburg, Ronél. "Communications Management in the Africa Context: Implications for Theory, Research, and Practice." *International Journal of Strategic Communication* 1, no. 1 (2007): 37–51.

Reus-Smit, Christian. "Emotions and the Social." *International Theory* 6, no. 3 (2014): 568–74.

Rheingold, Howard. *The Virtual Community: Homesteading on the Electronic Frontier*. Cambridge, MA: MIT Press eBooks, 2000. http://www.rheingold.com/vc/book/.

Riordan, Shaun. "Dialogue-Based Public Diplomacy: A New Foreign Policy Paradigm?," Netherlands Institute of International Relations 'Clingendael', Discussion Papers in Diplomacy no. 95 (November 2004): 1–17.

Riordan, Shaun. "Digital Diplomacy 2.0: Beyond the Social Media Obsession." *CPD Blog* (blog), April 25, 2016. http://uscpublicdiplomacy.org/blog/digital-diplomacy-20-bey ond-social-media-obsession.

Ritzer, George, and Pamela Gindoff. "Methodological Relationism: Lessons for and from Social Psychology." *Social Psychology Quarterly* 55, no. 2 (1992): 128–40. https://doi. org/10.2307/2786942.

Roschelle, Jeremy, and Stephanie D. Teasley. "The Construction of Shared Knowledge in Collaborative Problem Solving." In *Computer Supported Collaborative Learning*, ed., Claire O'Malley, 69–97. NATO ASI Series. Heidelberg: Springer, 1995. https://doi.org/ 10.1007/978-3-642-85098-1_5.

Rose, Frank. "The Art of Immersion: Why Do We Tell Stories?" *Wired*, March 8, 2011.

Rosenberg, Emily S., Akira Iriye, Jürgen Osterhammel, Charles S. Maier, and Tony Ballantyne. *A World Connecting: 1870–1945*. Cambridge, MA: Harvard University Press, 2012.

Rubenstein, Richard E. *Aristotle's Children: How Christians, Muslims, and Jews Rediscovered Ancient Wisdom and Illuminated the Middle Ages*. Orlando, FL: Harcourt, 2004.

Rumford, Chris, and Andrew Cooper. "Bordering and Connectivity: Thinking about Cosmopolitan Borders." In *Routledge International Handbook of Cosmopolitanism Studies*, 2nd ed., ed., Gerard Delanty, 277–86. New York: Routledge, 2018.

Rumi, Maulana Jalalu-'d-din Muhammad. *Masnavi I Ma'navi: Teachings of Rumi* (Book I, Story XIV), abridged and translated by Edward Henry Whinfield (London, 1887). Wikisource https://en.wikisource.org/wiki/Masnavi_I_Ma%27navi.

Rushkoff, Douglas. *Team Human*. New York: W. W. Norton & Company, 2019.

Russell, James A. "Is There Universal Recognition of Emotion from Facial Expression? A Review of the Cross-Cultural Studies." *Psychological Bulletin* 115, no. 1 (1994): 102–41. https://doi.org/10.1037/0033-2909.115.1.102.

Samovar, Larry A., Richard E. Porter, and Nemi C. Jain. *Understanding Intercultural Communication*. Belmont, CA: Wadsworth Publishing Company, 1981.

Sampson, Edward E. "The Debate on Individualism: Indigenous Psychologies of the Individual and Their Role in Personal and Societal Functioning." *American Psychologist* 43, no. 1 (1988): 15–22. https://doi.org/10.1037/0003-066X.43.1.15.

Saunders, Harold H. *Politics Is about Relationship: A Blueprint for the Citizens' Century*. New York: Palgrave Macmillan, 2006.

Saunders, Harold H. "The Relational Paradigm and Sustained Dialogue." In *Relational, Networked and Collaborative Approaches to Public Diplomacy*, ed. R. S. Zaharna, Amelia Arsenault, and Ali Fisher, 132–44. New York: Routledge, 2013.

Schmemann, Serge. "A New Rule Book for the Great Game." *New York Times*, April 12, 2017, sec. Books. https://www.nytimes.com/2017/04/12/books/review/chessboard-and-the-web-anne-marie-slaughter.html.

Schneider, Cynthia P. "The Unrealized Potential of Cultural Diplomacy: 'Best Practices' and What Could Be, If Only. . . ." *Journal of Arts Management, Law, and Society* 39, no. 4 (2009): 260–79.

Schoner, Gregor. "Embodied Communication: Looking for Systems That Mean What They Say," *Robohub*. March 14, 2014.

Schramm, Wilbur, Steven H. Chaffee, and Everett M. Rogers. *The Beginnings of Communication Study in America: A Personal Memoir*. Thousand Oaks, CA: Sage, 1997.

Schramm, Wilbur. *The Science of Human Communication: New Directions and New Findings in Communication Research*. New York: Basic Books, 1963.

Schulte-Rüther, Martin, Hans J. Markowitsch, Gereon R. Fink, and Martina Piefke. "Mirror Neuron and Theory of Mind Mechanisms Involved in Face-to-Face Interactions: A Functional Magnetic Resonance Imaging Approach to Empathy." *Journal of Cognitive Neuroscience* 19, no. 8 (2007): 1354–72.

Schultz, Teri. "State Department Magazine Courts Arab Youth." *Fox News*, September 1, 2003. http://www.foxnews.com/story/029339612200

Scolari, Carlos Alberto. "Mapping Conversations about New Media: The Theoretical Field of Digital Communication." *New Media & Society* 11, no. 6 (2009): 943–64.

Scollon, Ron, and Suzie Wong Scollon. "Face Parameters in East-West Discourse." In *The Challenge of Facework: Cross-Cultural and Interpersonal Issues*, ed., Stella Ting-Toomey, 133–57. Albany: SUNY Press, 1994.

Seargeant, Philip, and Caroline Tagg. *The Language of Social Media: Identity and Community on the Internet*. Basingstoke: Palgrave Macmillan. 2014.

Seeger, Matthew W. "Best Practices in Crisis Communication: An Expert Panel Process." *Journal of Applied Communication Research* 34, no. 3 (2006): 232–44.

Seib, Philip. *The Future of #Diplomacy*. Malden, MA: Polity, 2016.

Sending, Ole Jacob, Vincent Pouliot, and Iver B. Neumann. *Diplomacy and the Making of World Politics.* Cambridge Studies in International Relations 136. Cambridge: Cambridge University Press, 2015.

Sending, Ole Jacob, Vincent Pouliot, and Iver B., Neumann. "The Future of Diplomacy: Changing Practices, Evolving Relationships." *International Journal (Toronto)* 66, no. 3 (2011): 527–42.

Sennett, Richard. *Together: The Rituals, Pleasures and Politics of Cooperation.* New Haven, CT: Yale University Press, 2013.

Seo, Hyunjin, and Stuart Thorson. "Empathy in Public Diplomacy: Strategic Academic Engagement with North Korea." In *Intersections Between Public Diplomacy and International Development: Case Studies in Converging Fields*, ed., James Pamment, 19–34. Los Angeles: Figueroa Press, 2016.

Sergent, Kayla, and Alexander D. Stajkovic. "Women's Leadership Is Associated with Fewer Deaths during the COVID-19 Crisis: Quantitative and Qualitative Analyses of United States Governors." *Journal of Applied Psychology* 105, no. 8 (2020): 771–83.

Serrano-Puche, Javier. "Emotions and Digital Technologies: Mapping the Field of Research in Media Studies." MEDIA@LSE Working Papers, 2015. https://www.lse.ac.uk/media-and-communications/assets/documents/research/working-paper-series/EWP33.pdf.

Sevin, Efe. *Public Diplomacy and the Implementation of Foreign Policy in the US, Sweden and Turkey.* New York: Palgrave Macmillan, 2017.

Sewell, William H. "The Concept(s) of Culture." In *Beyond the Cultural Turn: New Directions in the Study of Society and Culture*, ed. Victoria Bonnell and Lynn Hunt, 35–61. Berkeley: University of California Press, 1999.

Shannon, Timothy J., and Colin Calloway. *Iroquois Diplomacy on the Early American Frontier.* Reprint ed. New York: Penguin Books, 2009.

Sharp, Paul. *Diplomatic Theory of International Relations.* New York: Cambridge University Press, 2009.

Shehata, Samer. "Why Bush's Middle East Propaganda Campaign Won't Work." *Salon*, July 13, 2002. https://www.salon.com/2002/07/12/propaganda_8/.

Sheikh, Aabid Majeed, and Saima Rashid. "Kautilya, the Indian Machiavelli; On War and Diplomacy in Ancient India." *Journal of Humanities and Education Development* 2, no. 1 (2020): 29–36.

Shelby, David. "US Starts New Arabic-Language Satellite TV Broadcast," The Coalition Provisional Authority (Archive), February 13, 2004, https://govinfo.library.unt.edu/cpa-iraq/pressreleases/20040214_satellite.html.

Shi-Xu. "Reconstructing Eastern Paradigms of Discourse Studies." *Journal of Multicultural Discourses* 4, no. 1 (2009): 29–48.

Shroff, Farah. "We Are All One: Holistic Thought-Forms within Indigenous Societies Indigeneity and Holism." In *Indigenous Philosophies and Critical Education*, ed., George Sefa Dei, 53–67. New York: Peter Lang, 2011.

Sinha, Durganand. "Changing Perspectives in Social Psychology in India: A Journey Towards Indigenization." *Asian Journal of Social Psychology* 1, no. 1 (1998): 17–31.

Sinha, Durganand. "Origins and Development of Psychology in India: Outgrowing the Alien Framework." *International Journal of Psychology* 29, no. 6 (1994): 695–705.

Sinha, Jai B. P., T. N. Sinha, Jyoti Verma, and R. B. N. Sinha. "Collectivism Coexisting with Individualism: An Indian Scenario." *Asian Journal of Social Psychology* 4 (2001): 133–45.

Sinha, Jai B. P., and Rajesh Kumar. "Methodology for Understanding Indian Culture." *The Copenhagen Journal of Asian Studies* 19 (2004): 89–104.

Slaughter, Anne-Marie. *The Chessboard and the Web: Strategies of Connection in a Networked World.* New Haven, CT: Yale University Press, 2017.

Smith, Anthony D. *Nationalism: Theory, Ideology, History.* New York: John Wiley & Sons, 2013.

Smith, Daniel, Philip Schlaepfer, Katie Major, Mark Dyble, Abigail E. Page, James Thompson, Nikhil Chaudhary, et al. "Cooperation and the Evolution of Hunter-Gatherer Storytelling." *Nature Communications* 8, no. 1853 (December 5, 2017): 1–9, DOI: 10.1038/s41467-017-02036-8.

Smith, Peter B., Hai Juan Huang, Charles Harb, and Claudio Torres. "How Distinctive Are Indigenous Ways of Achieving Influence? A Comparative Study of Guanxi, Wasta, Jeitinho, and 'Pulling Strings.'" *Journal of Cross-Cultural Psychology* 43, no. 1 (2012): 135–50.

Smith, William. *Dictionary of Greek and Roman Biography and Mythology.* London: via Perseus Digital Library, 1873.

Snow, Nancy. "Rethinking Public Diplomacy." In *Routledge Handbook of Public Diplomacy,* ed. Nancy Snow and Nicholas J. Cull, 2nd ed., 3–12. New York: Routledge, 2020.

Snow, Nancy. *The Arrogance of American Power: What US Leaders Are Doing Wrong and Why It's Our Duty to Dissent.* Lanham, MD: Rowman & Littlefield, 2007.

Stewart, Edward. *American Cultural Patterns: A Cross-Cultural Perspective.* Chicago: Intercultural Press, 1972.

Stewart, Edward C., and Milton J. Bennett. *American Cultural Patterns: A Cross-Cultural Perspective.* Yarmouth, ME: Intercultural Press, 1975.

Stokes, Benjamin. *Locally Played: Real-World Games for Stronger Places and Communities.* Cambridge, MA: MIT Press, 2020.

Streeck, Jürgen. "Embodiment in Human Communication." *Annual Review of Anthropology* 44, no. 1 (2015): 419–38.

Street, Brian. "Culture Is a Verb: Anthropological Aspects of Language and Cultural Process." In *Language and Culture: Papers from the Annual Meeting of the British Association of Applied Linguistics Held at Trevelyan College, University of Durham, September 1991,* ed., British Association for Applied Linguistics, 23–59. Bristol: Multilingual Matters, 1993.

Taras, Vas, Riikka Sarala, Paul Muchinsky, Markus Kemmelmeier, Theodore M. Singelis, Andreja Avsec, Heather M. Coon, et al. "Opposite Ends of the Same Stick? Multi-Method Test of the Dimensionality of Individualism and Collectivism." *Journal of Cross-Cultural Psychology* 45, no. 2 (2014): 213–45.

Taylor, Maureen, and Michael L. Kent. "Building and Measuring Sustainable Networks of Organizations and Social Capital: Postwar Public Diplomacy in Croatia." In *Relational, Networked and Collaborative Approaches to Public Diplomacy,* ed. R. S. Zaharna, Amelia Arsenault, and Ali Fisher, 103–16. New York: Routledge, 2013.

Thompson, Robert Farris, and J. Cornet. *The Four Moments of the Sun: Kongo Art in Two Worlds.* Washington, DC: National Gallery of Art, 1981.

Ting-Toomey, Stella. "Toward a Theory of Conflict and Culture." In *Communication, Culture, and Organization Processes,* ed. William B. Gudykunst and Leah P. Stewart, and Stella Ting-Toomey, 71–86. International and Intercultural Communication Annual, Vol. 9. Beverly Hills: Sage Publications, 1985.

Tobin, Vincent A. *Theological Principles of Egyptian Religion*. New York: International Academic Publishers, 1989.

Tobin, Vincent Arieh. "Mytho-Theology in Ancient Egypt." *Journal of the American Research Center in Egypt* 25 (1988): 169–83.

Todd, Kenneth P. *A Capsule History of the Bell System*. American Telephone and Telegraph Company, 1975. https://www.beatriceco.com/bti/porticus/bell/capsule_bell_system.html#The%20Corporation%20Grows:

Toensing, Chris. "Hi and a Low at the State Department." *The Daily Star*, August 23, 2003, sec. Opinion. http://www.dailystar.com.lb/Opinion/Commentary/2003/Aug-23/103843-hi-and-a-low-at-the-state-department.ashx.

Tomasello, Michael, Alicia P. Melis, Claudio Tennie, Emily Wyman, and Esther Herrmann. "Two Key Steps in the Evolution of Human Cooperation: The Interdependence Hypothesis." *Current Anthropology* 53, no. 6 (2012): 673–92.

Tomlinson, Kenneth Y. "Testimony of Kenneth Y. Tomlinson, Chairman, Broadcasting Board of Governors, Before the Committee of Foreign Relations, United States Senate, on American Public Diplomacy in the Islamic World," February 27, 2003. https://www.foreign.senate.gov/imo/media/doc/TomlinsonTestimony030227.pdf.

Triandis, Harry C. "Cross-Cultural Studies of Individualism and Collectivism." In *Nebraska Symposium on Motivation 1989: Cross-Cultural Perspectives*, ed., John J. Berman, 41–133. Lincoln: University of Nebraska Press, 1990.

Triandis, Harry C. *Individualism and Collectivism*. Boulder, CO: Westview Press, 1995.

Triandis, Harry C., Robert Bontempo, Marcelo J. Villareal, Masaaki Asai, and Nydia Lucca. "Individualism and Collectivism: Cross-Cultural Perspectives on Self-Ingroup Relationships." *Journal of Personality and Social Psychology* 54, no. 2 (1988): 323–38.

Tutwiler, Margaret. "Public Diplomacy: Reaching beyond Traditional Audiences, Testimony Before the House Appropriations Subcommittee on Commerce, Justice, State and the Judiciary," February 4, 2004. https://2001-2009.state.gov/r/us/2004/29111.htm.

Tylor, Edward B. *Primitive Culture: Researches into the Development of Mythology, Philosophy, Religion, Art, and Custom*. London: John Murray, 1871.

Urry, John. "Social Networks, Travel and Talk[1]." *British Journal of Sociology* 54, no. 2 (2003): 155–75.

U.S. State Department. "Muslim Life in America," 2003. http://usinfo.state.gov/products/pubs/muslimlife/homepage.htm.

Vagelpohl, Uwe. *Aristotle's Rhetoric in the East: The Syriac and Arabic Translation and Commentary Tradition*. Leiden: Brill, 2008.

Vallet, Elisabeth. *Borders, Fences and Walls: State of Insecurity?* New York: Routledge, 2016.

Van der Pluijm, Rogier, and Jan Melissen. *City Diplomacy: The Expanding Role of Cities in International Politics*. The Hague: Netherlands Institute of International Relations 'Clingendael,' 2007.

Van Dinh, Tran. *Communication and Diplomacy in a Changing World*. Norwood, NJ: Ablex, 1987.

van Ruler, Betteke, and Dejan Verčič. *Public Relations and Communication Management in Europe: A Nation-by-Nation Introduction to Public Relations Theory and Practice*. Boston: De Gruyter Mouton, 2008.

Van Ruler, Betteke, and Dejan Verčič. "Overview of Public Relations and Communication Management in Europe." In *Public Relations and Communication Management in Europe*, ed. Betteke van Ruler and Dejan Verčič, 1–11. Berlin: De Gruyter Mouton, 2008.

Venter, Elza. "The Notion of Ubuntu and Communalism in African Educational Discourse." *Studies in Philosophy and Education* 23, no. 2 (2004): 149–60.

Verčič, Dejan, Betteke van Ruler, Gerhard Bütschi, and Bertil Flodin. "On the Definition of Public Relations: A European View." *Public Relations Review* 27, no. 4 (2001): 373–87.

Villaneuva Rivas, Cesar. "Cosmopolitan Constructivism: Mapping a Road to the Future of Cultural and Public Diplomacy." *Public Diplomacy Magazine* Winter, no. 3 (2010): 45–56.

von Zimmermann, Jorina von, and Daniel C. Richardson. "Verbal Synchrony and Action Dynamics in Large Groups." *Frontiers in Psychology* 7, no. 2034 (2016): 1–10, https://doi.org/10.3389/fpsyg.2016.02034.

Vyasulu Reddi, Usha. "Communication Theory: An Indian Perspective." *Media Asia* 13, no. 1 (January 1986): 25–28.

Wachsmuth, Ipke, Manuela Lenzen, and Gunther Knoblich. "Introduction to Embodied Communication: Why Communication Needs the Body." In *Embodied Communication in Humans and Machines*, ed. Ipke Wachsmuth, Manuela Lenzen, and Guenther Knoblich, 1–28. Oxford: Oxford University Press, 2008.

Wagner, Roy. *The Invention of Culture*. Chicago: University of Chicago Press, 1975.

Waisbord, Silvio, and Claudia Mellado. "De-Westernizing Communication Studies: A Reassessment." *Communication Theory* 24 (2014): 361–72.

Wang, Georgette. "Paradigm Shift and the Centrality of Communication Discipline." *International Journal of Communication* 5 (2011): 1458–66.

Wang, Georgette, and Zhong-Bo Liu. "What Collective? Collectivism and Relationalism from a Chinese Perspective." *Chinese Journal of Communication* 3, no. 1 (2010): 42–63.

Wang, Jain. *Soft Power in China: Public Diplomacy through Communication*. New York: Palgrave Macmillan, 2010.

Wang, Jian. "Managing National Reputation and International Relations in the Global Era: Public Diplomacy Revisited." *Public Relations Review* 32, no. 2 (2006): 91–96.

Wang, Yiwei. "Relational Dimensions of a Chinese Model of Public Diplomacy." In *Relational, Networked and Collaborative Approaches to Public Diplomacy: The Connective Mindshift*, ed. R. S. Zaharna, Amelia Arsenault, and Ali. Fisher, 86–102. New York: Routledge, 2013.

Wang, Yiwei. "Public Diplomacy and the Rise of Chinese Soft Power." *The Annals of the American Academy of Political and Social Science* 616, no. 1 (2008): 257–73. https://doi.org/10.1177/0002716207312757.

Watson, Adam. *Diplomacy: The Dialogue Between States*. New York, NY: Routledge, 2013.

Watzlawick, Paul, Janet Beavin Bavelas, and Don D. Jackson. *Pragmatics of Human Communication: A Study of Interactional Patterns, Pathologies and Paradoxes*. New York: W. W. Norton & Company, 2011.

Wetherell, Margaret. "Cross-Cultural Studies of Minimal Groups: Implications for the Social Identity Theory of Intergroup Relations." In *Social Identity and Intergroup Relations*, ed., H. Tajfel, 207–40. Cambridge: Cambridge University Press, 1982.

Williams, Raymond. *Culture and Society, 1780–1950*. New York: Columbia University Press, 1958.

Wilson, Edward O. *The Social Conquest of Earth*. New York: Liveright Publishing, 2012.

Wiredu, Kwasi. *Cultural Universals and Particulars: An African Perspective*. Bloomington: Indiana University Press, 1996.

Witzel, E. J. Michael. *The Origins of the World's Mythologies*. Illustrated ed. Oxford: Oxford University Press, 2013.

Wong, Seanon S. "Emotions and the Communication of Intentions in Face-to-Face Diplomacy." *European Journal of International Relations* 22, no. 1 (2016): 144–67.

Wood, Julia T. *Interpersonal Communication: Everyday Encounters.* 8th ed. Boston, MA: Cengage Learning, 2015.

Woolf, Virginia. *Three Guineas.* Hogarth Critics ed. London: Hogarth Press, 1938.

Wright, Susan. "The Politicization of 'Culture.'" *Anthropology Today* 14, no. 1 (1998): 7–15. https://doi.org/10.2307/2783092.

Wu, Di. "Assessing Resource Transactions in Partnership Networks: US 100,000 Strong Network of Public Diplomacy." *Public Relations Review* 42, no. 1 (2016): 120–34.

Wu, Shali, and Boaz Keysar. "The Effect of Culture on Perspective Taking." *Psychological Science* 18, no. 7 (2007): 600–606.

Wu, Xu. "Doing PR in China: A 2001 Version—Concepts, Practices and Some Misperceptions." *Public Relations Quarterly* 47, no. 2 (Summer 2002): 10–20.

Wyne, Ali. "Anne-Marie Slaughter Tries to Make Sense of the New Global Order." *The New Republic*, September 22, 2017. https://newrepublic.com/article/144930/anne-marie-slaughter-tries-make-sense-new-global-order.

Yale Infant Lab. "The Infant Cognition Center | Yale University." 2021. https://campuspress.yale.edu/infantlab/.

Yang, Aimei, Anna Klyueva, and Maureen Taylor. "Beyond a Dyadic Approach to Public Diplomacy: Understanding Relationships in Multipolar World." *Public Relations Review* 38, no. 5 (2012): 652–64.

Yeh, Kuang-Hui. "Relationalism: The Essence and Evolving Process of Chinese Interactive Relationships." *Chinese Journal of Communication* 3, no. 1 (2010): 76–94.

Yoshikawa, Muneo Jay. "The Double-Swing Model of Intercultural Communication between the East and the West." In *Communication Theory: Eastern and Western Perspectives*, ed., D. Lawrence Kincaid, 319–29. New York: Academic Press, 1987.

Youssef, Nancy. "Music, All-Arabic Format Thrive; Some Say News Is Slanted." *Detroit Free Press*, March 11, 2003.

Yum, June Ock. "The Impact of Confucianism on Interpersonal Relationships and Communication Patterns in East Asia." *Communication Monographs* 55, no. 4 (1988): 374–88.

Yum, June Ock, "Confucianism and Communication: *Jen, Li*, and *Ubuntu*," *China Media Research* 3, no. 4 (2007): 15–22.

Zaharna, R. S. *Battles to Bridges: US Strategic Communication and Public Diplomacy after 9/11.* Basingstoke: Palgrave Macmillan, 2010. http://dx.doi.org/10.1057/978023 0277922.

Zaharna, R. S. "Culture, Cultural Diversity and Humanity-Centred Diplomacies." *The Hague Journal of Diplomacy* 14, no. 1–2 (April 22, 2019): 117–33.

Zaharna, R. S. "Emotion, Identity and Social Media: Developing a New Awareness, Lens and Vocabulary for Diplomacy 21." Working Paper. "Diplomacy in the 21st Century." Berlin: German Institute for International and Security Affairs, January 2017. https://www.swp-berlin.org/fileadmin/contents/products/arbeitspapiere/WP_Diplomacy21_No2_RS_Zaharna.pdf.

Zaharna, R. S. "Network Purpose, Network Design: Dimensions of Network and Collaborative Public Diplomacy." In *Relational, Networked and Collaborative Approaches to Public Diplomacy: The Connective Mindshift*, ed. R. S. Zaharna, Amelia Arsenault, and Ali Fisher, 173–91. New York: Routledge, 2013.

Zaharna, R. S. "The Soft Power Differential: Network Communication and Mass Communication in Public Diplomacy." *The Hague Journal of Diplomacy* 2, no. 3 (2007): 213–28. https://doi.org/].

Zaharna, R. S., Amelia Arsenault, and Ali Fisher, eds. *Relational, Networked and Collaborative Approaches to Public Diplomacy: The Connective Mindshift.* New York: Routledge, 2013.

Zappone, Tanina. "New Words for a New International Communication. The Case of Public Diplomacy." Europe China Research and Advice Network, 2012. https://www.academia.edu/5235863/New_Words_for_A_New_International_Communication._The_Case_of_Public_Diplomacy.

Zhang, Juyan, and Brecken Chinn Swartz. "Public Diplomacy to Promote Global Public Goods (GPG): Conceptual Expansion, Ethical Grounds, and Rhetoric." *Public Relations Review* 35, no. 4 (2009): 382–87.

Zhao, Kejin. "China's Rise and Its Discursive Power Strategy." *Chinese Political Science Review*, (April 19, 2016): 1–25, https://doi.org/10.1007/s41111-016-0027-x.

Ziegler, Ben. "How to Accelerate the Development of New Collaborative Relationships." *Collaboration Strategies and Solutions* (blog), July 21, 2015. http://collaborativejourn eys.com/how-to-accelerate-the-development-of-new-collaborative-relationships/.

Index

242   INDEX

male triangles, 114*f*
mutual adaptation, 118
public diplomacy and, 116, 117
reciprocity in, 111
relationality in, 107, 108*b*
relational universe and, 3
spiritual realm, 126
synchronous activities, 113
synchrony and, 118, 125–26, 146–49
synergy in, 120
yin-yang symbol, 32, 33*f*, 109
Holmes, Marcus, 100–1, 125
homo narrative, 134
homonoia, 15
Hudson, Lucian, 162
Huijgh, Ellen, 74
human capacity, cooperation and, 3–5
humanity. *See also specific topics*
  in Confucian philosophy, 11
  in Polynesian traditions, 11
  ubuntu, 11, 30
humanity-centered diplomacy
  connectivity and, 9–10
  diversity and, 9–11
  emotion in, 11
  functions of, 9–11, 161–63
  Good Country project, 10
  identity and, 16–17
  interconnectivity and, 11
  as issue-driven, 10
  problem-solving through, 5
  as process-oriented, 10–11
humanity-level perspective, on
    diplomacy, 153–55
  collaboration in, 154
  cooperation in, 154
  purpose of, 3
  social capital theories and, 155
  uses and gratification theory and, 153–54
human nature, collaboration in, as "social
    animal," 3
Al-Hurra, 23
hyper-cooperation, 5

Iacoboni, Marco, 100–1
I and Thou (Buber), 87–88
Ibn Khaldun, 29–30, 53
ICA. *See* International Communication
    Association
"I dance the other" (interpersonal
    synchrony), 150
identity
  for Boundary Spanners, 16–17, 67–70, 96–98

culture and, 16
emotional, 96–98
ethnic, 16
Holistic Logic and, 16–17, 122–24
humanity-centered diplomacy and, 16–17
Individual Logic and, 16–17
Medusa syndrome, 16
national, 16
preservation of heritages, 80
relational, 16–17
Relational Logic and, 16–17
in state-centric public diplomacy, 16
Igbo people, 51
immigration, 4
India. *See also* Hinduism
  relationality in, 52
indigenous diplomacies, 61, 105, 161
Individual Expressive Logic, 67–70, 71,
    77, 79–80
individualism
  agency, 69
  autonomy of, 46
  Boundary Spanners and, 58, 76–78
  bounded whole and, 47
  in communication, 14, 25–26, 29, 45–47
  de Tocqueville definition, 45
  Geertz definition, 46
  "habits of seeing" and, 58
  individual as separate, 46–47
  individuality as distinct from, 187n.74
  intercultural communication and, 27–28,
    41, 45–49
  justification of relations, 47–48
  methodological, 44
  the Other and, 47
  relationality compared to, 49
  relational life span, 49
  relationship creation and, 48–49
  relationships and, 48
  the Self and, 47
  separateness of, 46
  in U.S. culture, 45
  Western view of, 46
individualism-collectivism continuum,
    41, 49, 59
individualistic societies, collectivist
    traits in, 43
individuality
  for Boundary Spanners, 49–50, 58, 76–78
  individualism as distinct from, 187n.74
  whakapapa and, 49–50
individual-level perspective, on diplomacy,
    purpose of, 3